Modeling and Analysis of Real-Time and Embedded Systems with UML and MARTE

Modeling and Analysis of Real-Time and Embedded Systems with UML and MARTE
Developing Cyber-Physical Systems

Bran Selić

Sébastien Gérard

AMSTERDAM • BOSTON • HEIDELBERG • LONDON
NEW YORK • OXFORD • PARIS • SAN DIEGO
SAN FRANCISCO • SINGAPORE • SYDNEY • TOKYO

Morgan Kaufmann is an imprint of Elsevier

Acquiring Editor: *Andrea Dierna*
Editorial Project Manager: *Kaitlin Herbert*
Project Manager: *Punithavathy Govindaradjane*
Designer: *Mark Rogers*

Morgan Kaufmann is an imprint of Elsevier
225 Wyman Street, Waltham, MA 02451, USA

Library of Congress Cataloging-in-Publication Data
Selić, Bran.
Modeling and analysis of real-time and embedded systems with UML and MARTE: developing cyber-physical systems / Bran Selić, Sébastien Gérard.
 pages cm
Includes bibliographical references and index.
ISBN 978-0-12-416619-6 (alk. paper)
1. Embedded computer systems—Computer simulation. 2. UML (Computer science) I. Gérard, Sébastien.
II. Title.
 TK7895.E42S3985 2014
 006.2'2—dc23   2013027695

British Library Cataloguing-in-Publication Data
A catalogue record for this book is available from the British Library

ISBN: 978-0-12-416619-6

Printed and bound in the United States of America
14 15 16 17 18   10 9 8 7 6 5 4 3 2 1

For information on all MK publications visit our website at *www.mkp.com*

To Lillian, Andrew, Matthew, and Sandy
and
To Marie, Zélie, Nicole, and Jean-Marie

Contents

PART V EXTENDING MARTE

APPENDICES

Acknowledgments

The authors express their gratitude and indebtedness first and foremost to Professors Murray Woodside and Dorina Petriu of Carleton University in Ottawa, Canada, who made a major contribution to the text of chapter on performance analysis (Chapter 11), to Drs. Sara Tucci-Piergovanni and Chokri Mraidha for their key contributions to the chapter on schedulability analysis (Chapter 10), and to Dr. Richard Soley, Chairman and CEO of the Object Management Group, who graciously agreed to write the foreword. In addition, we would like to thank the staff of the Laboratoire d'Ingénierie dirigée par les modèles pour les Systèmes Embarqués (LISE) of the Commissariat à l'Énergie Atomique (CEA) LIST group in Gif-sur-Yvette, France, who contributed in various ways to this effort and, in particular (in alphabetical order): Arnaud Cuccurru, Frédérique Descreaux, Hubert Dubois, Agnès Lanusse, Ansgar Radermacher, François Terrier, Patrick Tessier, and Yann Tanguy.

The authors are also extremely grateful to those hardy expert reviewers, Frederic Mallet, Chokri Mraidha, and Rob Pettit, whose detailed comments, corrections, and suggestions have greatly improved the quality of the text. Any remaining errors and rough spots are the sole responsibility of the authors. Thanks are also due to our very supportive editors at Morgan Kaufmann (Elsevier), Andrea Dierni, and Kaitlin Herbert, who provided general guidance and also helped us navigate the intricacies of preparing the text for publication. We also acknowledge the contribution of Pavel Hruby, who prepared the Visio templates for UML 2, which were used in constructing most of the diagrams in the book.

Last but most definitely not least, we both owe unconditional thanks for the support of our respective families, who had to endure our absences and distractions while we worked on this manuscript. Hence, we dedicate this book to them.

Bran Selić
Nepean, Canada
Sébastien Gérard
Gif-sur-Yvette, France

Foreword

Early in this excellent tome you will find a terminological quibble, one of the myriad quibbles over terms found in the juvenile field of computer science. Should we say model-based engineering, model-based development, or model-driven development? There are really two arguments in that quibble:

1. Is it model-based or model-driven? These are functionally the same, based on the concept that complex organizations of systems should be based on (driven by) lower cost (and generally more abstract) models of those organizations.
2. Is it engineering, development, or (dare I say) architecture? In fact modeling should be used to drive development; it should be used to specify an architecture (after all, that is precisely what is done in the building trades); and the process of developing a working organization, device, or software program should be engineered based on a model.

Obviously, as the progenitor of the term, I like the term Model-Driven Architecture (MDA), the name that in 2001 pulled together the many streams of modeling-based development of software and other complex systems. Terminological quibbles aside, the importance of modeling of complex systems—whether software, ships, buildings, weapon systems, cabbages, or kings—is quite clear:

- Abstractions of complex systems are extraordinarily valuable in engineering processes for developing predictions of systems, from the usability of those systems to the likely failure modes and useful lifetimes of those systems.
- Abstractions of complex systems allow the pinpointing of subsets or parts of complex systems for analysis, and further the likely effects of integrating systems of systems.
- Abstractions of complex systems are generally much less expensive than the actual expressions of those systems (even in the case of software), and can thus serve as risk-mitigation approaches to the problems of large systems engineering.

None of this should be surprising to even the casual observer of engineering processes. Why, then, am I asked quite often why so many software developers do not model their systems before committing code to paper? The answer, of course, has more to do with human behavior than technology. It is a matter of training, of expectations, and of misunderstandings about the full costs of software development, and most importantly, it is the same reason that buggy whips were still made in quantity in 1910, when horse buggies were already on their way out as a primary method of transportation in favor of automobiles.

Modeling is key to engineering

While engineering has been developed over thousands of years—and as the authors of this book note—it *had* to be developed. That is, over the thousands of years of the creation of the engineering discipline, proven solutions have been developed, tested, and embedded in the body of knowledge of engineering. The authors of this tome state:

> *The use of models and modern model-based engineering technologies and related industry standards as a means of reducing accidental complexity in the development of real-time and embedded software is the primary theme of this book.*

In fact, it is more than the reduction of accidental complexity that models offer (see above), and it is far more than the development of real-time and embedded software.

A pedagogical example is relevant. On August 10, 1628, the great new warship Gustav Vasa (named after one of the greatest rulers of his time, Gustav Eriksson, otherwise known as Gustav I, King of Sweden) sailed proudly into its own home harbor and promptly sank into the Baltic mud, with the loss of 53 lives. Ships had been built for time immemorial all over the world, yet the nascent naval engineering field had not discovered how to compute the center of gravity of a large complex engineering system (like a ship), although it was certainly understood that a ship's center of gravity must always be below the waterline (or it will shortly find its way below the waterline, by process of sinking). This enormous, visible, deadly, and costly failure would spur (as all engineering failures do) a great leap in naval engineering, most importantly in modeling naval vessels. Further project management issues from the design and development of the Gustav Vasa (the untimely death of Henrik Hybertsson, the shipwright; the constantly changing specifications for the ship and its armaments; and most importantly a failed simulation of seaworthiness conducted before launch) contributed to a callosal failure, which was also a tremendously valuable failure that guaranteed better naval engineering in the future.

Engineered systems have always had a rather high level of expectation of success and correctness by the public at large; as engineering contributes to a better standard of life worldwide, it also engenders those expectations. Though civil engineers are aware that all engineered structures have some probability of failure, the public continues to be surprised when bridges fail; though naval engineers are aware of the same facts, the public continues to be surprised when ships sink. This gap can only be bridged by shared expectations of quality and cost, and quality and cost can only be brought into the engineering discipline through modeling.

Cyber-physical systems

There are various names for the connected nature of engineered systems that are largely (or entirely) dependent on correct underlying software systems:

- *Cyber-physical Systems*. Though this term directly brings together the cyber and physical worlds, it is quite a complicated term for the average person.
- *Internet of Things*. Though this term sounds fun for academics and other researchers, it seems too general to be acceptable.
- *Industrial Internet*. This term brings together the term most people understand to have changed the way we read, write, entertain ourselves, listen to music, and conduct many other activities (the Internet) with the largely unchanged way in which industrial systems are developed, delivered, and measured (consider the continuing use of ladder diagrams in discrete programmable control systems as a good example).

This move of industrial systems to the Internet only aggravates the need for correctness and completeness of software systems, pushing ever higher the expectation of correctness for cyber-physical systems.

Is a domain-specific language better than UML?

Given these expectations, how do we bring better development discipline to the software world, especially the real-time and embedded software world? And how to we deal with the bewildering blizzard of modeling languages? Is the Unified Modeling Language (UML) the best choice, or should we take a more domain-specific language (DSL) approach to ensure our designs are best matched to the system under development?

The reality is, of course, much simpler: the UML is just one of a large family of related modeling languages (including at least SysML, SoaML, UPDM, BPMN, UML for Systems on a Chip, and others), and is in fact a DSL (designed for use in software development, but used in other areas as well). The subject of this book, Modeling and Analysis of Real-Time and Embedded Systems (MARTE), is a DSL for designing, analyzing, and building embedded & real-time systems.

Implementations of the MARTE language are quite easy to find today, even if this book appears to be the first tome dedicated to its explication. Just as ships should never have been developed without understanding center of gravity issues after the failure of the Gustav Vasa, software-driven real-time and embedded systems should never again be built without a thorough analysis through the use of the MARTE language; to do so would simply be a negligent approach to engineering embedded systems. This makes this book indispensable for any engineer building the Industrial Internet of today and tomorrow, based on real-time and embedded systems.

May the Gustav Vasa sail again, this time without sinking!

Richard Mark Soley Ph.D.
Chairman and Chief Executive Officer,
Object Management Group, Inc.,
Brussels, Belgium

Preface

An honourable work glorifies its master—if it stands up

Lorenz Lechler, Instructions, 1516

Regardless of which statistics we are inclined to believe, there is little doubt that software systems all too often fail to "stand up."[1] There are many reasons for this, not the least of which is the often overwhelming complexity of such systems [4]. If we make a crude comparison with mechanical systems by equating a line of program code to a component in a machine, then even a simple 5,000-line program easily qualifies as a reasonably complex system in most people's judgment. Yet, there are numerous software systems in use today that incorporate millions and even tens of millions of lines of code.

In addressing complexity, it is helpful to distinguish between two types of complexity: (1) *essential complexity*, which is inherent to the purpose and nature of the system and is, therefore, unavoidable and (2) *accidental complexity*, that is, complexity that arises from the use of inadequate or ineffective methods and tools [2].

When it comes to real-time software systems, much of the essential complexity stems from the inescapable complexity of the physical world with which these systems interact. Needless to say, this world is highly concurrent, often unpredictable, interconnected in complex ways, and extremely diverse. Yet, the system and its software are required to cope successfully with at least some of these phenomena. Compounding our difficulties are resource limitations, such as limited processing speeds and limited amounts of memory, which further constrain our ability to address these issues. We have, over time, evolved a set of techniques and technologies to mitigate some of these difficulties, such as the use of mutual exclusion mechanisms for dealing with concurrency conflicts, or various redundancy patterns for dealing with failures. But, no matter how hard we try, these are essential characteristics of the problem, which cannot be eliminated by either process or technology.

Accidental complexity, on the other hand, is something that we can and, clearly, *must* strive to eliminate. Sadly, it is the authors' experience that real-time software development abounds with accidental complexity, perhaps because it is perceived as outside the mainstream of software engineering. It is typically developed using tools and methods that do not account for the specific problems of the real-time domain. A classical and notable example of this can be seen in the desire to ignore entirely the physical aspects of computing. For example, the well-known computing pioneer, Edsger Dijkstra, once wrote: "I see no meaningful difference between programming methodology and mathematical methodology," suggesting that software development should be a branch of applied mathematics [5]. This implies an idealized and, some would say, idealistic approach to software design, where physical factors are either ignored or deemed secondary. This line of thinking has led to development methods based on the simplifying but often inappropriate assumption that the time required to execute complex algorithms is negligible (the so-called "zero-time" assumption), or that there is a infinite

---

[1] The website http://www.it-cortex.com/Stat_Failure_Rate.htm maintains a collection of sources focusing on studies of software failure rates. Although there is some variance in the results across the different studies, they all indicate rates that would be deemed unacceptable in more traditional engineering disciplines.

supply of necessary resources available (memory, bandwidth, etc.). In fact, entire development methodologies have evolved that actively discourage any concerns with the physics of computing, which is reflected in oft-quoted but much misunderstood phrases such as "premature optimization" or "platform-independent design." Design issues related to the physical aspects of a computing system are typically bundled into a nebulous category referred to as "non-functional" issues, to be dealt with only *after* the "main" problem of functionality has been solved.

It is, of course, essential that a design realizes the desired functionality, but, as has often been pointed out producing the right output at the wrong time is still wrong. A program that takes 25 hours to predict tomorrow's weather is not particularly useful. However, any engineering problem needs to be addressed in its full context, which, at least in the case of real-time systems, necessarily includes the physical dimension of computing. After all, no matter how far we advance our software technologies, they will always require hardware to run. In a very pragmatic sense, computer hardware constitutes the raw material out of which our software systems are constructed. And, as with any technology, the raw material used and its properties must be accounted for and proper trade-offs made during system design.[2]

This incursion of the physical into the logical world of software is what distinguishes the design of real-time software most from other types of software. It requires that we extend our tools and methods beyond mathematics and enter the realm of *engineering*. Fortunately, engineering is a long-standing and well-developed discipline; it abounds with proven solution patterns that have evolved over thousands of years. One of the most fundamental and most useful of these is the use of *models and modeling* to support design. Models are used in many different ways in engineering, including, notably, helping us *predict* the key characteristics of designs before committing full resources to implementing them. This not only improves the overall reliability of our designs but also greatly reduces engineering risk and development time.

The use of models and modern model-based engineering technologies and related industry standards as a means of reducing accidental complexity in the development of real-time and embedded software is, in a way, the primary theme of this book.

About this book
Why this book

Interest in model-based methods for designing software has grown significantly since the introduction of the Unified Modeling Language (UML) and its adoption as an industry standard in the late 1990s. Quite naturally, this interest has extended to the real-time domain, resulting in the adoption of several real-time-oriented modeling language standards based on UML. The first of these, the UML Profile for Schedulability, Performance, and Time [12], was supplanted by the more advanced MARTE standard [13], which was aligned with the most recent major revision of UML, UML 2 [14].

MARTE, which stands for Modeling and Analysis of Real-Time and Embedded systems, is a *profile* of UML. A UML profile is a domain-specific interpretation of the general UML language that

---

[2]It is good to keep in mind a quote from a 2,000-year-old engineering text by the Ancient Roman engineer, Vitruvius: "All machinery is derived from nature, and is founded on the teaching and instruction of the revolution of the firmament."[18]

specializes some UML concepts to reflect domain phenomena and concerns. Because a properly defined profile is conformant to the rules and concepts of standard UML, it has the potential to reuse some of the existing UML tools, methods, and expertise. In the specific case of MARTE, the profile was not designed to displace UML but as a complementary domain-specific language.

MARTE provides broad coverage of the real-time domain and is the result of the collective work of numerous domain experts. The current version of the standard extends to almost 800 pages and is structured as a kind of reference manual with only a modicum of methodological guidance,[3] which is the standard format for all language specifications provided by the Object Management Group (OMG). Quite naturally, this presents an intimidating proposition for someone interested in learning about MARTE.

Consequently, this book is intended to provide a user-friendly introduction to the MARTE concepts and also to act as a methodological guide for their application in practice. It serves to identify and describe the key ideas behind MARTE, based on reduced and approachable (but nevertheless technically accurate) descriptions. However, beyond its core purpose as an introductory text, we expect that, because of its methodological content, the book will serve as a convenient user guide and reference even to expert MARTE users.

Modern model-based engineering for software development

The technical foundations for this book are the UML language and an approach to software development variously referred to as *model-based engineering*, *model-based development*, or *model-driven development* (we will use only the first of these in this book). Whatever we choose to call it, the essence of this approach is based on the use of models as an *essential* element of the development process. That is, it goes beyond the traditional exploitation of software models merely as a kind of power-assist and documentation facility. In particular, it means using models as an engineering tool for doing predictive analyses of key characteristics of proposed designs. In addition, given the unique nature of software, models of software systems can be used in a number of other ways, including, notably, computer-based code generation. This can greatly reduce the likelihood that design intent, which is captured in a model, will be corrupted during implementation. And, of course, it can also improve both productivity and overall design quality.

The OMG, UML, and MDA

The OMG[4] is an open not-for-profit computer industry consortium that develops and issues international standards for a wide range of computing-related technologies. It was established in 1989, focusing initially on distributed middleware standards, such as CORBA. However, with the increased interest in the object-oriented design methods that occurred in the mid 1990s, it broadened its scope to modeling and modeling languages for computer applications. The initial outcome of this expanded initiative was the Unified Modeling Language standard [14].

---

[3]This is by intent—specifications of this type generally avoid methodological aspects in order to remain open to a range of different approaches.

[4]http://www.omg.org

The original version of UML was primarily intended as a modest analysis and design support facility and, although it was supported by a semi-formal metamodel, its definition was not very precise. Nevertheless, despite such shortcomings, UML had a significant impact on the world of computing, indicating that there was a strong need for such a standard. As experience with UML grew, many of its users were interested in a more precise definition of the language that could be used for more advanced purposes such as automatic code generation and formal model analysis. As a result, a major revision of UML, UML 2, was released, characterized by a more precise and less ambiguous specification of its concepts. (This trend eventually led to a fully formal definition of a major subset of UML, called the Foundational Subset for Executable UML Models, or fUML [16].)

This trend to more formal modeling languages and greater exploitation of computer-based models culminated in a broadly based initiative to support model-based engineering with a corresponding set of industry standards. This is the Model-Driven Architecture (MDA) initiative, which covers a large number of modeling and related standards, including standards for model transformations, numerous UML profiles, and other modeling languages. The essence of MDA is to help raise the level of software design specifications by raising the level of abstraction covered by computer languages and, at the same time, to raise the level of computer-based automation to support those languages. MARTE is an integral part of the MDA initiative.

Prerequisites

As noted, MARTE is based on UML; it is a real-time extension of UML that directly supports concepts specific to that domain, such as semaphores, concurrent tasks, or schedulers and scheduling policies. Working with MARTE means working with UML, but with a slight real-time dialect. It is assumed, therefore, that readers have at least a basic familiarity with UML. There is no general tutorial material on UML in this book, although numerous examples of its usage are included. Readers who are unfamiliar with UML are advised to consult any of a number of introductory UML texts (e.g., [1], [11], and [17]) before approaching MARTE.

And, since this is a book for real-time system designers and developers, knowledge of and, ideally, some experience with the real-time domain and its various techniques is helpful. There are numerous excellent textbooks that provide good introductions to this domain, most notably the book by Burns and Wellings [3].

Complementary texts

To the best of the authors' knowledge, this is the first book to deal with the full breadth of MARTE and its usage. However, there are several texts that deal with the application of models and model-based methods that are complementary to this volume, including notably the comprehensive series of books by Gomaa [6–8]. The book by Lavagno et al. (2003) is a compendium of select articles from different authors on how to apply UML in a variety of different real-time problems [9].

What you will learn

The topics covered by the MARTE profile are grouped into two main categories: modeling and analysis. The former provides the capability to construct very precise models of real-time systems, including models that can be used for automatic code generation, while the latter deals with the ability to use MARTE to predict or validate important qualitative and quantitative characteristics of real-time system designs, such as timing and performance properties. This book covers both capabilities and explains not only what these capabilities are and how to use them, but also reveals the design rationale behind their realization in MARTE. This can help in making the most appropriate use of MARTE capabilities.

In addition, since each real-time system is unique in its own way, MARTE was designed to allow further specialization of its concepts to support the specifics of individual systems and projects. This capability is described in Chapter 12.

While the primary topic of this book is MARTE it also includes a chapter (Chapter 8) that describes the joint use of MARTE and the SysML language. SysML is another domain-specific UML profile adopted by the OMG, designed for use by systems engineers [15]. There is a natural synergy between these two domain-specific variants of UML. Namely, most real-time software is embedded within more complex technical systems, where it is typically given the role of controlling various electrical, mechanical, hydraulic, and other types of devices. The modern approach to the design of such systems, sometimes referred to as *cyber-physical systems*, is to deal with the system as a whole, rather than as a set of specialized parts that, once identified, are developed in isolation [10]. This fully matches the MARTE design philosophy, which recognizes that optimal design of complex systems involving heterogeneous technologies often requires design trade-offs between the different parts of the system.

Who should read this book

Broadly speaking, this text was targeted specifically at two types of readers. One category represents the *casual* reader, that is, a reader who is only interested in gaining basic understanding of MARTE and its capabilities. This could be, for example, a development team manager, a high-level system architect, or a researcher interested in learning about domain-specific languages for cyber-physical systems. Such a reader is likely to be interested mostly in introductory-level material. The second category comprises *practitioners*, that is, individuals who are directly responsible for designing, implementing, and analyzing software for cyber-physical systems and who are interested in finding out how to best take advantage of MARTE.

Accordingly, the text is structured to meet the needs of these two main categories of readers. The complete book is itself partitioned into introductory and detailed sections as are the individual chapters. The detailed parts are further subdivided into basic and more advanced topics, with the latter covering either less commonly used capabilities or delving into greater detail for those who are interested in such material.

Approach and structure of the book

This material in this book is split into five major parts, three of which correspond closely to the three major sections of the MARTE standard. However, in contrast to the standard, which uses a conventional reference manual format, we take a "how to" or use-case-driven approach. To that end, we selected a set of the most common design tasks encountered in real-time software design, and then describe various ways of realizing them using the appropriate concepts defined in the MARTE standard. The primary intent is to provide a more user-friendly view of MARTE compared to the standard itself, which has been fairly criticized for its complexity and lack of examples. Consequently, only a core subset of MARTE concepts and only the most common use cases are covered. The idea is to arm readers with sufficient knowledge to deal with the majority of standard design problems and, in cases where that may not be sufficient, to allow them to more easily navigate the full standard.

The first part, Introduction, contains a single overview chapter and serves as an introduction to MARTE. It starts with a prototypical (albeit somewhat simplistic) example to give readers an initial sense of how MARTE can be used. Following that, the purpose and the rationale behind the standard are explained and the primary use cases for it are identified. These use cases are used throughout the rest of the book to structure the detailed chapters.

Part II, Foundations, as its name suggests, describes the conceptual foundations of MARTE. Included here is an explanation of how the UML profile mechanism works. Experience has shown that this information is crucial for a proper understanding of profiles such as MARTE and how to make best use of them. Furthermore, it is also useful should there be a need to specialize MARTE for a particular domain or system (this is, in fact, one of the identified MARTE use cases), a topic which is covered in Part V. Also included in this part is an explanation of how MARTE extends UML to support various kinds of *physical values*, such as time-related information, resource limitations and capacities, etc. Needless to say, these play a crucial role in the design of any real-time system. Finally, concluding Part II is a description of two topics that are the very core of MARTE and which provide the essential bridge between the logical world of software and the physical world in which it must operate: the MARTE representations of time and resources.

Part III, Modeling with MARTE, explains how MARTE can be used to accurately model those parts of cyber-physical systems that involve software. As indicated earlier, this covers not only modeling of the application, but also modeling of the underlying platform, as well as specifying the relationships that exist between the two (i.e., deployment). Also included in this part is a description of how MARTE, which focuses on software, can be combined with the SysML language, which targets the broader issue of cyber-physical systems design.

The fourth part of the book, System Analysis Using MARTE, explains how MARTE can be exploited for analyzing designs in order to predict or validate their run-time characteristics, such as their performance and timing properties. MARTE provides a generic framework that supports a broad category of possible types of analyses that conform to a common pattern. Two of the most common of these, schedulability and performance, are directly supported by the standard and are described in this part of the book.

Finally, Part V deals with the more advanced topic of specializing MARTE for a particular purpose. A detailed example of such an extension is included, showing how MARTE can be extended to represent the AADL industry standard.

Three appendices complete the text. Appendix A provides an overview of the Value Specification Language (VSL), a textual language used primarily to specify quantitative information, including quantities involving physical dimensions such as time, weight, energy, etc. Appendix B contains a handy reference to the MARTE library of standard "non-functional properties." Appendix C provides a convenient quick reference guide to the MARTE concepts discussed in the book based on their primary purpose.

How to read this book

As noted earlier, this book targets two different categories of readers: (1) groups and individuals, such as development manages and systems engineers, who are not likely to personally construct MARTE-based models in their work but who still need to have a basic understanding of it and its capabilities, and (2) groups and individuals who will be using MARTE to build models representing their real-time systems. In the latter category, two levels are differentiated: general users and advanced users. Advanced users are those who need to exploit the full power of MARTE and, hence, need a deeper understanding of it. Information intended for this group of readers is explicitly identified by the word "[Advanced]" in the corresponding section titles. Of course, advanced users will most likely need to refer to the actual MARTE specification [13]. Nevertheless, these advanced sections may still be useful to such readers since they often provide explanations and rationale that may be missing or difficult to discern in the standard.

For "casual" readers in the first category, it is probably sufficient to just read the introductory chapter in Part I. If a bit more familiarity is desired, it is recommended to read the chapter on specifying non-functional properties (Chapter 3) as well as the chapter on modeling time and resources (Chapter 4).

New users of MARTE, both general and advanced, are advised to read the full material in both Part I and Part II before commencing on any of the remaining chapters. Also, MARTE users who are interested in doing model analysis should first read Chapter 9, which describes the general principles behind the analysis sub-profiles.

Once past these foundational chapters, readers can selectively read those sections in Parts III and IV that are relevant to their particular use cases and in whatever order suits their purpose best. Finally, Part V is intended for advanced users interested in customizing MARTE for their specific needs. This may occur more often than one might assume at first, especially in cases where there is a need for very precise specifications, such as using MARTE-based models for automated code generation or fine-grained and precise model analyses.

Typographical and diagramming conventions

To avoid possible confusion between user-defined names in models and "reserved" names, such as names of stereotypes and their attributes, the latter are written using a **bold** font, whereas user-defined names in *example models* are written using an Arial font. Note that, although many UML texts embed stereotype names between so-called guillemet quote marks (e.g., **«BinarySemaphore»**) we do not do so except in diagrams, which is where such marks are mandated by the rules of UML.

Also, to clearly distinguishes elements of the UML metamodel and MARTE stereotype definitions from user-defined models, these elements are depicted with a gray fill in diagrams in contrast to the white fill for user-defined models, as shown in Figure 1 below.

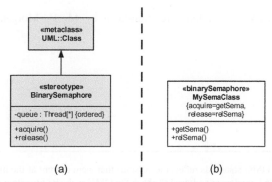

FIGURE 1 Formatting styles for (a) metamodel elements and stereotype definitions and (b) user model elements.

References*

The references to the various OMG standards reflect the versions that were current at the time of writing. However, since these standards are often updated, readers are advised to check the OMG web site (http://www.omg.org/) for possible newer versions.

[1] Booch G, Rumbaugh J, Jacobson I. The unified modeling language user guide, 2nd ed. Addison Wesley; 2005.

[2] Brooks Jr. F. Chapter 16 The mythical man-month (Anniversary Edition). Addison Wesley; 1995.

[3] Burns A, Wellings A. Real-time systems and programming languages: ada, real-time Java and C/Real-Time POSIX, 4th ed. Addison Wesley; 2009.

[4] Charette R. Why software fails. IEEE Spectr 2005;42(9):42–9.

[5] Dijkstra EW. Why American computing science seems incurable (EWD 1209), The Edsger W. Dijkstra Archive at the University of Texas, 1995, <http://www.cs.utexas.edu/~EWD/ewd12xx/EWD1209.PDF>.

[6] Gomaa H. Software modeling and design: UML, use cases, patterns, and software architectures. Cambridge University Press; 2011.

[7] Gomaa H. Designing software product lines with UML: from use cases to pattern-based software architectures. Addison Wesley; 2004.

[8] Gomaa H. Designing concurrent and real-time applications with UML. Addison Wesley; 2000.

[9] Lavagno L, Martin G, Selic B. UML for real: design of embedded real-time systems. Kluwer Academic Publishers; 2003.

[10] Lee E, Seshia S. Introduction to embedded systems—a cyber-physical systems approach, Lulu.com, also: <http://leeseshia.org>, 2003.

[11] Milicev D. (WROX Series) Model-driven development with executable UML. Wiley Publishing; 2009.

[12] Object Management Group, The, UML™ Profile for Schedulability, Performance, and Time Specification, Version 1.1, OMG document no. formal/2005-05-01, 2005.

[13] Object Management Group, The, A UML Profile for MARTE: Modeling and Analysis of Real-Time and Embedded Systems, Version 1.1, OMG document no. formal/2011-06-02, 2011.

[14] Object Management Group, The, OMG Unified Modeling Language™ (OMG UML), Superstructure, Version 2.4.1, OMG document no. formal/2011-08-06, 2011.

[15] Object Management Group, The, OMG Systems Modeling Language (OMG SysML™), Version 1.3, OMG document no. formal/2012-06-01, 2012.

[16] Object Management Group, The, Semantics of a Foundational Subset for Executable UML Models (fUML), Version 1.1, OMG document no. ptc/2012-10-18, 2012.

[17] Rumbaugh J, Jacobson I, Booch G. The unified modeling language reference manual, 2nd ed. Addison Wesley; 2004.

[18] Vitruvius, The Ten Books on Architecture (translated by M. H. Morgan), Dover Publications Inc., New York, 1960.

---

*The references to the various OMG standards reflect the versions that were current at the time of writing. However, since these standards are often updated, readers are advised to check the OMG web site http://www.omg.org for possible newer versions.

Introduction to MARTE

An Overview of MARTE

CHAPTER CONTENTS

1.1 INTRODUCTION

MARTE is a domain-specific modeling language intended for model-based design and analysis of real-time and embedded software of cyber-physical systems. It is designed as a supplement to UML, providing capabilities that are either inadequate or missing in UML. Since MARTE is defined as a profile of UML, the integration of the two languages is seamless. To better illustrate how MARTE complements UML and how it can be used, we include in this chapter a simple example demonstrating where and how it is used. However, we will first provide an answer to a question that is frequently asked when model-based engineering is proposed as an approach to software development.

1.2 Why model?

Models and modeling have been essential tools of engineering since pre-history. In fact, as pointed out by Joshua Epstein, anyone "who ventures a projection or imagines how some system or event would unfold is doing modeling"[2]. This clearly includes any design work, including the design of software. Of course, much modeling is implicit, done inside our heads. But, in the stringent world of formal engineering, it is generally necessary to validate our models, in order to explain and justify our design choices both to ourselves and to others. This requires that the models be rendered explicit, so that they can be reviewed, analyzed, validated, transformed, and manipulated in various other ways. Clearly, such models should be in a form that is understood by all stakeholders. The latter requirement is helped if the model is specified using some agreed-on standards, such as UML and MARTE.

We define an engineering model as: *a reduced representation of some system that captures accurately and concisely all of the essential properties of interest for a given set of concerns*. That is, a model is a selective representation that emphasizes the essential features of the modeled system while either omitting or hiding from view inessential information. Selective representation of information so that only the essentials are visible is a fundamental feature of any useful model, since it helps us cope with what might otherwise be overwhelming complexity. Of course, what is considered essential depends on the stakeholder, which means that different categories of stakeholders will require different models or views of a given system.

In engineering, models and modeling serve a number of related purposes:

- To *reason* about the problem and potential solutions
- To support *communication* and consensus between stakeholders (especially if they have conflicting requirements)
- To enable *prediction* of important properties of the modeled system
- To *specify* what is to be implemented; i.e., the use of models as blueprints for implementation, including computer-based models that may be used as "complete" system specifications that, in case of models of software, can be automatically translated into equivalent program code or executed directly on a computer.

Depending on which of these is the primary purpose of a model, the form and degree of detail provided in an application model will vary. The most detailed models are ones that are used as specifications, with the extreme case where the model is used to automatically generate an implementation requiring the most detail and precision. These types of models are known as *prescriptive* models. In contrast, *descriptive* models primarily serve the other three purposes and tend to be less detailed. A model used for prediction (e.g., by formal analysis methods) tends to be quite detailed for those aspects of the system used in the analysis, but has much less detail about other aspects and may even omit them completely. Models used for analysis and communication are typically the least detailed, since an excess of detail tends to impede understanding.

1.3 A simple example

To illustrate where MARTE can prove useful, consider a very simple `PreciseClock` software application. The purpose of this software system is to display the current time on a specialized LED display device with a high degree of precision. Specifically, we want the value displayed to be precise within 100 microseconds of the actual time as maintained by an internal hardware clock.

For the design of this system, we have chosen a straightforward design represented by the class diagram shown in Figure 1.1. Note that, as shown, this is just a straightforward UML model—we have yet to apply MARTE to it.

To avoid wasteful busy-wait loops, this system is designed as a concurrent application that is activated every 100 microseconds. To ensure adequate response time, it is required to complete *all* of its computations within that time interval. At first glance, this may not seem like much of a design challenge given the speed of modern computers, until we consider the possibility that other real-time applications may be running simultaneously on the same computing platform.

The application-specific part of this program is contained in the Displayer class. Since we have decided to make it a concurrent application, Displayer is an *active* UML class (indicated by the vertical bars on the side of the class box). Although UML does not associate the active class concept with any particular implementation technology, in practice this usually means that each instance of this class will be executing within its own dedicated operating system thread (e.g., a Linux thread or process). Instances of the Displayer class interact with two other entities: an instance of another active class, Timer, and an instance of the special hardware device, LEDDisplay. A Timer instance is created by the Displayer as part of its initialization and set to send a timeout signal every 100 microseconds back to the Displayer.[1] Upon the arrival of the signal, the Displayer instance computes the new value that is to be displayed, converts it to a string representing that value, and then synchronously invokes the display operation on the LEDDisplay device. The full life cycle of this application is described by the UML sequence diagram shown in Figure 1.2. Note the inclusion of the constraint TOT, which only *partially* captures our timing requirement. It states that the interval from the instant when the Timer instance is activated to the instant that the display operation is invoked must not exceed 100 time units.

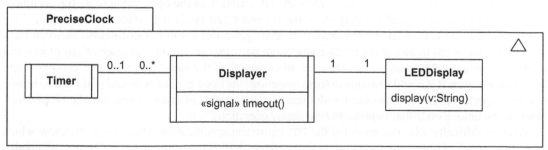

FIGURE 1.1

Class diagram of the elements of the **PreciseClock** application.

---

[1] The details of how the behavior of the Displayer class is specified are of no interest here and are omitted.

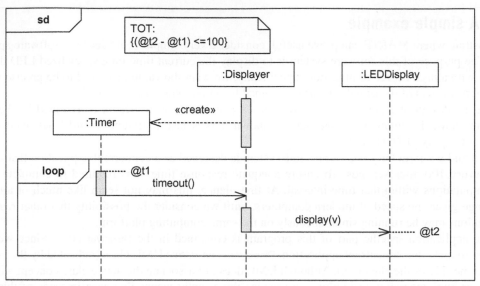

FIGURE 1.2

The required behavior of the **PreciseClock** application.

Note, however, that this model is merely a convenient high-level UML-based representation of what actually happens in the real system. For one, the Displayer task does not actually create a timer as the diagram in Figure 1.2 indicates. Instead, if we examined the technical details, we would see that the task merely invokes an underlying operating system function that actually creates the timer. However, although this is not a fully accurate representation, it may be both adequate and convenient for analysis and communication purposes, where such low-level technical detail is irrelevant. Similarly, LEDDisplay is not a software object with an explicit display function, as suggested by the sequence diagram, but is a hardware device that is accessed through an operating system mechanism that involves low-level interrupts and device drivers.

A model of this type may suffice as a high-level description of the application (e.g., for documentation, brainstorming, or analysis purposes), but it cannot satisfy all our needs. For example, if we wanted to generate code from such a model, the code generator could not distinguish between parts for which code needs to be generated (Displayer) from parts that are merely representations of external entities (Timer and LEDDisplay), since they are all examples of the same general UML class concept. Furthermore, even if it could distinguish them somehow, the code generator would still need to understand the special semantics associated with these model elements in order to generate the proper code (such as the unique code that implements the display operation).

Another difficulty with this model is the TOT constraint specification: How are we to know which time units (milliseconds? microseconds?) are associated with the value 100? We could, of course, agree on a default time unit, but this may become cumbersome and error prone should we need to specify values in the same model that are different orders of magnitude (e.g., from days to microseconds). In addition, such a model-specific convention could not be captured easily in UML in a way that could be recognized and exploited by external tools such as code generators.

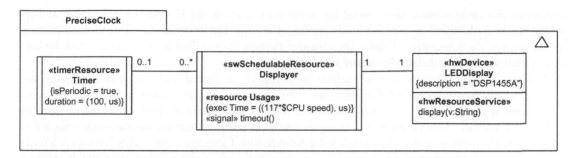

FIGURE 1.3

UML model of the **PreciseClock** application annotated using MARTE concepts.

Finally, perhaps the greatest problem that this type of UML model presents is that it cannot help us determine with a high degree of confidence that the required time constraint is guaranteed to be fulfilled.[2] Recall that there could be other applications executing on the same processor, which could get in the way of a timely response by either the Timer or the Displayer. Additional factors that need to be accounted for include the characteristics of the hardware clock that serves as a reference (e.g., accuracy, jitter, resolution), the efficiency of the underlying operating system in responding to clock interrupts, the execution time overhead of interrupt handlers, and any scheduling and dispatching overheads involved in executing the Timer and Displayer threads. These are all a function of the characteristics of the underlying platform and the coresident applications sharing that platform, which suggests that we need to include a model of the platform in addition to the application model.

We can use UML for this purpose, but, once again we run into the problem that standard UML does not recognize any special semantics associated with concepts such as interrupt handlers, schedulers, clocks, etc., and, thus, lacks the facility to formally capture these important characteristics in the model. This limits the utility of such models, since they cannot be precise enough to help us conduct trustworthy formal analyses or to automatically generate the appropriate code.

MARTE was designed to augment UML with these missing capabilities. For example, Figure 1.3 shows one possible MARTE-based version of the class diagram for the PreciseClock application. In this case, we have added the necessary annotations that identify what kinds of elements are represented by the classes in the diagram as well as some of their key characteristics. These annotations are packaged into units called *stereotypes* and are identified in diagrams by labels enclosed between paired guillemet quotation marks (e.g., «**timerResource**»). In most cases, these stereotypes include a list of additional properties and their corresponding values specified by a string between braces (e.g., "{isPeriodic = true, duration = (100, us)}").

Note that each of these annotations has well-defined and standardized semantics (as specified in the MARTE specification [7]). The Timer class is explicitly denoted as a periodic **TimerResource**,[3] a MARTE stereotype, with a period of 100 microseconds (specified by: **duration= (100, us)**). The

---

[2]Such "hard" guarantees are often required in many real-time and embedded systems, particularly in safety-critical applications.

[3]In this model and throughout the book, we will use the common convention of defining stereotype names with uppercase initial letters, but using lowercase initial letters when those same stereotypes are applied to model elements.

LEDDisplay device is marked as a special hardware device, using the **HwDevice** stereotype, and its display function identified as a special hardware-based service (**HwResourceService**) to distinguish it from a regular class operation. Finally, the Displayer element is identified as a concurrent task by tagging it with the **SwSchedulableResource** stereotype.

Note in particular that the timeout feature of Displayer is tagged with the **ResourceUsage** stereotype, which is a generic MARTE annotation for specifying the utilization factor of a resource. In this case, it is the amount of processor resources used by the timeout method, expressed in terms of CPU time consumed (**execTime**). In this example, instead of a literal value for the execution time, a formula is provided, specified using MARTE's Value Specification Language (VSL). This formula is a function of a VSL variable, CPUspeed,[4] which represents the relative speed of the underlying CPU. By using a variable here instead of a concrete value in this place, we have the opportunity to experiment with different values without changing the model or creating a different model for every value of interest.

Finally, we need to specify precisely the 100 microsecond time constraint. We can do this by adding a MARTE timed constraint (based on the **TimedConstraint** stereotype) to the behavior model, as shown in Figure 1.4. It states unambiguously that the *duration* between instants **t2** and **t1** is *required* to be less than or equal to 100 microseconds. (The stereotype **TimedInstantObservation** is used to associate a common reference clock with the two time instants.)

The platform itself can also be modeled using MARTE, which provides domain-specific stereotypes for precise modeling of a wide variety of computing platform resources, both hardware and software. These are described in more detail in Chapter 6. A simple platform model that could be

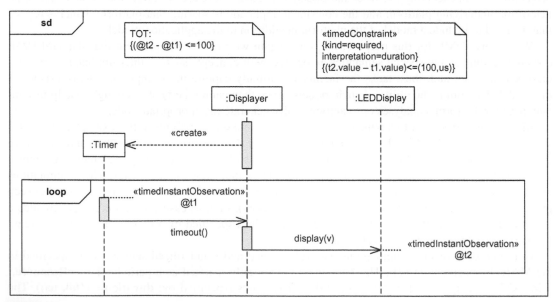

FIGURE 1.4

The interaction from Figure 1.2 with MARTE annotations.

---

[4] The dollar sign ($) prefixing the variable name indicates that this is where the variable is declared.

used with the PreciseClock application is shown in Figure 1.5. Note that the value of the **speedFactor** attribute associated with the **processingResource** stereotype, as applied to the Processor class, is defined by the VSL variable CPUspeed. It is the same variable that is referenced directly in the application model in Figure 1.3.

Finally, one last step may be needed to complete this model. But, before we do that, it should be noted that the two models in Figures 1.3 and 1.5 are related to two different concerns. The application model captures the software aspects of the application—intentionally decoupled from the underlying implementation technology. The platform model, on the other hand, is a technology-specific model, showing the hardware and software technologies that can be used to implement the application. If we are interested in understanding the impact that the platform technology can have on the application, we need to combine these two models into a single unified model.

This unification involves identifying elements that appear in both models, albeit in different form because they are represented from different viewpoints, and binding them in some way. For example, instances of the active Displayer class can be implemented by instances of platform class Thread. One way that this binding could be realized is to make Displayer a subclass of Thread. However, this is *not* recommended, because it mixes two different viewpoints in the same model. Furthermore, if the application is capable of running on different platforms, it would require a separate model for each platform, with the application elements cloned in each.

Instead, we choose a different approach to bind elements that are shared by the two models, based on the MARTE **Allocate** concept (see Chapter 7), as shown in the diagram in Figure 1.6.

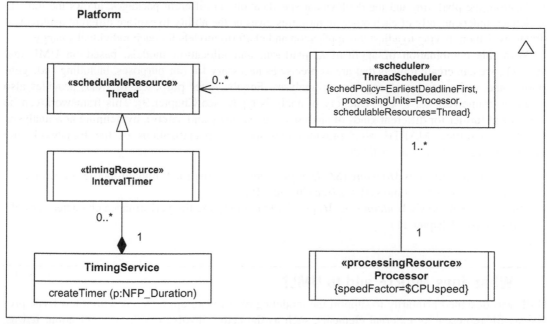

FIGURE 1.5

A MARTE model of a simple computing platform for the **PreciseClock** application.

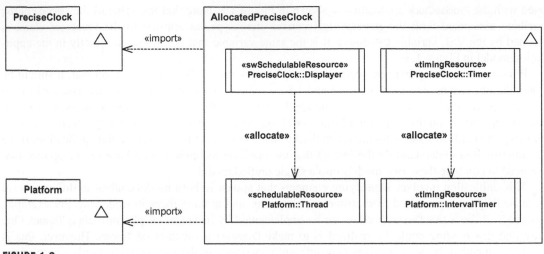

FIGURE 1.6

Allocating elements of the application model to corresponding platform model elements.

Note that, in order to keep the platform and application models as independent as possible, we have introduced a third model, AllocatedPreciseClock, in which to introduce the binding. If an alternative deployment is desired, a different allocation model would have to be defined. This approach, with the application, the platform, and the deployment specifications in different packages, allows the three to be defined independently of each other. In turn, this gives us the ability to explore different deployment strategies without having to adjust the application and platform models for each individual strategy.

With this combination of application, platform, and allocation models, based on UML and MARTE, we can create models that are as precise as necessary for our purposes, including code generation and various types of engineering analyses. For the latter purposes, MARTE provides also a generic framework for a wide category of analysis types (see Chapter 9). This framework can be specialized further for different kinds of analyses (e.g., security and safety), by defining new analysis-specific subprofiles. MARTE itself provides two specific specializations of the framework that exploits established analysis methods:

- *Schedulability Analysis Modeling (SAM)* profile: For analyzing the timing properties of certain common types of real-time systems (see Chapter 10).
- *Performance Analysis Modeling (PAM)* profile: For computing the performance characteristics of software (see Chapter 11).

1.4 What does MARTE add to UML?

UML was designed primarily to support the modeling of software applications with a few basic provisions for representing external elements, such as the actors involved with an application. It was, therefore, constructed with a very software-centric "logical" view of the world, with little attention given to the characteristics of the underlying computing technology. However, as noted earlier, in the domain of cyber-physical systems, including real-time and embedded applications, characterized by more onerous quality of service requirements, due consideration must be given to technological concerns, since they can play a fundamental role in the design.

MARTE was designed to fulfill that need. Specifically, it supplements standard UML with the following basic capabilities. These are of major importance in real-time systems design but are either missing or inadequately supported in the UML standard. These capabilities include the following:

- The ability to define and specify, as precisely as desired, different types of quantitative and qualitative measures[5] associated with a UML model and its various elements, as well as any functional relationships that may exist between them. For example, it may be necessary to specify the worst-case execution time of a code fragment or the required bandwidth capacity of a communications link.
- A precise, comprehensive, and flexible model of time, which can be adapted to suit application needs, including physically distributed systems.
- The ability to accurately model hardware *resources*, that is, model elements that represent entities with a physical underpinning, such as processors, memory, input and output devices, networks, and so forth.
- The ability to accurately model software resources specific to real-time and embedded software, such as threads, processes, or mutexes.
- The ability to accurately capture the relationships between software applications and the computing platforms that support them. This includes the ability to represent how elements of a software application are allocated (deployed) to various platform components, which is an important element in the design of distributed applications.

With these added capabilities and appropriate formal analysis methods and corresponding tools, it is often possible to automatically or semi-automatically predict or validate key performance indicators of a proposed design, long before committing to its implementation. This enables early detection of design flaws thereby greatly reducing engineering risk. As already mentioned, to that end, MARTE provides the following additional important capabilities:

- A general framework for supporting various kinds of engineering analyses along with two practical customizations of that framework: one for analyzing the real-time characteristics of certain categories of multitasking applications (known as "schedulability" analysis) and another for computing performance-related properties such as end-to-end delays, average response and waiting times, etc. It is, of course, possible to supplement these with additional customizations for other types of analyses, such as risk, availability, or security.

1.5 Conceptual foundations and design principles

MARTE replaces an earlier standardized UML profile called the *UML Profile for Scheduling, Performance, and Time* (SPT) [6]. This profile was based on the initial version of UML (UML 1.3),

---

[5]The term "non-functional property" is often used for this; however, even though it is also used in the MARTE standard itself, we generally prefer to avoid it. We feel that, with its vague and negative connotation, it creates the misleading and often dangerous impressions that such properties are inherently less important than so-called "functional" properties. (In principle, concepts should be named based on what they are and not based on what they are not.)

and covered a narrower scope. While MARTE has retained the general conceptual foundations and the organizational structure of its predecessor, it has significantly enhanced both, providing much more expressive and more powerful modeling facilities. Unfortunately, this has also resulted in a more complex and bulkier specification, with the undesirable consequence that it is more difficult to identify and understand its basic paradigms and organizing principles. Therefore, the purpose of the following sections is to describe the salient conceptual frameworks and design principles that drove much of the contents of MARTE. Readers interested in a deeper study of MARTE may find this material particularly useful before delving into the details of the actual specification.

1.5.1 **Foundational concepts: Applications, platforms, and deployment**

Software people often forget—or prefer to forget—that it takes hardware to make software useful. While the well-known design principle of writing software to be independent of computing hardware makes eminent sense, we must keep in mind that it is an ideal that is not always possible to achieve in practice. This is because all hardware has limits: it is not infinitely fast, there is only a finite quantity of it, and, it has imperfections that sometimes cause it to misbehave. Consequently, computations can be late, applications can run out of memory, and electronic circuits can fail. This is simply a reflection of the laws of physics imposing themselves on the highly abstract logical world of software. In a very real sense, it can be said that hardware is the raw material out of which software applications are constructed. And, like any construction material, its physical characteristics can have a significant impact on the end product.

So, how can we account for these undesirable but often unavoidable limitations of hardware when designing software? Clearly, to achieve this we must understand the following:

- The structure and physical characteristics (e.g., capacity, speed, and reliability) of the hardware *platform*.
- The relationship between elements of the application and elements of the platform; i.e., the *deployment* of software to hardware.

Hence, the world view of MARTE can be summarized simply by the diagram in Figure 1.7.

While standard UML also supports modeling of both deployment and platforms, in addition to application modeling this is often far from adequate, as illustrated in Section 1.1.

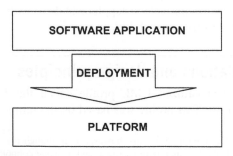

FIGURE 1.7

MARTE world view.

It is worth noting here that the concept of platform is a relative one: for instance, a software application may rely on a framework, such as Microsoft's.Net[6] or JavaBeans™ from Oracle,[7] as its platform. However, a framework of this type typically requires an operating system as its platform, and so on. In other words, an application may serve as a platform for a higher level application, which means that a platform is not exclusively a hardware-based concept. In general, *a platform is any combination of external software and hardware resources required by a software application to run successfully.* Of course, the hardware platform invariably lies at the bottom of all such platform hierarchies and its physical properties necessarily affect the performance and characteristics of all the other platforms sitting on top of it. Therefore, it is fundamental to be able to accurately represent the hardware elements and their physical characteristics, and MARTE provides a rich set of concepts for this purpose. Moreover, given the pace of innovation in hardware, it also provides the ability to specialize these further or to introduce new ones.

1.5.2 Foundational concepts (1): Resources, brokers, services, usages

MARTE addresses the issue of capturing platform limitations through its core concept of a *resource*. A dictionary definition of this word states that it represents "a source of supply, support, or aid, especially one that can be readily drawn upon when needed."[8] As we all know, however, resources can run out and, even if they are "readily" available, there may not be enough of them to suit our needs. This is the situation that all engineers must address, regardless of the specific nature of their disciplines. Many different kinds of engineering analyses can be reduced to answering the question: Will the available resources be sufficient to satisfy the system requirements? That is, will the supply of resources meet demand?

Consequently, MARTE uses the well-known *client-server* pattern for modeling the relationship between an application and the underlying platform. This may in some cases involve three parties: a *client*, that is, the application element that needs resources; a *resource broker*, responsible for managing and dispensing resources under its control and which represents the server; and the actual *resources*. Of course, in cases, where the client accesses a resource directly, the broker is omitted.

For example, when an application component, such as the AppTask class instance shown in Figure 1.8, needs to dynamically create a new instance of some utility class (e.g., ClassX), the request is eventually routed to the platform's HeapManager. This is the broker responsible for managing the heap resource. In this example, the heap is represented by an instance of the Memory class. By tagging it with the **HwMemory** stereotype, we can specify the size of the heap (4096 MB in this case). If the HeapManager determines that there are sufficient memory resources available to fulfill the request, a block of memory of the appropriate size is allocated to the application.

Servicing any resource request invariably consumes some resources. In MARTE, the consumption of resources is referred to as a *resource usage*. Obviously, the type of usage depends on the type of resource. For example, each dynamic object creation consumes some memory and some CPU time. We can specify precisely how much of a resource is used, by tagging the appropriate model element with the MARTE **ResourceUsage** stereotype. This stereotype includes a number of optional parameters, including how much memory is required by a service request (**allocatedMemory**). In the UML

---

[6]http://www.microsoft.com/net.
[7]http://docs.oracle.com/javase/tutorial/javabeans/index.html.
[8]http://dictionary.reference.com/browse/resource?s=t.

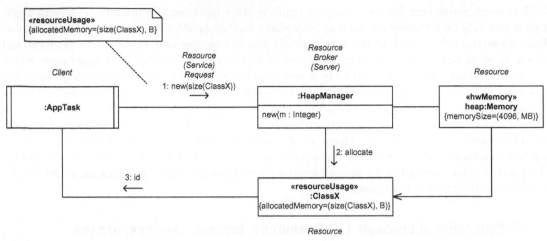

FIGURE 1.8

The general **client-server resource** pattern of MARTE and resource usage.

communication diagram shown in Figure 1.8, we have chosen to represent the **new** operation of HeapManager as a kind of resource usage, tagged it as such, and specified the execution time that the operation takes (specified by a VSL expression). Similarly, we have also represented the allocated memory block for ClassX as a resource usage, and specified the amount of memory allocated.

On the client side, we use the **ResourceUsage** stereotype to specify the resource *demands*. In our example, we have associated the usage with the new message passed between the application task and the heap manager, specifying the amount of memory required.

In summary, the concepts of resources and their services, combined with the ability to precisely specify the supply and demand sides of resource usage, are the means by which MARTE handles the physical aspects of running software. This general pattern appears in various different customized forms throughout MARTE, adjusted to individual resource types.

1.5.3 Foundational concepts (2): Physical data types and values

As can be seen from the examples in this chapter, to support meaningful engineering analysis, it is necessary to support the representation of various physical qualities, such as duration, speed, and memory capacity as well as their values. To this end, MARTE includes a handy library of *physical data types* for capturing a wide variety of such qualities, as well as the VSL language for specifying precisely and unambiguously their values and, if required, functional dependencies that may exist between different values. A value of a physical type includes not only a quantity but also specifies the corresponding physical unit, and may optionally include additional qualifiers about the value, such as whether it represents an estimate or a measurement, or its degree of precision.

1.5.4 Foundational concepts (3): Time and timed behavior

Inherently, time plays a crucial role in real-time and embedded software applications and needs to be properly accounted for in many kinds of engineering analyses. Therefore, the ability to accurately specify time, its conceptual model (i.e., whether it is represented as logical, physical, discrete, continuous, relative, or absolute time), its sources and devices (i.e., clocks and timers), and its passage and its measurement, is a defining feature of MARTE. Furthermore, MARTE allows time and its progress to be associated with model elements that represent dynamic behavior, such as operation invocations, messages, state machine transitions, actions and activities, and so forth. For example, there is in MARTE a concept (stereotype) called **RtFeature** ("real-time feature"), which can have associated time-related properties, such as absolute or relative deadlines. With that, MARTE can explicitly associate various model elements with the time that they consume or require, something that is not possible with basic UML. Namely, the standard UML model of time assumes a single ideal physical clock, whose beat implicitly orchestrates the behavior of modeled systems.

1.5.5 Foundational concepts (4): Class/instance unification [Advanced]

Contrary to UML, which uses different concepts to represent classes and instances of classes, MARTE often uses the exact same stereotype for both. Most notably, the MARTE **Resource** concept (stereotype), which is the common ancestor of a very large variety of specialized resource types, can be applied to model elements that represent classifiers (**UML::Class**, or **UML::Interface**) as well as to elements that represent instances of such classifiers. The latter can appear in many different forms: as object instances, links, class attributes, parts in structured classes, roles in collaborations, and lifelines. This is a convenience intended to avoid possible confusion that might result from having two (or more) stereotypes with different names but with exactly the same attributes.

Applying this kind of multipurpose stereotype to a class usually defines a category of instances with shared attributes, such as specific resource *types* (e.g., **StorageResource**, **ProcessingResource**, and **CommunicationResource**), and except for possible defaults, the values of the stereotype attributes are left undefined. Conversely, when they are applied to model elements that represent instances, at least the attributes applicable to that instance would typically be assigned values, which can be used in analysis.

Given that real systems consist of instances rather than classifiers, most analyses are performed on models or parts of models that represent instances of applications. For example, a typical class model would not specify exactly how many hops are encountered in a given path through a network (other than to say that there may be "many" (i.e., 0..*)), but the exact number is obviously necessary for calculating the overall delay.

1.5.6 Core design principle (1): Support for concern-specific representations [Advanced]

Many engineering analyses need to represent a system from a different viewpoint than the one that is captured in its UML-MARTE design model. For instance, a particular model that we want to analyze for its timing properties may not actually include an explicit clock element. So, if the characteristics of this clock (e.g., resolution and drift) are required to perform the analysis, where do we put this information? One possibility, of course, is that we add a clock element to the model—even though it was not required in the original model. However, you can imagine what kind of cluttered model we could end up with, if we were to add elements for each kind of analysis that we want to perform. Alternatively, we could construct a new analysis-specific model. But, this too can be problematic since it involves duplication and a possible profusion of models, all of which need to be maintained and kept in sync with each other as the respective designs evolve.

In some cases, a better approach might be to include the missing elements *implicitly*, by associating their properties with directly related model elements. For our clock example, the clock attributes can be attached to an event that is a direct consequence of the beat of the clock. This approach is widely supported by many MARTE stereotypes, with the intent of reducing the amount of changes to a model required to enable model analysis (in the ideal case, no changes would be required). For example, the **Clock** stereotype can be applied not only to object instances (instances of the UML concept **InstanceSpecification**) and class attributes (instances of **UML::Property**) but also to instances of **UML::Event**. Similarly, the **RtFeature** stereotype mentioned earlier can be applied to operations, receptions, invocation actions, messages, signals, and even ports. Even though these are conceptually quite different kinds of things, in such cases they will all have the same interpretation because they are tagged with the same stereotype.

1.5.7 Core design principle (2): Composite stereotypes [Advanced]

To reduce the number of stereotypes, many MARTE stereotypes combine features from a variety of potential specializations into a single concept. Consider, for example, the **ResourceUsage** stereotype discussed earlier and shown in Figure 1.9.

It is unlikely that all of these attributes will ever be required at the same time. For instance, the **execTime** attribute may be needed for timing analysis, while **powerPeak** and energy are likely to be used only for energy consumption calculations. On the other hand, **execTime** and **allocatedMemory** might be combined in some cases. The number and type of possible combinations of attributes can be significant and depends on the type of analysis desired. Rather than define a different stereotype for each such combination, as a pragmatic measure, they are all combined into the same concept. Fortunately, their attributes are all optional (since their lower multiplicity bounds are zero) and only the ones that are of interest need be used (even in cases where the attributes are not optional, the ones that are not used will default to a value of null.).

1.5.8 Core design principle (3): Modularity for scalability [Advanced]

The MARTE specification is quite large (close to 800 pages), which may intimidate some potential users. But, as stated by Albert Einstein, "Everything should be made as simple as possible, but no

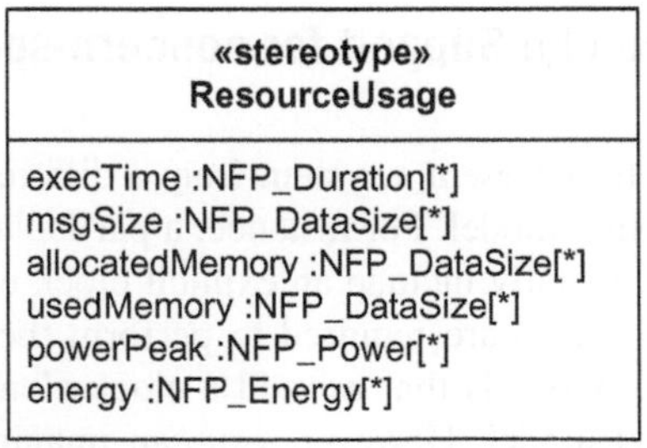

```
            «stereotype»
            ResourceUsage
    ───────────────────────────────
    execTime :NFP_Duration[*]
    msgSize :NFP_DataSize[*]
    allocatedMemory :NFP_DataSize[*]
    usedMemory :NFP_DataSize[*]
    powerPeak :NFP_Power[*]
    energy :NFP_Energy[*]
```

FIGURE 1.9

The definition of the MARTE::**ResourceUsage** stereotype.

simpler."[9] Due to the intended broad scope of the specification, the complexity of designing and analyzing real-time and embedded systems, and the diversity of mechanisms used in their realization, the number of essential concepts that needed to be covered by MARTE was necessarily large. Moreover, much of the bulk of the specification is due to ensuring very precise definitions and including numerous examples and illustrations. Fortunately, this concern was recognized from the start, so that the structure of MARTE was designed to be highly modular. As a result, users need only concern themselves with those parts of the spec that are relevant to their needs, safely ignoring the rest. This also applies to the definition of the profile, which is equally modular, so that only those subprofiles that are needed can be applied to a model.

To assist MARTE users, the specification has crisply defined units of reuse that can be combined in a minimal manner to fit some precise set of concerns (the Conformance section of the specification provides the complete list of units [7]).

1.6 Standard use cases for MARTE

MARTE is rich and extensible enough to be used in many different ways. However, here we identify several of the most common use cases. These are described separately but they can be and often are combined either by performing them in succession or concurrently, depending on the circumstances on hand and the chosen development process (e.g., [8]). For example, the application and platform models could be developed in parallel or in sequence.

1.6.1 Use case (1): Application modeling

This use case occurs either when an *application modeler* is attempting to design a real-time application model from scratch or is modifying an existing one, or, alternatively, when it is necessary to reverse engineer an existing software program by constructing a model.

Most real-time applications have some type of strict physical constraints such as response times, load capacities (e.g., requests handled per unit of time), and resource usage (e.g., memory capacity and CPU performance) that they must meet. In such cases, MARTE is used to specify such constraints directly and to associate them with appropriate model elements. Furthermore, since practically all such constraints are either directly or indirectly dependent on the capacities and capabilities of the underlying platform, MARTE is also used to specify the required platform resources and their quality of service characteristics.

For example, a real-time banking application may need to handle a specific minimal number of transactions per second, while ensuring that the response times are kept to acceptable levels. These may, in turn, impose requirements on memory capacity (to handle queued requests) and CPU and disk performance. Furthermore, to avoid concurrency conflicts, application designers may need to specify where mutual exclusion must be provided, including, possibly, the particular nature of the mutual exclusion mechanisms to be used (e.g., semaphore, monitor, or critical region). None of these categories are recognized in standard UML but they are all directly supported by MARTE constructs.

---

[9]There is some doubt that this quote actually originated with Einstein although it is usually attributed to him (see http://quoteinvestigator.com/2011/05/13/einstein-simple/#more-2363).

Note the dependency between the requirements imposed on the application from a user point of view (e.g., transactions per second) and the platform requirements specified in the model (e.g., CPU performance). A key design challenge for application modelers is to determine whether the specified platform requirements will support the stated application requirements; that is, will the combination of the chosen design and the required platform resources and their specified qualities of service be sufficient to meet the application needs? This type of question (if it is asked at all[10]) is often answered by an informal analysis of the model dependent on the experience of the design team and supplemented possibly with some rough back-of-the-envelope calculations. However, because of the intricate interdependencies between various elements of a complex design and their characteristics, this approach is far from reliable and has led to numerous project failures in practice.

A more reliable alternative is to seek an answer by taking advantage of appropriate formal analyses methods that are based on proven theoretical foundations. Practical examples of such methods are queuing theory [3], used to compute the statistical performance characteristics of a software application, and schedulability theory [4], for computing the timing properties of an important category of real-time applications. However, even this approach can be problematic because individual analysis methods typically operate on analysis-specific models. This means that the UML-MARTE model needs to be converted before it can be analyzed. If this transformation from one modeling language to another is performed by informal means, due to the differences in the concepts between the two modeling languages, the result may be an analysis model that is not an accurate representation of the original. The analysis method specialist may be an expert in the analysis-specific language, but is unlikely to be an expert in UML-MARTE, and, of course, the converse holds for the application modeler.

MARTE deals with this situation by defining a generic conceptual framework for model analysis that facilitates *automated* transformation of UML-MARTE models into models suited to various types of analyses. Once such transformations for a particular type of analysis are defined and validated, they can be reused any number of times, saving time and effort and eliminating the troublesome human intervention in the process. A further advantage of this approach is that it practically eliminates, or at least reduces, the need for sophisticated analysis expertise, which is typically difficult to find and can be expensive. The use of such automated transforms in practice is discussed in Section 1.6.4.

The MARTE concepts used for modeling real-time software applications and corresponding usage guidelines are described in Chapter 5.

1.6.2 Use case (2): Modeling platforms

This use case is initiated and performed by *platform modelers*, specialists responsible for designing and maintaining application platform models. The skill set involved may vary, depending on whether the platform is a software or a hardware platform.

Platforms are constructed to support one or more applications. Hence, in a way, they are the inverse of an application, since platforms are service providers whereas applications are (platform) service users. Note, however, that since a software platform may itself require an underlying

---

[10]Sadly, it is too often the case in practice that this question is put off until implementation testing (since, as noted before, "non-functional" requirements are often deemed secondary to "functional" ones), by which time it may be too late to do anything about it except at great expense.

platform, it can also be viewed as a kind of application. Still, in the context of this book, the main difference between platform and application design is that the former focuses mostly on managing and providing resources (and resource services) to be used by applications. MARTE provides extensive mechanisms for modeling resources and resource management for both software and hardware platforms, as well as more general concepts for modeling platforms at a higher system level, i.e., with no hardwired assumptions about implementation technology choices.

The MARTE concepts used for modeling platforms for real-time software and corresponding usage guidelines are described in Chapter 6.

1.6.3 Use case (3): Specifying deployment

This task is performed by a *deployment modeler*, who is responsible for defining a deployable system model, which specifies the allocation of application components to elements of the platform that are responsible for realizing them. The inputs to this process are an application model and a platform model and the output is a new model that includes the two input models and a mapping specification between the application and the platform.

MARTE provides a relatively straightforward specialized general language for specifying deployment. However, defining deployment for an application is not always as simple as specifying which code modules are to be loaded on which processors. In this basic case, it is sufficient to represent the application as a set of code modules. In more complex cases it is often necessary to view the application in terms of its run-time entities and specify how these are to be allocated to the appropriate platform components. For example, it may be required to move application components dynamically between platform elements based on the current state of the system. Since there is great variety in the way that deployment needs to be specified, it is often necessary to extend the general MARTE deployment language to provide a more refined and more precise capability. The process of extending MARTE in this and other ways is covered by a separate use case in Section 1.6.7.

The MARTE concepts used for modeling deployment and corresponding usage guidelines are described in Chapter 7.

1.6.4 Use case (4): Analyze model

As explained earlier, one of the major advantages of models over code is that they are more easily analyzed by formal, automatable, methods simply because, by definition, they include less information that needs to be processed. This use case complements any of the modeling use cases and may even be performed directly by either an application modeler or a platform modeler. We will refer to the stakeholder who initiates this use case generically as the *analyst*.

The analyst is interested in getting predictions from the model. Once the desired analysis type has been selected (e.g., schedulability analysis), it is typically necessary to provide an analysis-oriented model (*analysis model*) to be used in the analysis. This typically consists of the core design model but extended with additional model elements, which contain data that characterize the specific case of interest. For instance, schedulability analysis will require a model that not only includes the system to be analyzed but also models of external entities that interact with the analyzed system as well as their characteristics (e.g., arrival rates and load characteristics). It may not be necessary to construct a new analysis model for every individual analysis. Instead, a single generic model can be constructed to be reused in multiple analysis runs, but with different input values provided in each run (refer to the use case in Section 1.6.6).

Once the analysis model is in place, the corresponding model translation must be invoked to convert the UML-MARTE model into one that is understood by the analysis tool. The result of this operation (preferably automated or at least computer aided) is an analysis model, which is then passed (*a priori* automatically) to the specialized analysis engine[11] for processing. The analyst may be required to configure the analysis engine to suit the problem at hand (for example, to define the desired precision of the degree of precision of the results), although, again, if the tooling allows it, much of this process can be automated, or at least computer aided (particularly if human intervention is required in the process). Once the parameters of the analysis are defined, the analysis itself is performed, and the results examined by the analyst. The results may be fed back to the modeler with appropriate interpretation in terms of the original input model. (If a suitable inverse model transformation from the analysis model back to UML-MARTE is available, and the tools are appropriately coupled, then this last step can also be automated.)

Based on the results of the analysis, it may be necessary to change the input model and redo the analysis. Or, the same type of analysis with the same input model may be repeated but with different values for the analysis parameters, as, for example, when evaluating different architectural alternatives. Tracing the analysis results back to the model elements that influence them is one of the more challenging aspects of this use case and it often requires extensive experience with and understanding of both the system and the analysis method.

The general principles behind the MARTE approach to model analysis are described in Chapter 9. Chapter 10 covers the special but common case (at least for real-time software) of schedulability analysis with MARTE, while Chapter 11 deals with analyzing the performance characteristics of models.

1.6.5 Use case (5): Create a new analysis profile

As noted previously, MARTE provides two default specific analysis frameworks: either performance or schedulability. For other kinds of analysis or in cases where the default frameworks are insufficiently refined, it may be necessary to define a new custom framework or to refine an existing one, starting preferably with the generic analysis framework provided by MARTE. This is the responsibility of the *analysis expert*.

The first step consists of selecting (or designing) a suitable analysis method or set of methods and, if available, at least one corresponding computer-based tool for performing the analysis. Each analysis method focuses on certain characteristics of the system being analyzed while ignoring the rest. It is the job of the analysis expert to determine how these features of interest are to be extracted from UML-MARTE models that are used as input to the analysis. In some cases, this information can be extracted directly or indirectly (e.g., by computation) from the values of existing features of the design model. However, in other cases, the necessary information may need to be added to a model. In that case, either the analysis framework of MARTE already includes the required concepts, or an analysis expert has to define an extension of MARTE (see Section 1.6.7). For example,

---

[11]It is assumed here that the actual analysis is performed by a computer program, but, it is also possible for it to be done by human experts. The former, is, generally speaking, preferable.

analysis of safety-critical systems typically requires computing the so-called "safety integrity level (SIL)" of a system, which is a complex function of a number of different parameters of that system. Since MARTE does not provide an out-of-the-box safety analysis capability, new safety-related concepts and relationships have to be added to the profile and fitted within its general analysis framework [9]. Typically, this is done in a modular fashion, as a separate optional increment to MARTE, thereby leaving the standard unchanged.

When the domain concepts have been added, it is then necessary for the analysis expert to define a model transform for converting the UML-MARTE model (along with its new concepts) into a corresponding model in the analysis-specific language understood by the analysis tool. Preferably, an inverse transformation would be defined as well, so that the results of the analysis can be automatically converted and presented in terms of the UML-MARTE model, reducing the need for analysis-level expertise.

If an analysis tool is available, it is the responsibility of the analysis expert to ensure proper integration of that tool with the UML authoring tool such that human intervention is minimized. While the implementation of this may be delegated to the tool developers, the overall design of the workflow and user interface of the integrated system should remain with the analysis expert who understands best how the system is used.

The general principles behind the MARTE approach to model analysis are described in Chapter 9. This provides the necessary background for defining a new profile. Note that such an extension necessarily requires extension of MARTE itself. This "included" use case is covered in Chapter 12.

1.6.6 Use case (6): Configure product variant

In the Analyze Model use case described in Section 1.6.4, we noted that it is possible to start with a generic (i.e., parameterized) analysis model from which we can extract case-specific models simply by changing one or more parameter values. This is merely a special case of a very general problem of extracting a meaningful model from a generic *product line* model. A product line model specifies a collection of different variants through some form of parameterization. UML provides a number of mechanisms such as subtyping, templates, and various kinds of parameters, which support the definition of product line models. However, MARTE provides an additional mechanism that is particularly useful in model analysis (as explained earlier), but can be convenient in other situations as well. This is achieved through a component of MARTE called the VSL, which includes the ability to include variables when specifying the values of parameters and features in a model. Different particular models can then be extracted from a single generic model simply by substituting different values for the variables in evaluating the corresponding expressions. For example, by defining the parameters of a Poisson distribution that characterizes the arrival rate of some event generator element as VSL variables, it is possible to generate many different analysis models from just a single generic model.

The task of selecting the required values for such variables is the responsibility of the *configuration expert*, who could be the analyst from the Analyze Model or, more generally, anyone responsible for generating a concrete model from a generic product line model.

Configuring a product variant usually involves specialized tools and methods. One approach to this based on a combination of UML and MARTE is described in the journal paper by Behjati et al. [1]. An overview of VSL and its use are provided in Appendix A.

1.6.7 Use case (7): Extend MARTE

As noted, MARTE provides a very rich vocabulary of concepts directly derived from a variety of different software and hardware domains related to real-time system design. Yet, given the relentless pace of domain specialization, it is often insufficient. New concepts, new devices, and new analysis methods are constantly emerging and there is a consequent and ever-present need to extend MARTE. This task falls to the *domain language expert*.[12]

Extending the language typically involves adding new subprofile modules that extend the standard (without modifying it) or extend a previously defined subprofile. Like any profile, a MARTE subprofile consists of a set of stereotypes and related constraints (preferably written in OCL). The stereotypes may be defined as either subclasses of existing stereotypes or extensions of UML meta-classes. The resulting new language elements can be used for modeling purposes or analysis or both. Once a profile has been defined, it is realized within a UML authoring tool and tested on suitable examples. When it is deemed adequate it is distributed to users and incorporated into their tools for use.

Methods of extending MARTE with corresponding examples are described in Chapter 12.

1.7 Tool support for MARTE

A number of commercial and open source tools support the MARTE profile. An updated list of UML and related tools is maintained by the Object Management Group (OMG) at http://www.omgmarte.org/node/31.

The **Papyrus** UML tool,[13] developed under the leadership and guidance of the Laboratoire d'Ingénierie dirigée par les modèles pour les Systèmes Embarqués of the CEA, and LIST at Gif-sur-Yvette in France, is an example of an open source tool that supports MARTE that is used by a number of industrial organizations. It was also used to validate a number of the examples presented in this book.

Other up-to-date information related to MARTE, including tutorials and discussion forums, is located at http://www.omgmarte.org/.

1.8 SUMMARY

MARTE is an industry-standard language that complements standard UML. Like all profiles, MARTE refines standard UML concepts to provide their real-time interpretations. In effect, MARTE is a domain-specific modeling language for specifying and analyzing real-time and embedded software applications and systems. Specifically, it includes provision for the following:

• Accurate and precise modeling time and temporal relationships
• Accurate and precise modeling of real-time software applications and their qualitative and quantitative characteristics

---

[12]It can be argued that this should be the responsibility of a MARTE or UML expert, since it involves extending a computer language, but, it is generally much easier for domain experts to learn how to extend MARTE than it is for a language expert to learn about the intricacies of a particular specialist domain.
[13]http://www.eclipse.org/papyrus.

- Accurate and precise modeling of many different kinds of hardware and software resources that constitute the computing platforms for applications including their qualitative and quantitative properties
- Specifying the deployment of applications to platforms
- Predicting key characteristics of designs, such as timeliness and performance, through computer-aided analysis

Because MARTE is defined as a proper profile of UML, it can in principle be used with any UML tool and it can take advantage of widely available UML expertise. Moreover, as is the case with any profile, it can be combined with other complementary profiles, such as the SysML profile for system engineering (Chapter 8).

In addition, while offering a wealth of domain concepts, MARTE is highly modular and configurable. This means that only those parts of it that are of interest to the case on hand need to be used while the rest can be ignored. This is well suited to the real-time and embedded domain, which is quite diverse and constantly evolving. MARTE is also highly extensible (Chapter 12), which means that it can be specialized or extended to support highly idiosyncratic as well as newly emerging technologies.

References

[1] Behjati R, Yue T, Briand L, Selic B. SimPL: a product-line methodology for families of integrated control systems. J Inf Softw Technol 2012 (in press, accepted for publication, available on line at: <http://dx.doi.org/10.1016/j.infsof.2012.09.006>.

[2] Epstein J. Why model? Keynote address delivered at the 2nd World Congress on Social Simulation (WCSS-08), Fairfax, VA; 2008.

[3] Kleinrock L. Queueing systems, volume 1: theory. : Wiley Interscience; 1975.

[4] Klein M, et al. A practitioner's handbook for real-time analysis: guide to rate monotonic analysis for real-time systems. : Kluwer Academic Publishers; 1993.

[5] Mraidha C, Tucci-Piergiovanni S, Gérard S. A MARTE-based methodology for schedulability analysis at early design stages Sangiovanni-Vincentelli A, Zeng H, Di Natale M, Marwedel P, editors. Embedded systems development: from functional models to implementations. : Springer London, Limited; 2013.

[6] Object Management Group, The, UML™ Profile for Schedulability, Performance, and Time Specification, Version 1.1, OMG document no. formal/2005-05-01, 2005.

[7] Object Management Group, The, A UML profile for MARTE: Modeling and analysis of real-time and embedded systems, Version 1.1, OMG document no. formal/2011-06-02, 2011.

[8] Radermacher A, Mraidha C, Tucci-Piergiovanni S, Gérard S. Generation of schedulable real-time component implementations in IEEE Conference on Emerging Technologies and Factory Automation (ETFA), 2010, p. 1–4.

[9] Yakymets N, Jaber H, Lanusse A. Model-based systems engineering for safety analysis of complex systems Presentation given at the Model-Based Safety Assessment Workshop (MBSAW 2012), <http://mbsaw2012.labri.fr/slides/talk-11-02.pdf>; 2012.

Foundations

PART

II

An Introduction to UML Profiles

2

CHAPTER CONTENTS

2.1 INTRODUCTION

In this chapter, we briefly review the *profile* concept of UML and how it works [5]. A basic understanding of the rationale behind this mechanism and its principles of operation can be very helpful in making effective use of profiles such as MARTE. It is, therefore, recommended that readers unfamiliar with profiles read the full chapter before proceeding further.

There is still some controversy about the UML profile approach [5], and alternative solutions are being considered [1,2]. However, despite some undeniable technical shortcomings, profiles are very widely used in practice, including for the definition of MARTE.

In simplest terms, a UML profile is a facility for augmenting UML models with supplementary information. Typically, this is information that cannot be expressed directly using standard UML. This mechanism can be used in either of two ways:

1. *It can be used to extend the UML language.* For example, UML does not provide an explicit semaphore concept, but it is possible to add it by *overloading* an existing UML concept, such as Class. The result is a special kind of Class that, in addition to its standard Class semantics, incorporates semaphore semantics.
2. *It can be used to attach additional information to models needed for ancillary purposes* such as model analyses or code generation. Such an annotation can be used, for instance, to specify the worst-case execution time of some operation of a class, which might be needed for analyzing the timing characteristics of an application.

These annotations must conform to a formally defined specification: the *profile*. Profiles are constructed according to the strict rules of standard UML, the foremost of which is that *a profile must be fully consistent with the (abstract) syntax and semantics of standard UML*. Thus, a semaphore extension of the Class concept in some profile is still a proper UML Class, which means that it is subject to all the formal language rules that apply to Classes. However, it may also be subject to additional nonconflicting rules specific to semaphores, such as that it must provide special operations for acquiring and releasing the semaphore. It may also include additional properties, such as a queue for storing pending acquisition requests.

This fundamental property of profiles means that a valid profile is simply a specialization of standard UML. As a consequence, *a modeling tool that works with standard UML models is equally capable of working with profile-based models*. This is very important, since it can greatly reduce the cost of supporting profiles as it allows UML tools to be reused. It also has the advantage that UML expertise can be directly reused when working with profile-based models.

2.2 The two kinds of profiles

The two different ways of using profiles leads to two different kinds of profiles:

1. Language profiles
2. Annotation profiles

In the first case, the profile mechanism is used to create either a stand-alone, full-fledged domain-specific language, such as SysML [6], or, as is the case with MARTE, a "utility" language that is designed to augment UML or some other language profile by extending it with new domain-specific concepts.

Annotation profiles, on the other hand, are used to attach supplementary information to a model and its elements, typically involving concepts that cannot be conveniently expressed using standard UML. These types of profiles are primarily intended for analyzing models. The two analysis subprofiles of MARTE, Schedulability Analysis Modeling (SAM; Chapter 10) and Performance Analysis Modeling (PAM; Chapter 11), are typical examples of annotation profiles. For instance, the PAM profile provides facilities to attach information about the expected arrival rate to a message in a sequence diagram, which is required to compute the performance characteristics of the associated design. To take advantage of an annotation profile, we first need to *apply* the desired profile to the model, after which the concepts in the profile become available for use. The annotations attached to a model are analogous to a transparent overlay being placed on a projected slide, resulting in a view that combines both the original and the extra annotations. It is even possible to apply multiple profiles simultaneously, provided they do not conflict in some way (e.g., name or constraint conflicts).

One interesting and very useful feature of annotation profiles is that they can also be *unapplied* from a model. This effectively removes the supplementary annotations associated with that profile, leaving the underlying model in its original unannotated state. This permits multiple different annotations to be applied successively to the same model, enabling different kinds of analyses to be performed.

Consider, for example, the sequence diagram fragment in Figure 2.1, showing a database read message arriving at a database server, where it is processed and a reply returned. This is a typical client-server pattern. It is, of course, not possible to compute the performance characteristics of such a system based purely on this model, since we are missing information. We need to know at least the processing capacity of the server as well as the arrival rate of read requests.

However, if we apply the PAM profile to this model, we can use it to overlay the required performance information. To that end, we will *apply* the **PaStep** stereotype from that profile to both the incoming message and to the execution occurrence block. This stereotype represents a computational step, that is, an action utilizing the CPU resource. The **hostDemand** attribute of this stereotype specifies how much CPU time is consumed by such a step—information that is required for performance analysis. The resulting model following the application of the MARTE profile and the addition of the required annotations is shown in Figure 2.2.[1]

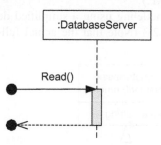

FIGURE 2.1

An unadorned UML sequence diagram fragment showing a database read request.

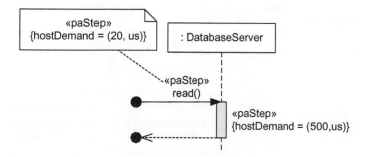

FIGURE 2.2

The annotated version of the model in Figure 2.1 with performance data included.

---

[1] Readers who are curious as to why two different forms of referring to the same stereotype, one starting with uppercase letter (**PaStep**) and the other with a lowercase letter (**paStep**), will find the answer in Section 2.3.5.

In this particular example, we can conclude based on the annotations that the CPU time required to execute this behavior fragment is equal to (20 microseconds + 500 microseconds) = 520 microseconds.

If we subsequently "unapply" (i.e., remove) the PAM profile from this example model, we revert to the model shown in Figure 2.1. Of course, the same profile can be reapplied later, if necessary.

2.3 How profiles work

To understand how profiles work, it helps to understand how they are defined [5]. This requires some understanding of how UML itself is defined.

2.3.1 Metamodels[2]

Modeling languages such as UML are defined using a technique called *metamodeling*. The mechanism used for this is familiar to anyone who has used class modeling in UML. In essence, the concepts of a modeling language are specified using class models. In other words, we use models to define modeling languages, which is why such models are called *metamodels*. (In contrast, programming languages are typically specified using *grammars*, which are usually expressed through some variant of Backus-Naur Form or BNF.)

We illustrate the idea of metamodeling using a simplified definition of the UML Class concept using the class diagram in Figure 2.3 (Note that the actual full-blown specification is significantly

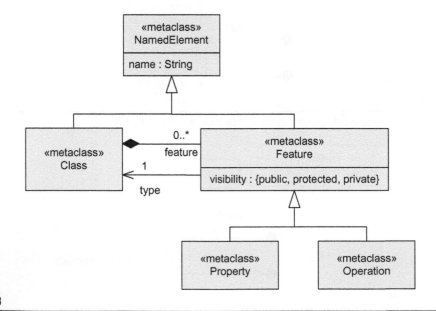

FIGURE 2.3

A simplified metamodel definition of the concept of a UML **Class**.

---

[2]Readers familiar with the UML metamodel can safely skip this section.

more complex, but we are more interested here in explaining how the mechanism works rather than focusing on the UML metamodel).

The root of this metamodel is the abstract **NamedElement** concept, defined by a (meta)class with a single **String** attribute called **name**. The **NamedElement** metaclass is the common parent of all language concepts that have a name, including, in this case, **Class**, **Feature**, as well as the subclasses of **Feature**, **Property**, and **Operation**. The metamodel tells us that an instance of the **Class** concept may own zero or more **Feature**s. **Feature** is an abstract metaclass that has a **visibility** attribute and is associated with a **type**, which has to be a kind of **Class**. It is further specialized into a **Property** metaclass, representing structural features, and an **Operation** metaclass for behavioral features. Further details, such as the definition of **Operation** parameters, are not shown in this diagram.

The entire UML language is defined by diagrams of this type supplemented with additional textual explanations and, in some cases, formal constraints (usually written in OCL) that impose certain restrictions on how to construct a model [4].

An example of a user model element, Person, which conforms to the definition of **Class**, is shown in the simple class diagram in Figure 2.4. Person is a class with a single public attribute, id, of type String.

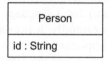

FIGURE 2.4

An example of a class conforming to the metamodel definition specified in Figure 2.3.

To fully comprehend how models and stereotypes work, it is also helpful to know how this type of diagram element is actually stored inside the computer. This internal representation is based on the language definition and is depicted in Figure 2.5. We can see that, in this case, there is one instance of the **Class** concept representing the Person class, and one instance of the **Property** concept representing the id attribute of Person. There is also a second instance of **Class** representing the String class, which is the type of the id attribute.

2.3.2 The stereotype concept

The central concept in the profile mechanism of UML is the *stereotype*. This is a special kind of metaclass that is used to define an extension of an existing UML concept or of another stereotype. To explain how it works, we consider the example of adding the concept of a binary semaphore to the UML language using the profile approach.

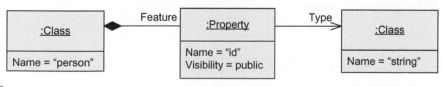

FIGURE 2.5

The internal model repository representation of the model element shown in Figure 2.4.

A binary semaphore is a special kind of object used to synchronize the execution of concurrent threads [7]. It typically provides some kind of "acquire" operation, by which access is obtained to it, and an inverse "release" operation, by which it is released after having been acquired. The acquire operation has special semantics: If at the time the invocation is made the semaphore has already been acquired by a different thread and has not yet been released, then the calling thread is suspended and put on a queue of waiting acquire requests. It remains suspended until a release operation is invoked and until all acquire requests that preceded it (if any) have been serviced. Once the thread has completed its exclusive activity, it invokes the release operation to free up the semaphore.

The first step in defining a language extension of this type is to decide which UML concept to extend. Recall that *all* profile-based extensions *must* be based on an existing UML metaclass, to ensure that the profile is compatible with UML semantics [3]. Basing a language extension on a UML concept implies that the new concept assumes (inherits) all the semantic and syntactic properties of its *base metaclass*. It may, of course, add new properties (attributes, operations, etc.), specify a graphical icon for the stereotype, and, possibly, impose some constraints on the characteristics that it inherited from its base metaclass.

For our binary semaphore, we choose to extend the UML Class concept, because it has the characteristics that we need for representing our semaphore. That is, classes in UML represent templates for constructing objects that can have their own operations and attributes. Choosing an appropriate base metaclass (UML concept) for a language extension is the single most important decision involved and must be done very carefully. It is crucial to choose a concept that has all the right semantics and syntax and, equally important, has no undesirable or conflicting semantics. For instance, it would be highly inappropriate to use the UML Package concept as a base metaclass for our semaphore, because packages do not have any run-time semantics. (Fortunately, UML is a fairly general language and it is almost always possible to find an existing UML concept on which to base a desired extension. For instance, standard UML concepts such as Class or Property are malleable enough to cover a wide spectrum of domain-specific concepts. Difficulties arise mostly in cases where a new concept has semantics that do not have an equivalent in UML.)

Figure 2.6 shows how the semaphore extension, **BinarySemaphore**, is defined using the profile mechanism.[3] The new concept appears in the form of a *stereotype*, which extends a base metaclass,

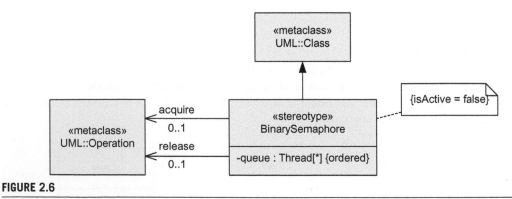

FIGURE 2.6

Example of a simple binary semaphore stereotype definition.

---

[3]Readers should be aware that the **BinarySemaphore** stereotype is not part of MARTE, but is introduced for its illustrative value. MARTE uses different stereotypes for modeling semaphores as explained in Section 5.3.2.

the UML **Class** concept in this case. A stereotype is similar to a regular metaclass in that it defines the features (properties, operations) associated with the new concept. The line with a filled triangular arrowhead emanating from the stereotype and pointing to the base metaclass is called an *extension*. It has some similarity to the standard UML generalization relationship in that it implies inheritance of characteristics, but it differs from a generalization in a few key aspects that we will explain later.

This stereotype defines the requisite **acquire** and **release** operations and it also adds a private **queue** attribute for maintaining the ordered list of pending thread requests.[4] This definition may be supplemented with constraints. In this case, since semaphores are passive objects, we associate an OCL constraint with the stereotype requiring that the **isActive** Boolean attribute inherited from the UML Class concept must always be **false**.

To facilitate visual identification of domain-specific concepts, there is an option to associate a user-defined icon with a stereotype. For example, for our binary semaphore, we might choose an icon, such as the one shown in Figure 2.7, which is reminiscent of a traffic light. This icon can then be used in different ways when constructing models, as explained in Section 2.3.4.

2.3.3 First-class language concepts

At this point someone might ask the seemingly obvious question: Why didn't we simply define a regular class in the model to represent our semaphore, as in Figure 2.8? After all, aren't classes the mechanism by which we define the concepts that characterize an application? Do we really need to go through the bother of actually extending the definition of the UML language itself?

The answer lies in the fact that a binary semaphore is *not* a regular class, since it has unique semantics associated with its synchronization role. Furthermore, given its specific nature, there may be additional constraints on how such elements can be used. These special properties are not shared with other kinds of classes, yet this distinction cannot be discerned in the specification in Figure 2.8.

FIGURE 2.7

A user-defined icon for the **BinarySemaphore** stereotype.

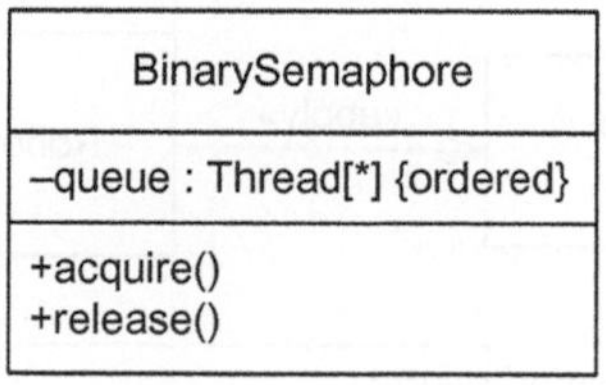

BinarySemaphore
–queue : Thread[*] {ordered}
+acquire() +release()

FIGURE 2.8

A binary semaphore modeled by a simple user-define UML class.

---

[4]In practice, the **queue** attribute would most likely be implicit, since it may never actually be directly referenced elsewhere in the model. However, we include it here for illustrative purposes.

(It would be inappropriate and impractical to deduce such special semantics based on the name of a model element, since that is error prone (e.g., misspelling) and limits users from choosing their own naming conventions.)

There are situations where it is crucial to be able to differentiate such special elements. For instance, if we want to generate code from these models, a semaphore and its properties need to be distinguished from regular user-defined classes to ensure that the correct code is generated. Similarly, some tool that analyzes a model to determine whether all acquired semaphores are eventually released will need to distinguish calls to the **acquire** and **release** operations from calls to regular operations.

The difference between a stereotype and a user-defined construct built out of the concepts of the language is that a stereotype represents what we will refer to henceforth as a *first-class* concept. That term means that it is a concept that is *built into the language* and is, thus, part of the definition of the language rather than being limited to a specific user model.

2.3.4 Profile packages

A stereotype such as **BinarySemaphore** would most likely be grouped with others related to the same domain, such as a **Thread** stereotype (UML does not have an explicit thread concept), into a special kind of package called a *profile*. This is a package that contains a collection of related stereotype definitions. To make use of the stereotypes in a model, it is necessary to first formally *apply* the profile to that model. This is an operation performed either on a full model or on selected parts of a model. A *profile application* is conceptually similar to a UML package import in the sense that it makes available all its definitions for use within the package (or model) to which it has been applied.

For example, the package diagram in Figure 2.9 shows an example in which the full MARTE profile is applied to an application model called `RobotController`.[5]

2.3.5 Using stereotypes in models

In diagrams, the use of stereotypes is typically indicated by the name of the stereotype between so-called *guillemets* (« and »), which are used as quotation marks in some languages, such as French or Russian. In those cases, the graphic used for a stereotype is the same as the graphic for the base class of the stereotype. However, it is also possible to use the stereotype icon, if it is defined, either in place

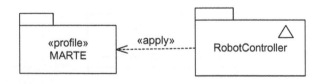

FIGURE 2.9

Applying the MARTE profile to an application model.

---

[5]Diagrams such as this are rarely encountered in practice. Instead, the application of profiles is usually performed by direct manipulation of the model via the navigator panel of the modeling tool.

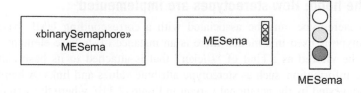

FIGURE 2.10

Examples of different stereotype notational forms.

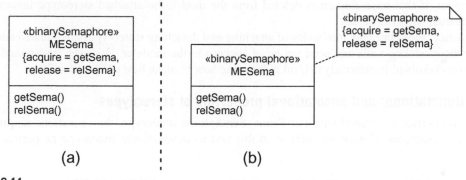

(a)   (b)

FIGURE 2.11

Notational variants for showing the values of stereotype properties.

of the regular element notation or as a symbol embedded within the name compartment within the graphic. These notational variants are illustrated in Figure 2.10.

There is a long-standing informal convention, supported by most UML tools, by which the first letter of the stereotype name, *when the stereotype is applied to an element*, is in lower case, even if in the definition of the stereotype the name begins with an upper case letter (e.g., "**binarySemaphore**" instead of "**BinarySemaphore**"). We adhere to this convention throughout the book.

When stereotypes have operations and properties, as is the case with most stereotypes, the values of the stereotype properties can be included below the name of the element (or immediately after the stereotype label), or, if preferred, they can be shown in a separate note element, labeled by the name of the stereotype. Figure 2.11 illustrates the two techniques for our example binary semaphore stereotype. Another example, depicting the assignment of values to stereotype properties for elements in a sequence diagram, is given in Figure 2.2.

As a practical measure, when assigning values to stereotype properties, it is not necessary to specify values for all the properties that are defined, but only those that are of interest for the situation on hand. Properties with unassigned values and without predefined defaults automatically default to the "null" (empty) value.

2.3.6 Under the hood: How stereotypes are implemented[6]

Recall that every stereotype must be associated with a corresponding UML base element. Thus, whenever a stereotype is used in a model, there is an instance of its base element accompanying it. A stereotype can be viewed as a kind of "sticker" that is attached to its base element, containing stereotype-specific information, such as stereotype attribute values and links. A helpful way of thinking about this is suggested by the notational variant in Figure 2.11b, where the stereotype information is shown as a note attached to the base element (the Class MESema).[7] However, a technically more precise representation of the repository structure is shown by the model fragment in Figure 2.12.

This may seem unduly complex at first glance, but it is necessary to allow stereotypes to be dynamically unapplied (i.e., removed) from a model without affecting that model. This structure achieves that. Another of its useful features is that, since the stereotype is (logically) owned by the base element, if that base element is deleted from the model, the attached stereotype instance will also be deleted from the model.

In practice, these intricate mechanics of attaching and detaching stereotypes are handled automatically by the modeling tools and need not be of concern to the modeler. However, understanding the mechanisms involved is extremely helpful in knowing how to make best use profiles.

2.3.7 Denotational and annotational properties of stereotypes

The two properties associated with our **BinarySemaphore** stereotype, the operations **acquire** and **release**, are examples of what we refer to in this text as *denotational* stereotype properties. These

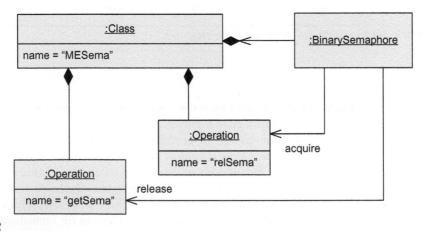

FIGURE 2.12

The method of attaching stereotypes to their base metaclass instances.

---

[6] This topic may, at first, appear as an advanced topic. However, the authors' experience is that this information is quite helpful for a proper understanding of how profiles work in UML. Therefore, we encourage readers to familiarize themselves with this aspect.

[7] Another helpful analogy is to think of stereotypes as akin to the label tags that airlines attach to checked luggage; the tags contain information specific to the trip being taken and can be safely removed when no longer needed without affecting the luggage itself.

types of properties *do not introduce any new features to the base class, but provide a reinterpretation of already existing features based on a particular domain-specific viewpoint.* In that particular case, the two attributes are used to associate (denote) a specific semantics with operations that are defined in the user model. The semantics of **acquire** and **release** are defined by the semantics of the stereotype. However, in case of the MESema class, which has the operations getSema and relSema, it is not possible to know which of them corresponds to **acquire** and which one to **release**. Furthermore, this user-defined class may have additional operations defined that do not have the special semantics associated with them. Hence, it is necessary to formally *bind* the special semantics to the appropriate properties of the stereotyped element. This is achieved by setting the value of the stereotype attributes to the names of the appropriate user-class features, as shown in Figure 2.11. This binding allows us to correctly interpret these otherwise indistinguishable operations.

Annotational stereotype properties, on the other hand, are used to extend the set of characteristics of the base class with properties that are not part of standard UML. Consider the case of a **Thread** stereotype as defined in Figure 2.13. **Thread** extends the standard UML Class concept by adding a new annotational property called **priority**, whose value defines the priority of the thread. It also constrains the base concept by forcing the **isActive** feature of the UML Class concept to always be **true**.

This stereotype adds the concept of both threads and priorities, which does not exist in standard UML. Examples of the use of annotational properties in a user model can be seen in Figure 2.14.

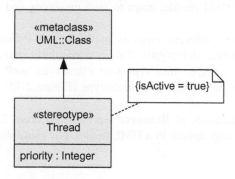

FIGURE 2.13

A **Thread** stereotype with an annotational attribute priority and a constraint.

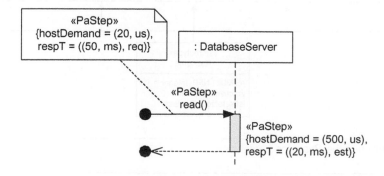

FIGURE 2.14

Example of a stereotype applied to two different kinds of base metaclasses.

2.3.8 Multibased stereotypes

Note that the **PaStep** stereotype in Figure 2.14 is applied to two different kinds of base elements: a message element (the `read` message) and an execution occurrence element on the `DatabaseServer` lifeline. A message in UML is represented by the metaclass **Message**, while the execution occurrence block is represented by an instance of the **BehaviorExecutionSpecification** metaclass. So, which of these two is the "true" base class of the **PaStep** stereotype and how is it possible to attach the same kind of stereotype to two different types of elements?

In fact, the UML stereotype mechanism *does* allow a stereotype to extend *multiple base metaclasses*. This is intended as a practical measure, which avoids excessive duplication of stereotype definitions. Consider that, without this capability, for the previous example we would need to define two different stereotypes for **PaStep**, one that extends **Message** and the other that extends **BehaviorExecutionSpecification**. But, *both stereotypes would have to define the same properties*, which would duplicate effort and create potential maintenance problems.

Multiple base metaclasses are particularly useful in annotation profiles (see Section 2.2). These profiles are typically used to overlay a domain-specific interpretation on a UML model. For example, the PAM profile reinterprets a UML model as a queuing network, whereas the SAM profile views it as a schedulability pattern. The concepts in such domain-specific languages do not necessarily map one to one to UML concepts. Thus, the notion of a "step" in performance analysis, represented by the **PaStep** stereotype in the PAM profile, maps to both messages and execution occurrence blocks in UML.

Because MARTE supports different analysis methods and different viewpoints of systems, it makes heavy use of multibased stereotypes. This is particularly manifested in the fact that *many MARTE stereotypes extend concepts that represent classes as well as concepts that represent instances*. A notable example is the **Resource** stereotype (Figure 2.15), which serves as the root of many MARTE concepts.[8]

All the various base metaclasses of **Resource** represent different forms in which the relatively abstract notion of a resource may appear in a UML model. For example, in instance form, it may be

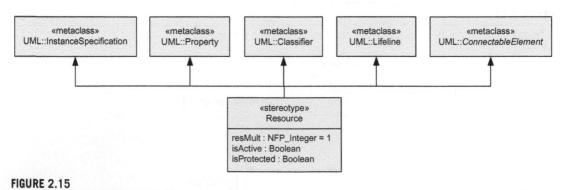

FIGURE 2.15

The MARTE definition of the *Resource* stereotype.

[8]Section 4.2.2 describes this stereotype in depth.

represented by a **Lifeline** in a sequence diagram, a **Property** in a class definition, an object or link (**InstanceSpecification**) in an object diagram, or a part in a structure diagram or role in a collaboration (**ConnectableElement**). Alternatively, it can appear in classifier form (e.g., **Class**, **Interface**, **Component**, **Node**) in a class diagram.

Note that MARTE takes advantage of the fact that a stereotype that extends a base metaclass that has subclasses automatically extends all subclasses. Yet again, this is a mechanism intended to avoid duplication of stereotype definitions. An example of this can be seen in Figure 2.15, where **Resource** extends two different abstract UML concepts: **Classifier** and **ConnectableElement**. This means that the **Resource** stereotype and its specializations (e.g., **StorageResource**, **ProcessingResource**) can be applied to any subclasses of these two concepts.

2.4 Conventions related to the use of profiles

The UML profile mechanism leaves some room for interpretation on a number of common modeling issues. To avoid confusion in such cases, we introduce here three conventions that apply throughout the text.

2.4.1 Default values of omitted stereotype properties

It is often the case that we are not interested in specifying the values of all properties of a MARTE stereotype, but only those that are of interest to the case on hand. For example, the **NFP_Duration** stereotype has a total of eight properties, but, in the majority of cases, we are only interested in just one of these: the value. It would be tiresome and impractical to force users to specify all eight values every time this stereotype is used. Consequently, in this text *we assume that unspecified values of stereotype properties are either empty (the value "null") or automatically set to their default values, if such defaults are defined*.

2.4.2 Transitivity of class stereotypes to elements representing instances

Consider the example depicted in Figure 2.16a. In this case, the **SwMutualExclusionResource** stereotype is applied to the UML Class `BinSema` in Figure 2.16a and, in a sequence diagram fragment from the same model shown in Figure 2.16b, to a lifeline associated representing an instance of this class, `sem1`.

However, how should the final fragment form the same model shown in Figure 2.16c be interpreted? Intuitively, one might assume that the lifeline in that fragment also represents a semaphore—even though it is not itself stereotyped as such—by virtue of the fact that its defining type, `BinSema`, already has the stereotype applied. The question asked is: Does the application of a stereotype to a classifier automatically imply that all instances typed by that classifier are also (implicitly) stereotyped?

Since both standard UML and MARTE are silent on this point, as a practical measure in this book we adopt the convention that when a stereotype is applied to a classifier that the stereotype characteristics are transferred to all its instances by default. But, it is crucial to stress that this is strictly a local convention that is not standardized. For example, some code generators may not adopt this convention. Hence, readers are warned not to presume that it applies universally.

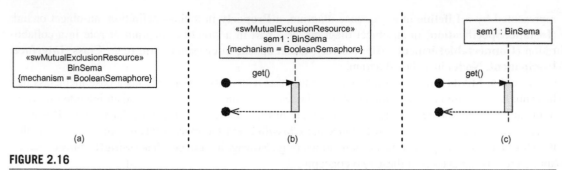

FIGURE 2.16

Application of the same stereotype to a class element and to an "instance" element.

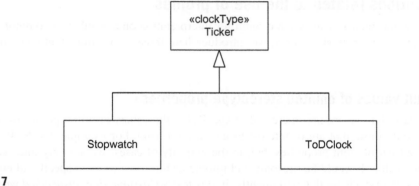

FIGURE 2.17

Inheritance of stereotype applications to subclasses.

Note, however, that this convention does not completely free us from having to stereotype model elements that represent instances of classes that have already been stereotyped. This is because it may happen that different instances of the same class will have different values for specific stereotype attributes. Since stereotype attributes cannot appear independently of their stereotypes, in those situations it is necessary to stereotype those instance elements as well, so that the proper values can be assigned to their attributes. But, even in such cases, we will assume that any default values of stereotype attributes (such as the value of the **mechanism** attribute in Figure 2.16a) are automatically transferred to the instance, except when they are explicitly overridden in the instance.

2.4.3 Inheritance of stereotype applications

A similar issue is whether stereotypes applied to classes also automatically apply to their subclasses. For instance, if the **ClockType** stereotype is applied to the user-model Ticker class shown in Figure 2.17, does it also apply to its subclasses Stopwatch and ToDClock? To avoid duplication of effort, *we assume that a stereotype application to a class is implicitly applied to all of its direct and indirect subclasses.* In other words, it is not necessary to annotate the two subclasses of Ticker with the **ClockType** stereotype, because the annotation is automatically transferred to them.

2.5 Model libraries for profiles

In UML, a *model library* is a UML package specially designated via the system-defined stereotype **ModelLibrary** as a module that contains model fragments, which are potentially useful in multiple models. Many UML profiles incorporate such libraries for specifying domain-specific concepts. These are typically used both in the definition of the profile itself as well as in user models that make use of the profile. As a case in point, the MARTE profile includes an entire collection of such libraries for various modeling purposes. One of these is the **BasicNFP_Types** library with data types used for specifying nonfunctional properties (see Chapter 3). A typical example of such a type is **NFP_Duration**, which is used to specify time values expressed in terms of physical time units, such as seconds or microseconds. This type is used extensively in the definition of the MARTE profile for all stereotype attributes that represent durations. It is also used in user models that take advantage of MARTE.[9]

2.6 Specializing profiles

MARTE extends the UML standard by providing new concepts that are commonly encountered in real-time and embedded applications. However, there are very many different idiosyncratic realizations of these domain-specific concepts. For example, almost every real-time operating system has its own variant of the concurrent thread concept. It would clearly be impractical to cover all interesting variants in a single MARTE standard—its almost 800 pages are intimidating enough as it is. Fortunately, it is possible to refine the MARTE standard itself. Better yet, because of its highly modular structure, it is possible to pick and choose which subsets of the standard to specialize, leading to relatively compact extensions.

The mechanism by which this is achieved is quite simple and fully aligned with the rest of UML: *stereotype definitions can be subclassed*. For example, we could decide to specialize the **Resource** stereotype depicted in Figure 2.15 by defining a special **ActiveResource** stereotype as shown in Figure 2.18, which restricts the **isActive** attribute to **true**. (Note that the relationship between the two stereotypes is a UML Generalization and not an Extension.)

This type of refinement process can be carried on recursively until the desired level of language refinement is reached, as depicted symbolically in Figure 2.19.[10]

2.7 SUMMARY

The purpose of UML profiles is to extend standard UML to support key concepts specific to a given application domain. This is achieved by refining standard UML concepts using the *stereotype*

---

[9]The topic of extending profiles is discussed in more detail in Section 2.4 and also in Chapter 12.

[10]Note that this is not a UML class or package diagram, but merely an informal illustration of the relationships between the metamodel and profiles using a UML-like notation for the relationships.

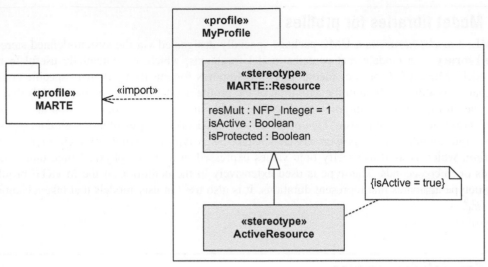

FIGURE 2.18

Example of specializing a MARTE stereotype.

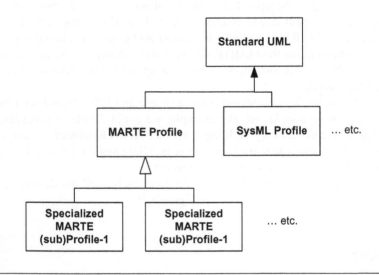

FIGURE 2.19

An example hierarchy of UML language refinements (profiles).

mechanism. A stereotype is a specialization of one or more existing UML concepts (or of other stereotypes), such that it is semantically and syntactically compatible with those concepts. This ensures that the new language constructs defined in a profile are consistent with standard UML, allowing direct reuse of UML-based tooling, information, and expertise. A collection of related stereotypes are grouped into a common package called a *profile*, which captures the definition of the domain-specific

UML variant. When a profile is *applied* to a UML model, the domain-specific concepts defined in the profile become available within that model.

Two types of profiles can be constructed: *language* profiles add new concepts to UML, or, in some cases, displace corresponding UML concepts, while *annotation* profiles are used to provide domain-specific reinterpretations of UML models. An example of a language profile is the Systems Modeling Language, SysML [6]. It is designed to be used as a full-fledged, self-contained language by systems engineers for modeling at the system level. An example of an annotation profile is the SAM profile, which is actually a module within the MARTE profile. This profile is used for analyzing the schedulability characteristics of UML models in the real-time and embedded domain. By applying such a profile to a model along with the necessary data, it may be possible to predict key properties of a planned design using domain-specific analysis methods.

Effective use of UML profiles such as MARTE is greatly enhanced if users have some understanding of how the profile mechanism works. The main principles of operation and rationale behind the profile concept are described in this chapter.

References

[1] Greenfield J, et al. Software factories: assembling applications with patterns, models, frameworks, and tools. Wiley; 2004.

[2] Kelly S, Tolvanen J-P. Domain-specific modeling: enabling full code generation, 1st ed. Wiley_IEEE Computer Society; 2008.

[3] Lagarde F, Espinoza H, Terrier F, Gérard S. Improving UML profile design practices by leveraging conceptual domain models. In: Proceedings of the twenty-second IEEE/ACM international conference on Automated software engineering, Atlanta, Georgia, USA; 2007. p. 445–48.

[4] Lagarde F, Terrier F, André C, Gérard S. Constraints modeling for (Profiled) UML models. In: Akehurst D. Vogel R, Paige R, editors. Model driven architecture–foundations and applications, 4530. Berlin Heidelberg: Springer; 2007. p. 130–43.

[5] Object Management Group, The, OMG Unified Modeling Language™ (OMG UML), Superstructure, Version 2.4.1, OMG document no. formal/2011-08-06, 2011. (Clause 18 provides the specification of the UML Profile mechanism.)

[6] Object Management Group, The, OMG Systems Modeling Language(OMG SysML™), Version 1.3, OMG document no. formal/2012-06-01, 2012.

[7] Silberschatz A, Galvin P, Gagne G. Operating system concepts essentials. John Wiley & Sons; 2011.

MARTE Foundations: Specifying Non-functional Properties

3

CHAPTER CONTENTS

> All things come to those who wait.
> Sometimes they just come too late.
> **Westlife, Before it's too late**

> *Time has been systematically removed from the theories of computation, since it is viewed as representing the annoying property that computation takes time.*
> **Professor Edward Lee, University of California at Berkeley**

3.1 INTRODUCTION

As the quote by Ed Lee above epitomizes, there is a persistent desire among some software theoreticians to deny the physical nature of computing. For example, Edsger Dijkstra, one of the true giants of computer science, argued that, in his view, there should be "no meaningful difference between programming methodology and mathematical methodology" [2],[1] In such a world view, quantity is

---

[1] For this reason, Dijkstra bemoaned the use of interrupts because it introduced concurrency and, consequently, non-determinism into software. However, it seems that he did not recognize that concurrency and non-determinism are fundamental and unavoidable in practically any software that actively interacts with the physical world.

an abstract concept expressed by pure numbers, stripped of any physical connotation. However, for software that interacts with the physical world, this does not hold: the difference between responding to an event within 5 milliseconds (ms) and 5 seconds could mean the difference between success and catastrophe. There are numerous well-known (and expensive) software disasters, such as the failure of NASA's Mars Climate Orbiter, which can be traced directly to difficulties in specifying physical quantities in software [3]. (In that particular case, the root cause of this multimillion dollar failure was traced to the undetected use of incompatible measurement units in different software modules.)

The fact is that most modern software languages, including practically all of those used in real-time systems, leave the issue of how to specify physical quantities to the programmer. UML was designed in this spirit. Even in its representation of time, there is no standard physical time unit defined. One can talk about an event occurring at instant "5," but we do not even know whether this represents some abstract measure (i.e., "logical" time) or a physical one, let alone what unit (seconds, milliseconds, hours?) is intended. Of course, users can devise individual solutions to this, and, for example, agree on a time unit, such as, say, a millisecond. However, these are not first-class concepts (see Section 2.3.3), which means that they are not part of the standardized language. Without a standardized means for expressing physical quantities, it is not possible to deal with such information in a general manner. New tools, such as code generators or model analyzers, would have to be designed or existing ones modified for each specific way of expressing such values.

To avoid this problem, MARTE provides a standardized facility for specifying physical quantities, which are, somewhat unfortunately, referred to as *nonfunctional properties* (NFPs).[2] More specifically, MARTE provides the following capabilities:

- A standard library (the *MARTE model library*) of *physical data types* that represent physical dimensions, such as volume, energy, duration, mass, and so forth [1].
- The ability to specify concrete literal values for such physical data types (e.g., "5 s").
- The ability to extend the library of physical data types with new domain-specific and application-specific types.

The example in Figure 3.1 illustrates the type of expressive power that is made possible by these library types. It shows a fragment from an activity diagram in which an occurrence of a UML

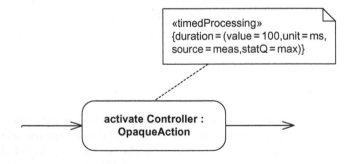

FIGURE 3.1

The use of MARTE non-functional types to specify the precise execution time of an action.

---

[2]We have already commented on the inappropriateness of this term to represent system qualities in Chapter 2, but it is pretty much hardwired in the MARTE spec (and in practice) so that it is not always possible to avoid it.

OpaqueAction (**activateController**) is tagged with the **TimedProcessing** MARTE stereotype. This stereotype is used to identify behaviors that have a non-zero duration. It includes an attribute, **duration**, which can be used to specify a time value. In this example, the value is an instance of the standard MARTE model library data type called **NFP_Duration**, which includes a number useful qualifiers that not only specify the duration itself but also provide some additional information about it. Consequently, we can determine that this particular action has a maximal duration of 100 ms and that this value was obtained by measurement (as opposed to being an estimate).

These library data types can also be used in conjunction with the Value Specification Language (VSL), which is described in Appendix A. This not only enables the specification of complex values, but also allows definition of complex functional dependencies between the values of various elements in a model that would be difficult or even impossible to express directly in basic UML.

3.2 The modeling of physical data types in MARTE

In physics, quantities are expressed as values of some standardized unit. For instance, depending on the chosen *system of units*, mass may be expressed in kilograms or pounds, length in meters or feet, etc [1]. What is needed, therefore, is not only a standardized set of physical units, but also a means for converting from one system of units to another as well as between different units within the same system (e.g., converting from feet to miles).

Different units measure different things: length, duration, mass, etc. To ensure dimensional consistency between different measurement units, MARTE first introduces the notion of *dimension*. This is represented through a special stereotype, **Dimension**, which extends the UML enumeration concept. A dimension in MARTE is, in essence, a linear list (i.e., enumeration) of named units belonging to a given standard physical dimension. Classical physics recognizes three fundamental dimensions: *length* (L), *mass* (M), and *time* (T). These can be combined to represent other more complex units, such as speed (length over time), area (mass squared), and so on. To these three base dimensions, MARTE adds a fourth, *data* (D), which is used to measure information.

Figure 3.2 shows the set of standard dimension types defined in the MARTE model library. It is possible to extend this set, as explained in Section 3.4.

Note the use of the **Unit** stereotype to identify the enumeration literals that represent measurement units. This stereotype has three attributes:

- **baseUnit** — An optional attribute representing a unit that serves as a base for this unit.
- **offsetFactor** — An optional attribute specifying a numerical offset for computing the value of this unit relative to the base unit (this attribute is used if the unit and the base unit start from a different point of origin, such as is the case between the Celsius and Fahrenheit temperature scales).
- **convFactor** — An optional attribute representing the quantitative relationship to the **baseUnit** (e.g., a centimeter (cm) is one one-hundredth (1E-2) of a meter (m)).

The **Dimension** stereotype has three annotational attributes:

- **symbol** — An optional attribute that denotes the character that identifies the *base* physical dimension (L, M, T, or D); this attribute is only used for basic dimensions.
- **baseDimension** — An optional attribute used only for *derived* dimensions that, along with **baseExponent**, identifies the relationship between this dimension and one or more base

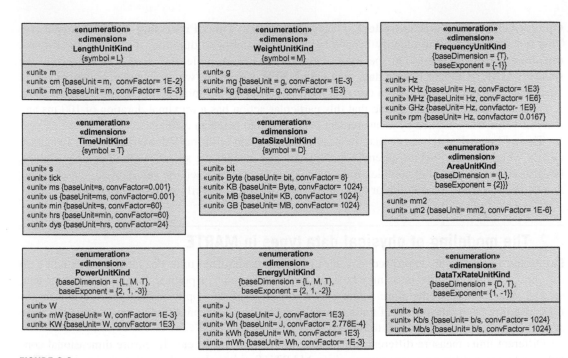

FIGURE 3.2

The standard set of dimensions and measurement units defined in the MARTE model library.

dimensions from which it is derived. It is in the form of an ordered list of base dimension symbols. For example, the data transmission rate kind (**DataTxRateUnitKind**) is based on amount of data (D) and time (T).

- **baseExponent** — An optional attribute used only for derived dimensions that identifies the relationship between this dimension and one or more base dimensions from which it is derived. It takes the form of an ordered list of exponent values corresponding to the relationship to the base dimensions listed in the **baseDimension** attribute. Thus, **DataTxRateUnitKind** is expressed as amount of data (proportional to D; i.e., an exponent value of 1) *divided* by time (inversely proportional to T; i.e., with an exponent value of − 1).

The actual physical values are modeled by specialized UML data types, called *NFP types*, represented by the standard MARTE stereotype, **NfpType**. This stereotype supports three kinds of denotational attributes:

- **valueAttrib** — This attribute points to the attribute of the data type that contains the value of data type. This is usually a numerical quantity (integer or real), although, in some cases, it can be a string.
- **unitAttrib** — This attribute points to the attribute of the data type that contains the physical measurement unit corresponding to the values. This is always an enumeration literal tagged with the **Unit** stereotype described previously.
- **exprAttrib** — This optional attribute points to the attribute that contains a VSL expression to be used for various purposes as explained later in this section.

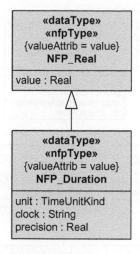

FIGURE 3.3

MARTE model library definition of the **NFP_Duration** data type.

For example, to represent a time interval (duration), MARTE first defines an intermediate type, **NFP_ Real**. This is a general type used as a base for any physical data types whose values can be represented by real numbers. To complete the specification, MARTE then refines **NFP_Real** into the **NFP_Duration** data type, which has a **unit** attribute of the appropriate type (**TimeUnitKind** in this case), as well as additional **clock** and **precision** attributes. (In practice, the latter two attributes are usually left undefined.) The definition of **NFP_Duration** is shown in Figure 3.3.

Figure 3.4 depicts the standard physical data types defined in the MARTE library. As explained in Section 3.4, it is possible for modelers to extend this set with custom physical types.

Note the use of a common abstract data type, **NFP_CommonType**, which includes a number of optional annotational attributes that are shared by all other physical types. These include:

- **expr** — This attribute, typed by **VSL_Expression**, is used when it is desired to specify the value using an *expression* instead of a value literal. As might be expected, the type of this expression must match the type of the **value** attribute. This provides the capability to define functional relationships between the values of different attributes. For example, the value of a "force" attribute could be defined by an expression that specifies a product of a "mass" and an "acceleration" attribute. This is particularly useful for the case of derived attributes, since the expression can capture the precise derivation rule. It can also be used to define initial values of data types.
- **source** — This is typed by the **SourceKind** enumeration type (see Figure 3.4) and is used when it is required to specify *how* the data item was obtained. **SourceKind** provides the following options (enumeration literals):
  - **est** — The value is an estimate.
  - **meas** — The value represents a measured value.
  - **calc** — The value was obtained by some calculation.
  - **req** — The value represents a required quantity.

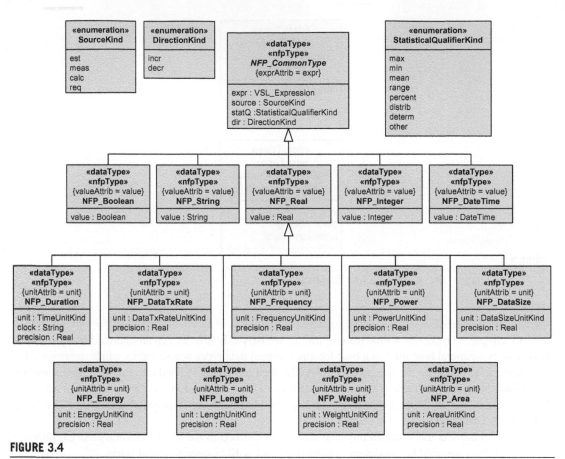

FIGURE 3.4

MARTE model library standard physical data types.[3]

- **statQ** — This parameter is used in cases where the value is a *statistical quantity* and is used to further qualify its nature. It is typed by the **StatisticalQualifierKind** enumeration type (see Figure 3.4), which includes the following choices:[4]
  - **max** — maximum value
  - **min** — minimum value
  - **mean** — mean value
  - **variance** — statistical variance value
  - **percent** — percentile value
  - **range** — the value represents a range of possible values
  - **distrib** — the value is described by a probability distribution (see Section 3.5)
- **dir** — This parameter is used to support *qualitative comparisons* between two different values of the same value type. It is typed by the enumeration **DirectionKind** (see Figure 3.4), which defines

---

[3]This diagram shows slightly simplified definitions of these data types; it also omits some less frequently used types.
[4]The full definition includes several other possibilities.

two possibilities: **incr** (increasing) and **decr** (decreasing). The literal **incr** means that higher values represent higher quality (e.g., reliability), whereas **decr** implies that lower values are of higher quality (e.g., failure rates).

With these added capabilities, it is possible to specify not only values and units, but also additional pertinent information such as the source and nature of data. If any of these attributes are not required, they can simply be left undefined using the VSL "null" literal (e.g., **(value= 50, unit= cm, precision= -)**) or, more simply, by not listing the attributes that are not required.

3.3 How to use the MARTE standard physical types

The physical types from the standard MARTE library can be used like any other data type in the model, such as using them to specify the types of class attributes. However, since they are part of the MARTE standard, they do have the added advantage of being first-class language concepts whose unique application-independent semantics can be readily distinguished by modelers as well as tools that support MARTE.

One of the most common uses for these physical types is to specify concrete values of model parameters. This requires a convenient way of expressing such values, usually in textual form. This is easily done using VSL. The following are example VSL expressions that specify the values of physical data types:

```
(value = 5, unit = m) // 5 meters (length)
(5, m)                        // shorthandform of preceding example[5]
(100, mg)                     // 100 milligrams (weight)
(2, MB)                       // 2 megabytes (data size)
(3, ms)                       // 3 milliseconds (time duration)
(5, Mb/s)                     // 5 megabits per second (data
                              transmission)
```

Note that each of these literals consists of a < value, unit> pair or, more generally, a *tuple*, since as explained previously, it is possible to have additional information associated with the value itself.

3.3.1 Time types, time values, and time expressions

For obvious reasons, time plays a key role in real-time systems and the ability to specify time values precisely is an important capability of MARTE. Hence, we will further elaborate on how to represent such values using MARTE library types and VSL.

To specify time, it is necessary to at least specify a *numerical quantity* and a *unit of measurement* (e.g., 5 s, 3 days). However, we often require more complex specifications, such as time expressed in terms of some standard calendar (e.g., 12/3/2003). The following MARTE library types are related to time values:

---

[5]This shorthand form is supported by most VSL parsers and only applies to certain types that are defined in the standard MARTE model library.

- **DateTime** is a primitive type for specifying time instant values in a format based on the standard western calendar. The general format for literal values belonging to this type is as follows:

```
<datetime-literal> :: = ( <date-string> [<daystring>] ) |
                        ( <time-string> [<date-string>] [<day-string>] ) |
                        ( <day-string> )
<time-string> :: =  <hr> [':' <min> [':' <sec> [':' <centisec>] ] ]
<hr> :: = '00'..'23'
<min> :: = '00'..'59'
<sec> :: = '00'..'59'
<centisec> :: = '00'..'99'
<date-string> :: = <year> '/' <mon> '/' <day-of-mon>
<year> :: = '0000'..'9999'
<mon> :: = '01'..'12'
<day-of-mon> :: = '01'..'31'
<day-string> :: = 'Mon' | 'Tue' | 'Wed' | 'Thr' | 'Fri' | 'Sat' | 'Sun'
```

The following are all examples of valid **DateTime** literals:

```
2011/08/12              --August 12, 2011
2012/09/04 Tue          --Tuesday, September 4,2012
01:30:45                --1:30:45am
Mon                     --Monday
12:00                   --noon
14:39 2011/06/07        --2:39pm on June 7, 2011
23:59:59:99 2010/02/28  --the instant 1 centisecond prior to
                        --midnight on February 28, 2010.
```

- **NFP_DateTime** is an extended form of the **DateTime** type for specifying time instant values with some additional capabilities of optionally providing supplementary information. The actual value is stored in its **value** attribute, which is of type **DateTime**.
- **NFP_Duration** is used to type elements that represent intervals in time and, like **NFP_DateTime**, it has the ability to optionally include supplementary information about the nature of the value. It includes the following attributes:

  - **value** is a **Real** number specifying the actual duration expressed in terms of the units specified by the **unit** attribute.
  - **unit** is an attribute of the type **TimeUnitKind** that specifies the time units (seconds, microseconds, etc.) for a duration value.
  - **source** is an optional feature inherited from NFP_CommonType described in section 3.2.
  - **statQ** is another optional feature inherited from NFP_CommonType.
  - **precision** is an optional attribute of type **Real**, which is used to define the precision of the specified value, in terms of units specified by the **unit** attribute.

In addition to these, two additional attributes are provided to be used in cases where the duration is used to represent a variable time interval. In that case, the **value** attribute typically represents the average duration of the interval and the following two attributes capture its extremes:

- **worst** is an optional **Real**-valued attribute, which can be used to specify the longest (worst) possible value of the interval.
- **best** is an optional **Real**-valued attribute, which specifies the shortest (best) duration of the interval.

Literals belonging to this type are specified using the standard VSL consecutive labeled pairs notation of the form:

```
( < attr-name> = < attr-value > , < attr-name> = < attr-value > ,…)
```

For example, a *required* value of 5 milliseconds would be represented as follows:

```
(value = 5, unit = ms, source = req)
```

(Note that, since most of the attributes are optional, only the desired attributes need be included.)

A short form, which drops the attribute labels and equal signs, is supported by most MARTE tools. In this case, only the value and unit attributes are specified, with the remainder defaulting to null. Thus, a 10 microsecond literal can be specified simply as:

```
(10, us)
```

In a model, time values are specified through time expressions, that is, expressions which, when evaluated, return a time value. To this end, UML provides the concept of a **TimeExpression**. This is merely a refinement of the standard UML concept of a value expression used to specify literal values and expressions. As explained below, **TimeExpression** is the primary mechanism for associating time values with events and other time-related phenomena that can appear in interaction models (UML sequence and communications diagrams). It has the following two main attributes:

- **observation**, which is used to link the expression to one or more observations[6] of events that occurred during an execution.
- **expr**, which is used to store the actual time expression.

Unfortunately, standard UML does not define a standard syntax for these types of expressions, except for expressions consisting of a single term, that is, a literal or reference to a time value. To allow for more complex expressions, MARTE uses the VSL language (see Appendix A), which, as elaborated below, can be used to specify the content of time expressions.

TimeExpression is based on the so-called simple time model of UML, which uses an implicit concept of a clock. But, in situations where it is necessary to express time values relative to an explicit reference clock, then it is necessary to tag the time expression with the MARTE **TimeValueSpecification** stereotype. This is a kind of timed element stereotype, which means that it can be associated with an explicit reference clock.

VSL provides special facilities for expressing time values and relationships. Specifically, it recognizes the UML (and MARTE) time-related concepts of observation, instant, and duration as first-class

---

[6]The concept of an "observation" is covered in more detail in Section 4.2.6.

elements. Thus, it is possible to refer directly to the name of an observation in a VSL time expression. It also supports the notion of repeated event occurrences, such as periodic events, so that it becomes possible to discuss temporal relationships between such occurrences. Finally, it also introduces the notion of "jitter in time," a specification of potential temporal variations of a duration or time of occurrence.

In VSL, time *instant* values are restricted to the **DateTime** type (note that this limits the maximum resolution between two instants to 1 centisecond). Consequently, VSL expressions involving instants, are also of this type. In an expression, a time instant can be referred to either by its corresponding observation name, by its literal value, or by a VSL variable of the appropriate type. Optionally, in case of instants corresponding to recurring event occurrences, it is possible to attach a selector to differentiate individual samples. For example, t1[i] represents the *i*th occurrence of an event marked by observation t1, while t1[i + 2] specifies the second occurrence following the occurrence t1[i]. This allows writing of expressions such as:

```
(t1[i + 1] - t1[i]) < (5, ms)
```

which is a constraint that requires the interval between two successive occurrences of t1 to be less than 5 milliseconds.

It is often convenient to specify the time value of an event occurrence relative to the occurrence of some earlier event. VSL supports this by allowing instant expressions, which include a positive offset expressed as a duration. The following is an example of an expression that denotes an instant that occurs 7 microseconds after instant t1:

```
t1 + (7, us)
```

Durations, on the other hand, are assumed to be of type **NFP_Duration**. Like instants, durations can also have attached observations that can be used in VSL time expressions. The following example constraint specifies that the duration of the execution occurrence of some behavior, labeled by observation d1, must be in the range between 150 and 200 nanoseconds:

```
(d1 > = (150, ns)) and (d1 < = (200, ns))
```

3.4 Adding new physical data types [Advanced]

If the standard MARTE library does not include the desired physical data types, it is possible to define custom types. This involves a number of steps and requires some understanding of the underlying metamodel of MARTE's NFP types.

1. Defining the appropriate physical units and their concrete representation (e.g., seconds, grams, etc.)
2. Defining the unit type (dimension) of physical units required (e.g., energy, length, volume etc.)
3. Defining the desired physical type, that is, the combination of value and unit that represents the desired physical quantity

We explain how this is done by using an example of a Temperature type, which can be expressed using either the centigrade (Celsius) or the Fahrenheit scale.

3.4.1 Step 1: Defining the physical units and their concrete representation

We first need to define the units we are interested in including in our models. Let us assume that in our example we are interested in only two types of units: degrees Celsius (designated by the literal "C") and degrees Fahrenheit (designated by the literal "F").

There exists, of course, a well-known relationship between these two types of measures, defined by the following:

$$TC = (TF - 32)*5/9 \text{ or, conversely: } TF = TC*1.8 + 32$$

where TC is the numerical value of the temperature expressed in degrees centigrade and TF is the equivalent expressed in degrees Fahrenheit.

To support numerical analyses of models where it may be required to convert from one system of units to the other, we will incorporate this information into the definition of our units. To that end, we first need to choose one of these to serve as the *base unit*. Which unit is chosen for this purpose is usually an arbitrary decision since the units are formally coupled through relationships such as the one above. In our example we chose Celsius as the base unit, which means that we will use the second of the two expressions to derive the Fahrenheit unit.

As explained earlier, a "unit" in MARTE is represented by a UML enumeration literal. However, we need to differentiate it from other types of enumeration literals so that it is understood unambiguously (by users and by tools) that this literal represents a physical unit. Furthermore, we also want to be able to specify the functional relationship between the units, so we need to associate some additional information with the literals.

MARTE provides a convenient stereotype for this purpose called **Unit** (see Section 3.2). This stereotype can be applied to UML model elements that are either **EnumerationLiteral**(s) or subtypes of it. This stereotype has three optional attributes:

- **baseUnit** — An attribute specifying another unit that is the base unit for this unit. For the Fahrenheit unit in our example, this will be a reference to the Celsius (C) unit.
- **offsetFactor** — An attribute specifying an offset for computing the value of this unit relative to the base unit. In the example, for the Fahrenheit unit this factor will be + 32.
- **convFactor** — An attribute specifying the conversion factor of this unit relative to the base unit. For the Fahrenheit unit, this will be 9/5 (=1.8).

The "C" and "F" units will be defined as enumeration literals of the enumeration that defines the unit type in the following step.

3.4.2 Step 2: Defining the unit type (Dimension) of the physical type

The unit type, or *dimension*, is specified simply as an enumeration of units. However, to ensure that its semantics are clear and differentiated from other types of enumerations, we need to stereotype this enumeration with the predefined MARTE **Dimension** stereotype. In our example, we define a new **TemperatureUnitKind** enumeration as shown in Figure 3.5.

Note that each of the enumeration literals is stereotyped as a unit and that the corresponding functional relationship between the two is specified in the definition of the Fahrenheit unit. We now have all that is necessary to define the new physical data type.

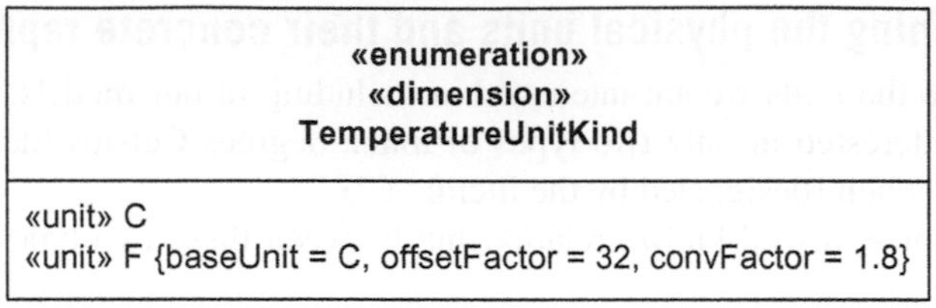

```
                ┌─────────────────────────────────────────────────┐
                │                  «enumeration»                  │
                │                   «dimension»                   │
                │                TemperatureUnitKind              │
                ├─────────────────────────────────────────────────┤
                │ «unit» C                                        │
                │ «unit» F {baseUnit = C, offsetFactor = 32,      │
                │           convFactor = 1.8}                     │
                └─────────────────────────────────────────────────┘
```

FIGURE 3.5

The **TemperatureUnitKind** dimension definition.

3.4.3 Step 3: Defining the new physical type

This step is accomplished with the help of two types of elements provided by the MARTE profile:

1. The MARTE **NfpType** stereotype — This abstract stereotype defines the general format of NFP types and, as noted previously, helps to distinguish physical data types from other kinds of data types that may exist in a model.

2. A specific *physical value type*, which is a one of a set of convenience data types defined in the MARTE library. Each of these types is stereotyped as a MARTE **NfpType** and each contains a unique **value** attribute. They are all subtypes of the same abstract class, **NFP_CommonType** described earlier, and differ only in the type (i.e., **Real**, **Boolean**, **String**, etc.) of their **value** attribute. These utility types are used as bases from which to derive the desired physical data type via specialization. A new physical data type typically adds a **unit** attribute—typed by the appropriate unit type (see Section 3.4.2)—to complement the **value** attribute it inherited from its parent. The end result is a new **NfpType** data type with the requisite < **value**, **unit** > pair.

The following physical value types are predefined in the MARTE library, each having a **value** attribute set to the appropriate type[7]:

> NFP_Boolean {value : Boolean}
> NFP_String {value : String}
> NFP_Integer {value : Integer}
> NFP_Real {value : Real}
> NFP_DateTime {value : DateTime}

In summary, the procedure to define a new physical data type involves:

a. Selecting the appropriate physical value type, based on the kind of value to be specified
b. Creating a new subclass of that type and adding the corresponding **unit** attribute

For our example, we will choose the **NFP_Real** physical value type as our base class, because we want to be able to express non-integer temperature values. We can now define our physical type, Temperature, as shown in Figure 3.6. Note that we have chosen to include an optional **precision** attribute.

This data type can now be used to specify the type attributes of various elements in an application model, which have a temperature characteristic, such as the ProcessorChip class in Figure 3.7.

---

[7]This is only a partial list of the most widely used types.

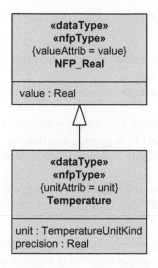

FIGURE 3.6

Defining the new Temperature physical type as a specialization of **NFP_Real**.

ProcessorChip
type : String minTemperature : Temperature maxTemperature : Temperature clockSpeed : NFP_Frequency dissipation : NFP_Power

<u>cpu : ProcessorChip</u>
type = "Pentium III 500E" minTemperature = (0, C) maxTemperature = (85, C) clockSpeed = (500, MHz) dissipation = (16, W)

FIGURE 3.7

An example of use of the **Temperature** physical type defined in Figure 3.6.

This class includes two attributes minTemperature and maxTemperature, which use the newly-defined **Temperature** physical type, and which define the operating temperature range. Figure 3.7 also shows an example of an instance of this class which might appear in an object diagram.

3.5 Specifying probabilistic values for physical data types [Advanced]

In some situations, it may be useful to specify that the value is a probability that conforms to a particular probability distribution function. For example, the following VSL expression defines a value that conforms to the Poisson distribution with a mean value of 3.2:

```
(value = poisson(3.2), statQ = distrib)
```

The function **poisson()** is defined as an operation of the **NFP_CommonType** data type, which is the common supertype of all the physical data types. Note that, if the optional **statQ** attribute is used, as shown in this example, it should be set to **distrib** for consistency.

The following common probability distributions are defined as operations of the **NFP_CommonType**[8]:

- **bernoulli (prob : Real)** — The Bernoulli distribution; **prob** defines a probability, which is a real number between 0 and 1 (inclusive)
- **binomial (prob : Real, trials : Integer)** — A binomial distribution with a probability and number of trials (**trials**) parameters
- **exp (mean : Real)** — An exponential distribution with a given **mean** value
- **gamma (k : Integer, mean : Real)** — A gamma distribution
- **normal (mean : Real, stdDev : Real)** — A normal distribution with given **mean** and standard deviation (**stdDev**) values
- **poisson (mean : Real)** — A Poisson distribution with a given **mean**
- **uniform (min : Real, max : Real)** — A uniform distribution between a minimum (**min**) and maximum (**max**) values

Additional distributions can be supported by creating a subclass of the desired physical type and defining a new probability distribution operation for it. Note, however, that it is not always necessary to define the actual implementation of the distribution in the model, particularly in cases where the evaluation is to be performed by some external analysis tool. Such tools often use their own definition of these distribution functions and only need to be told the types and parameter values of the case on hand.

3.6 Specifying required and offered values

As described in Section 1.5.2, much of MARTE is based on the fundamental client-server pattern. The most prominent example of this pattern is the relationship between a software application—the client—and its supporting platform—the server. To be able to determine whether a particular server can support its clients, it is necessary for the client to specify its *required* qualities of service and for servers to specify the quality of service that they *offer*. If this data is provided explicitly and precisely, it becomes possible to perform engineering analyses; in effect, to determine whether the supply meets demand.

A primary and relatively general means of specifying the required and offered qualities of service in MARTE is via the **NfpConstraint** stereotype and its associated **ConstraintKind** enumeration (see Figure 3.8).

This stereotype can be attached to a constraint to specify a required or offered quality of service. The **kind** attribute, which is of type **ConstraintKind**, is used to identify whether the constraint represents a **required**, **offered**, or **contract** value. Constraints with **kind = required** are used to specify required qualities of service and constraints with **kind = offered** are used to specify offered (provided) qualities of service. Constraints with **kind = contract** are used to specify relationships between a required quality of service and an offered quality of service (typically, these are contracts where the offered quality of service must be greater than or equal to what is required).

---

[8] The full definition includes a few additional but less frequently used distribution operations.

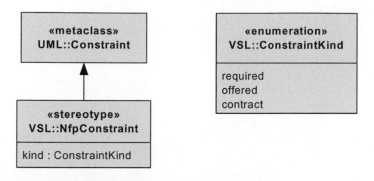

FIGURE 3.8

The **NfpConstraint** stereotype and the **ConstraintKind** enumeration definitions.

The most common use of **NfpConstraint** is through its time-related specialization, the **TimedConstraint** stereotype, for specifying timing data. This is covered in Section 4.2.7.

3.7 SUMMARY

Real-time software systems often need to be very precise about physical quantities such as deadlines, intervals, and resource characteristics (performance, throughput, power consumption, dissipation, etc.). This type of data is useful not only during analysis but also for specifying design constraints and design intent. Unfortunately, standard UML does not support the specification of such values.

MARTE compensates for this deficiency by providing a standard model library which provides:

- A set of generally useful *physical data types*, which represent physical quantities, such as area, energy, duration, mass, and so forth.
- The ability to specify concrete literal values for such physical data types.
- Means to extend the standard library with new custom physical types.

These types are intended to be used in conjunction with VSL, but can also be used with other languages such as the standard UML action language, Alf.

References

[1] Bureau international des poids et mesures, Le Système international d'unités. 8e éd. Sèvres, France, BIPM; 2006, p. 92. <http://www.bipm.org/utils/common/pdf/si_brochure_8_fr.pdf>.
[2] Dijkstra EW. Why American computing science seems incurable (EWD 1209), The Edsger W. Dijkstra Archive at the University of Texas; 1995. <http://www.cs.utexas.edu/~EWD/ewd12xx/EWD1209.PDF>.
[3] National Aeronautics and Space Administration (NASA), The, Mars Control Orbiter—Mishap Investigation Board: Phase I Report (November 10, 1999). <ftp://ftp.hq.nasa.gov/pub/pao/reports/1999/MCO_report.pdf>.

MARTE Foundations: Modeling Time and Resources

CHAPTER CONTENTS

4.1 INTRODUCTION

There are two basic concerns that figure much more prominently in the design of real-time software than in other types of systems:

1. **Timeliness** — This is the ability to respond to events in the environment in a "timely" manner. How that characteristic is defined can vary greatly, depending on the application. It is, of course, just one of a set of *qualities of service (QoS)* that characterize a real-time software system. But regardless of whether we are dealing with soft, hard, or firm real-time systems, time and its passing invariably play a fundamental role in the design and realization of such systems.

2. **Resources** — The laws of physics dictate that program execution requires physical resources, such as processors and memory. For real-time software difficulties can arise due to the *finiteness* of resources, either because there may not be enough of them (e.g., insufficient memory), which often forces them to be shared, or because their characteristics may be limited in some way (e.g., slow processors, limited bandwidth, unreliable hardware). In a very real sense, resources

61

constitute the raw material out of which software applications are constructed, and, as in all engineering, its characteristics can have a significant impact on the characteristics of the end product.

Practically all of MARTE is built on these two foundational notions: *time* and *resources*. These are the two core concepts that connect the conceptual, or logical, world of software to the physical world in which it operates. In this chapter we explain how these two core concepts are modeled in MARTE.

4.2 Modeling with time and clocks

Time is a tyrant: it is the only physical dimension over which we have absolutely no control. It flows relentlessly and the most we can do is to monitor its flow and, when necessary, try to synchronize our actions relative to the occurrence of particular time instants, such as deadlines.

The model of time supported by standard UML is rather elementary; a single reference time source is assumed to exist that is equally and instantaneously accessible by all run-time entities. Unfortunately, its accuracy, resolution, and other key characteristics remain undefined. The concepts of observable time instants and time intervals with durations are defined, but no facility is provided for specifying concrete physical values for them. This idealized model is inadequate for many real-time software systems, which can have stringent timeliness requirements. This holds in particular for physically distributed real-time systems in which different parts of the system may be using different sources of time measurement. MARTE addresses these deficiencies and a significant portion of it is dedicated to modeling various mechanisms (resources) for measuring time, relationships between system behavior and time, and for specifying time values.

4.2.1 Two alternatives for dealing with time values

Because of its ephemeral nature, our access to time is indirect. It requires the medium of clocks—mechanisms that measure and register the progress of time. In general, a clock provides a *time reference*, which can be used to order the execution of behaviors. Unfortunately, even the most accurate physical clocks are imperfect, suffering from flaws such as finite resolution and jitter. This becomes a particularly thorny issue in geographically distributed systems, where multiple time references exist, which, due to their physical nature and the inherent limitations of communications mechanisms, preclude perfect synchronization. This can lead to incorrect orderings of time-sensitive behaviors, which, in turn, can cause system failures.

In time-sensitive applications, where the *accuracy* of time specification is a primary concern, it must be possible to explicitly represent and quantify the relevant characteristics of clocks (e.g., their resolution, offset, rollover value). To this end, MARTE provides the ability to not only accurately model clocks and their characteristics, but to also to associate the times of occurrence of events and behaviors with explicit reference to the clocks by which they are recorded.

On the other hand, there are numerous cases where a precise and detailed representation of clocks and time is unnecessary and would be unduly burdensome if forced on the modeler. In those situations it may be sufficient to simply assume an ideal centralized clock, which serves as the *implicit* reference for all specified time values.

Since each model of time has its use cases in practice, MARTE supports both:

1. The *explicit clock reference approach*, in which timing information is expressed relative to an explicit clock whose characteristics may be precisely defined.
2. The *implicit clock reference approach*, in which timing information is based on an assumed central ideal time reference.

Note that the latter approach does not preclude explicit representation of clocks in a model, but their characteristics are typically not specified nor are any time values explicitly associated with them.

The choice of approach is up to the modeler. It is important to note, however, that *this choice does have downstream implications in terms of which MARTE constructs can be used when dealing with time*. For example, if an explicit reference clock approach is used, then, for capturing the time associated with an event occurrence, the **TimedInstantObservation** stereotype should be used, since it allows an explicit reference clock to be specified. Otherwise, the standard UML **TimeObservation** concept is used. Hence, choosing the approach is an important decision that needs to be made early in the modeling process.

In this chapter, we focus mostly, but not exclusively, on the explicit reference clock approach and its associated MARTE concepts. As noted, this approach is suitable for situations where the characteristics of clocks (i.e., their imperfections) may have significant impact as well as cases where there may be multiple time references. The alternative approach based on an implicit clock is described in more detail in Section 5.5.1.

4.2.2 **MARTE models of time**

In MARTE, time is represented simply as an ordered and unbounded progression of time instants. This progression may be represented either as *discrete* or *continuous* (sometimes referred to as the *dense* model of time). However, to support various models of time used in software engineering and computer science, MARTE recognizes and provides three different alternative conceptualizations of time:

- The *logical (or causal)* time model is non-metric, concerned only with the relative ordering of events and their causal relationships. It is a very abstract model of time and is useful in certain types of qualitative (as opposed to quantitative) analyses, such as determining whether deadlocks are possible in a system.
- The *synchronous (or clocked)* model of time is another non-metric view of time, in which it is assumed that system responses to inputs are computed at regular time intervals, which are tied to the beat of a reference clock. Furthermore, the computation times of the responses are assumed to be negligible relative to the interval between successive clock ticks, so that the outputs can be considered as simultaneous with the inputs (this is referred to as the *synchrony hypothesis* [2]). One of the major advantages of this model is that the degree of nondeterminism can be greatly reduced since all proximate occurrences are compressed into a single time instant. This can simplify state-space exploration analyses by orders of magnitude.
- The *physical* model of time comes closest to time as we experience it: as a monotonic progression of time instants. In contrast to the synchronous time model, behavior is not necessarily assumed to occur instantaneously.

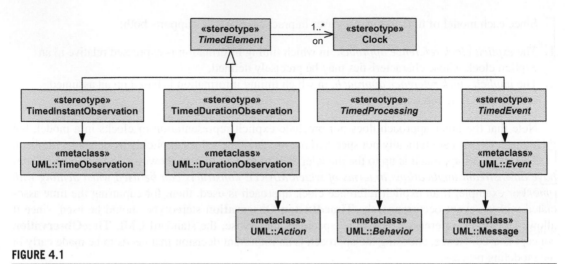

FIGURE 4.1

The **TimedElement** stereotype and its subtypes.

The physical model comes closest to reality, such as we understand it. The logical and synchronous models abstract out most of its physical aspects of time and are, therefore, not considered further in this and subsequent chapters. Readers interested in these logical models of time should consult references [1] and [3] as well as the time modeling section of the MARTE specification [4].

The ability to precisely specify literal values of physical time (instants and durations) is provided in MARTE through the VSL language (see Appendix A) and through its physical data types, notably **NFP_Duration** and **NFP_DateTime**, as described in Section 3.3.1.

4.2.3 Base concepts for explicit reference clock modeling

For the explicit clock reference approach mentioned earlier, the key MARTE abstraction is the concept of a "timed element," which captures the concept of a model element that is indelibly associated with a reference clock.[1] This is captured in the form of an *abstract* stereotype (**TimedElement**), which serves as the common parent of a variety of different time-related stereotypes including (Figure 4.1):

- **TimedInstantObservation** — For modeling instants that occur at a particular point in time; this stereotype is applied to event occurrences of various types (described in Section 4.2.6.1).
- **TimedDurationObservation** — For modeling time intervals of time, usually associated with two complementary event occurrences (Section 4.2.6.2).
- **TimedProcessing** — For modeling computations and other processes that take time to complete (Section 4.2.6.2).
- **TimedEvent** — For modeling event *types* that occur at a particular point in time, such as periodic clock beats (Section 4.2.8).

---

[1] More precisely, MARTE allows multiple clocks to be associated with a timed element (each clock with a value corresponding to its perspective), but a single clock is by far the most common case.

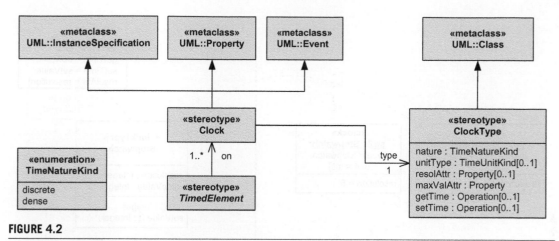

FIGURE 4.2

The **Clock**, **ClockType**, and **TimedElement** stereotypes and their base classes.

The meaning and application of these stereotypes is described in more detail in the following sections. In all cases, the relevant reference clock is specified by the **on** attribute of the stereotypes, which they inherit from **TimedElement** (Figures 4.1 and 4.2). An example of the use of this attribute is shown in Figure 4.10.

4.2.4 Modeling clocks

If the implicit approach is chosen, the simplest but least detailed way of modeling clocks with MARTE is to use its **ClockResource** stereotype. This is merely a way of labeling an element in the model to indicate that it represents a kind of clock. However, no additional characteristics of that clock, such as its resolution or accuracy, can be specified with this method. This means that it is not particularly well suited for any kind of precise formal analysis of the timing properties of a system.

For more detailed and more precise modeling of clocks, MARTE provides two related stereotypes: **ClockType** and **Clock**, whose definitions are depicted in Figure 4.2.

An example of the use of these two stereotypes is shown in the two model fragments in Figure 4.3.[2] In the left fragment are two object instances, sw1 and sw2, both of which are tagged with the **Clock** stereotype, meaning that they represent *instances* of a clock. In this case, they both happen to be instances of the same *clock type* called Stopwatch, which is shown in the model fragment on the right. The link between the instances and their type is made through the value of the **type** attribute of the **Clock** stereotype applied to the instances. The Stopwatch class is stereotyped as a **ClockType** and it serves to define the shared characteristics of all clock instances of this type. Note that, despite being of the same type, the two clocks shown here have different resolutions (1 and 5 milliseconds, respectively).

As this example illustrates, the **ClockType** stereotype can be used to tag those UML classes that represent clock *type* definitions. These are used to specify the general characteristics of a particular

---

[2]The curved dashed lines in the diagram are informal annotations overlaid on the UML diagram indicating "pointer-like" relationships.

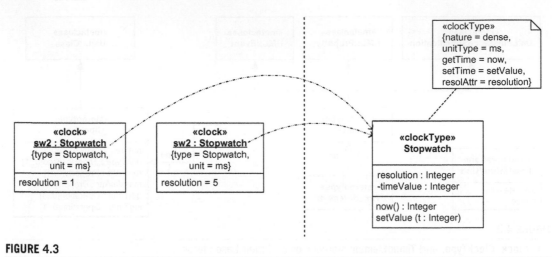

FIGURE 4.3

Examples of the use of the **Clock** and the **ClockType** stereotypes.

type of clock, such as its accuracy and resolution. The **Clock** stereotype, on the other hand, must always be linked to a particular **ClockType** and is used to tag model elements that represent instances of that type. It can be applied to model elements of the type **InstanceSpecification** (as shown in Figure 4.3) or to *properties* of classifiers, such as the parts of a structured class (as in Figure 4.4), or to the roles of a collaboration. The type corresponding to a clock instance is specified by the **type** attribute of the **Clock** stereotype. As explained previously, this is a mandatory attribute, so that an appropriate **ClockType** stereotype must be defined whenever the **Clock** stereotype is used in a model.

The **ClockType** stereotype has a number of generally useful attributes, all of which are optional. This means that modelers modeling clocks need only concern themselves with specifying the values of those features that are of interest to them. The following are the most commonly used features of this stereotype:

- **nature** is used to identify whether time is modeled as continuous (*dense*) or *discrete*. For software applications, which live in the discrete world of digital computers, it is usually safe to assume that time is discrete and, hence, the attribute and its value need not be specified explicitly.
- **unitType** is an optional attribute used to identify the *type* of units that the value of the clock represents. This has to be a kind of UML enumeration and is normally set to the predefined enumeration type **TimeUnitKind** included in the MARTE standard model library **MARTE::TimeLibrary** (see Section B.5 in Appendix B).
- **maxValueAttr** is a denotational attribute[3] that identifies the attribute of the tagged class that specifies the maximum possible value of the clock before it wraps around.
- **resolAttr** is a denotational read-only attribute that is used to identify the user-defined attribute of the tagged class that specifies the resolution of the clock. This is normally an integer value that represents a multiple of the unit specified by the attribute denoted by **unitType**. For example, in Figure 4.3 this attribute points to the **resolution** attribute of the Stopwatch class. Note that this does

---

[3]For a definition of "denotational" attribute, see Chapter 2.

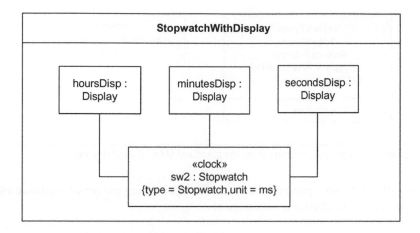

FIGURE 4.4

Example the **Clock** stereotype used to tag a part (sw2) in a structured class.

not specify the value of the resolution, but merely identifies the attribute whose value actually specifies the resolution. This allows different instances of the type to have different resolutions, as is the case with the clocks sw1 and sw2.

• **getTime** is a denotational attribute used to identify the user-defined operation of the class used to read the current value of the clock. For instance, this information can be used to determine when the application is asking for the current time of the system. In the example in Figure 4.3 this attribute points to the now() operation of the Stopwatch class. A sophisticated timing analysis program might use this information to determine when an executing application is accessing the current time. For example, a synchronous call to this operation could occur in a sequence diagram.

• **setTime** is another denotational attribute that is used to identify the operation that sets the value of the clock.

In addition, the **ClockType** stereotype provides facilities for modeling additional characteristics of clocks, such as their accuracy, offset relative to a reference clock, etc. Further details can be found in the MARTE specification [4].

As explained, individual clock instances are indicated by applying the **Clock** stereotype to a model element that represents a clock. Examples are included in both Figures 4.3 and 4.4. The following two stereotype attributes are the ones used most often:

• **type**, which points to the appropriate **ClockType** element. Note that the value of this attribute usually, but not necessarily, matches the type of the property, as is the case in Figure 4.3 in which the type of the instances is equal to their clock type (Stopwatch).

• **unit**, which is an enumeration literal value from the type defined by the **unitType** attribute of the clock's corresponding clock type. As noted, this is usually set to the **TimeUnitKind** enumeration defined in the standard MARTE Time Library, so that the value of this attribute is set to one of the **TimeUnitKind** literals (e.g., **ns, us, ms, s**).

A slightly more detailed representation can be obtained using the **HwClock** stereotype (Section 6.4.7.2), which includes a clock **frequency** attribute (of type **NFP_Frequency**). But, this is intended

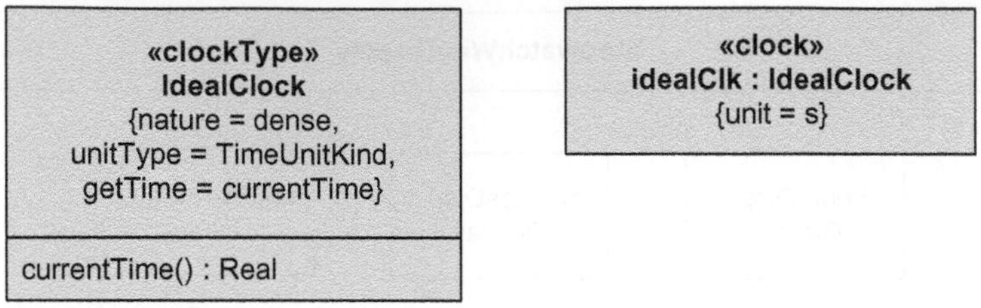

```
┌─────────────────────────────┐     ┌─────────────────────────────┐
│        «clockType»          │     │          «clock»            │
│        IdealClock           │     │    idealClk : IdealClock    │
│      {nature = dense,       │     │         {unit = s}          │
│   unitType = TimeUnitKind,  │     └─────────────────────────────┘
│   getTime = currentTime}    │
├─────────────────────────────┤
│   currentTime() : Real      │
└─────────────────────────────┘
```

FIGURE 4.5

The ideal reference clock type and instance from the standard MARTE model library.

to be used primarily in detailed platform modeling for representing the actual hardware clock mechanisms used to drive discrete electronics components.

4.2.5 The ideal clock

The standard MARTE model library provides a utility element that represents an "ideal" clock and a corresponding clock instance (see Figure 4.5). This represents a dense-time clock with no jitter and perfect accuracy. It is mostly intended for cases when we want to use the explicit clock reference stereotypes (e.g., **TimedProcessing**, **TimedEvent**), which require explicit reference clocks, but when we are not concerned with the detailed characteristics of those clocks. While this is reminiscent of the implicit reference clock approach (see Section 4.2.1), which assumes an ideal clock, it is still possible that there may be other reference clocks in that same system that are not ideal. In fact, in most such situations, the characteristics of those clocks are expressed relative to the ideal clock.

4.2.6 Associating behavior with time

Behavior occurs through time and, in real-time software, it is often important to be precise about when things occur or when they should occur, and how long they take or should take. In this section, we examine how MARTE can be used to associate time with behaviors.

4.2.6.1 Specifying times of event occurrences

In UML, an *event occurrence* is defined as an *instantaneous* change of state in the system, which means that, from a temporal perspective, they have only a time of occurrence, but no duration. Event occurrences should be distinguished from *event types*, which are classifiers that represent *categories* of event occurrences rather than individual event occurrences. UML includes explicit support for the following types of events[4] (see Figure 4.6):

- Signal sending events occur at the instant a signal send action completes and a signal message is dispatched to the designated receiver. In a sequence diagram, this occurrence is represented by the point of origin of the outgoing signal send message (points @t2 and @t10 in Figure 4.6). In the model, this is captured by an instance of the UML **MessageOccurrenceSpecification** element.

---

[4]UML also recognizes so-called "change events," which are typically used to specify triggers in state machines. However, it does not provide the ability to directly represent an individual occurrence of a change event, so we do not consider it further here.

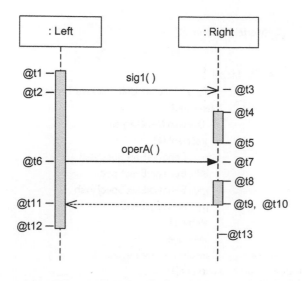

FIGURE 4.6

Different types of event occurrences in an interaction (represented by a sequence diagram).

- (Operation) call events occur in the course of the execution of an operation invocation action and represent the instants when a message carrying the operation call data is sent to the designated receiver. In the diagram, this is represented by the point of origin of the outgoing call event message (point @t6 in Figure 4.6) and is captured in the model by an instance of the **MessageOccurrenceSpecification** model element.
- Message reception events occur when a signal or operation call message arrives at the receiving location. Note that it is important to distinguish this event type from the start of execution type of event explained below. In the sequence diagram, this event occurrence is represented by the termination point of a signal or operation call message (points @t3, @t7, and @t11 in Figure 4.6). The corresponding model element is, once again, an instance of the UML **MessageOccurrenceSpecification** element.
- There are two special cases of receive event occurrences: *object creation* and *object destruction*. These are distinguished from regular communications receptions based on the type of message associated with the MessageOccurrenceSpecification. Namely, if the **messageSort** attribute of the message that owns the end is set to **MessageSort::createMessage**, it represents an object creation event occurrence. If it is set to **MessageSort::deleteMessage**, then it is an object destruction occurrence.
- Behavior execution start events occur at the instant when a behavior starts executing. While this may coincide with a message receive event, it does not always have to, since additional processing and queuing may occur between message reception and the start of the corresponding execution. In a sequence diagram, an execution start is represented by the point on the lifeline at which the execution occurrence specification starts (points @t1, @t4, and @t8 in Figure 4.6). The corresponding model element is an instance of the UML **ExecutionOccurrenceSpecification** element.
- Behavior execution completion events occur when a behavior completes its execution run. In a sequence diagram, this occurrence is represented by the point on the lifeline

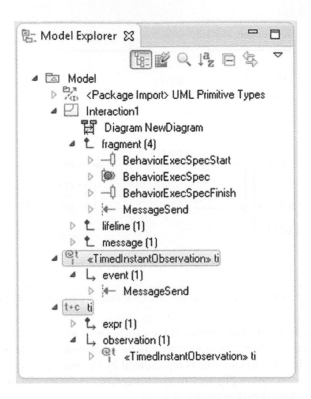

FIGURE 4.7

An example of a model navigator/explorer in the Papyrus UML modeling tool.

at which the execution occurrence specification terminates (points @t5, @t9, and @t12 in Figure 4.6). The corresponding model element is, again, an instance of the UML **ExecutionOccurrenceSpecification** element.

- The occurrence of arbitrary time instants can also be represented, such as instant @t13 in Figure 4.6, by inserting an instance of the more general UML concept **OccurrenceSpecification** in the appropriate position in the list of occurrences of a lifeline.

With the exception of arbitrary time instants, the above event occurrences are typically automatically created by a modeling tool as the diagram is being created, so that the modeler does not have to add them explicitly. But to associate timing information with these event occurrences typically requires direct manipulation of the model by the modeler since most tools do not provide direct support for this in a diagram editor. In most UML tools, this is achieved with the help of the model navigator/explorer facility and a corresponding properties editor for setting up the values of the various attributes. An example of such a model explorer for the Papyrus UML tool[5] is shown in Figure 4.7.

In UML, timing information can only be associated with occurrences that have been explicitly designated as "observed" within the model. It is the modeler who chooses which event occurrences

---

[5]http://www.papyrusuml.org/.

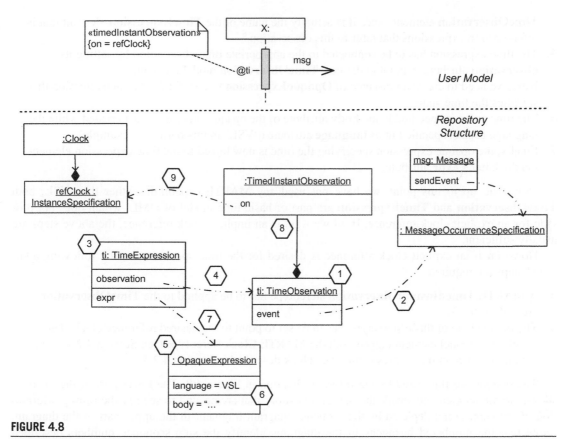

FIGURE 4.8

Example of the model structures that need to be created to associate a time observation with an event occurrence (a message send in this case). The numbered hexagons correspond to the step numbers in the text.

will be "observed" by first creating an observation element and then binding it to the appropriate event occurrence. In most modeling tools this requires a sequence of tool manipulations that conform to the following (see Figure 4.8):

1. It is necessary to first create an instance of a UML **TimeObservation** model element.
2. Once created, the newly created time observation element needs to be bound to the corresponding event occurrence. This is usually an instance of a UML **MessageOccurrenceSpecification** if the occurrence is a message send or receive, or an instance of a UML **ExecutionOccurrenceSpecification** if it is a start or completion of an execution. The linking is done by setting the **event** attribute of the time observation element to point to the appropriate event occurrence element.
3. To specify the time value associated with the occurrence, it is first necessary to create an instance of the UML **TimeExpression** element (for hosting the value). To avoid possible confusion, *it is strongly recommended to give this expression the same name as the name of its corresponding*

TimeObservation element, since it is actually the name of the **TimeExpression** element that is referenced in expressions that refer to this observation.[6]

4. The time expression has to be connected to the appropriate time observation by setting its **observation** attribute to point to the new **TimeObservation** model element.

5. Next, we need to create an instance of **OpaqueExpression** to contain the actual expression that specifies the time value.

6. The time value is specified in the **body** attribute of the opaque expression just created while the language used is specified in its **language** attribute ("VSL" in this particular example).

7. Finally, the opaque expression specifying the time is now linked to the time expression element via the latter's **expr** attribute.

Note that, up to this point, we have not used any MARTE capabilities other than VSL; both **TimeObservation** and **TimeExpression** are part of basic time model of UML, which does not provide for an explicit clock reference. If all we want is an implicit clock reference, the above steps are usually sufficient.

However, if an explicit clock reference *is* desired for the time specification, the following additional steps are required:

8. A MARTE **TimedInstantObservation** stereotype has to be applied to the **TimeObservation** created in step 1.

9. The **on** attribute of this\e stereotype has to be set to point to the desired reference clock. This should be a model element tagged with the MARTE **Clock** stereotype (see Section 4.2.4). One common choice in these cases is the ideal clock described in Section 4.2.5.

These steps are illustrated by the informal diagram in Figure 4.8. The lower part of the diagram shows the model elements inside the model repository that are needed to specify the timing information of the signal send depicted by the sequence diagram fragment in the upper part of the diagram. (Note that the numbered hexagons in the diagrams identify the step sequence numbers described above and are not part of the actual diagram, but are included here to assist the reader in matching the steps to the model.)

4.2.6.2 Specifying durations

MARTE also provides facilities for specifying durations, which quantify the time between two instants in an interaction. The key facility here is the **NFP_Duration** library type (see Section 3.3.1). Different kinds of durations are of interest, notably:

* Durations of behavior executions (e.g., worst-case execution times),
* Intervals between event occurrences.

When dealing with sequence diagrams, the basic approach specifying durations in UML interaction models is comparable to that used for instants (described in Section 4.2.6.1).[7] Instead of

---

[6] This is necessary because the **TimeObservation** model element does not by itself represent a value (i.e., it is not an element that is associated with any kind of type). So, it cannot be used in an expression that requires a value.

[7] The UML concept of a **DurationObservation** has additional facilities that can be used in these types of situations; however, in keeping with the introductory nature of this text, we omit discussion of these capabilities.

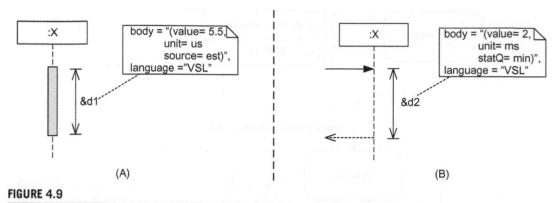

FIGURE 4.9

Examples of duration specifications.

TimeObservation, the UML **DurationObservation** element is used and **Duration** replaces **TimeExpression**. Like **TimeObservation**, **DurationObservation** has an **event** attribute. The difference is that, instead of pointing to just one event occurrence like a time observation, a duration observation should point to two: the initial and final occurrences. (Note that the two occurrences do not have to be on the same lifeline, as shown in the example in Figure 4.12.) For example, in the model fragment on the left-hand side of Figure 4.9, the duration observation would include both the start of execution event occurrence and the end of execution event occurrence, respectively (the gray rectangle on the left lifeline). The value of the duration between these two event occurrences is then specified by the **body** attribute[8] of the time expression linked to the **Duration** model element, analogous to the way that **TimeExpression** is used to specify the value of a **TimeObservation**.

If an explicit reference clock is desired then the **TimedDurationObservation** stereotype should be applied to the duration observation, analogous to how **TimedInstantObservation** is used for instant values based on a specific clock. This stereotype includes an **on** attribute for specifying the reference clock, which it inherits from the **TimedElement** stereotype.

The left-hand side of Figure 4.9 depicts an example of a duration observation attached to an execution occurrence element, whose duration is estimated at 5.5 microseconds, while the right-hand side illustrates a case where it is specified that the duration between two time instants on the same lifeline is at least 2 milliseconds. The values are expressed here using an opaque expressions (i.e., UML **OpaqueExpression** elements) specified in the VSL language (see Appendix A) and the library type **NFP_Duration** (see Section 3.3.1). (Note that, for convenience, we have used a comment-like notation for showing the values of the duration elements directly in the diagrams. However, in most UML editors, these values can only be seen in the appropriate property editors rather than in the diagrams.)

The concept of an observation is really only meaningful in the context of an execution model, and should, therefore, only be used with interaction models that represent systems in execution. However, there are cases where we would like to express durations *independently of any particular execution context*, such as specifying the estimated execution time of some behavior or action.

As explained, two ways of specifying this are supported by MARTE: the explicit clock reference approach and the implicit one.

---

[8]This attribute is inherited from the metaclass **ValueSpecification**, which is a superclass of **TimeExpression**.

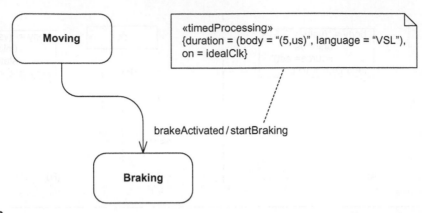

FIGURE 4.10

Using the **TimedProcessing** stereotype to define the execution time of a behavior (**startBraking**).

For the explicit clock reference approach, MARTE provides a timed element stereotype called **TimedProcessing**. This stereotype can be attached to instances of UML actions and behaviors (e.g., state machines, activities) to specify their potential execution durations. The stereotype includes a **duration** attribute, which can contain a time expression (**TimeExpression**) that specifies the execution time of that behavior. For example, we can use the **TimedProcessing** stereotype to tag the behavior startBraking, which is the behavior associated with a transition in a state machine, as shown in the diagram fragment in Figure 4.10. In this case, we are using it to specify the execution time of that behavior, which is probably the most common case.

The use of the **TimedProcessing** stereotype for specifying durations requires that we explicitly specify a reference clock, such as the ideal clock. For the implicit clock case, a different approach is used, as explained in Section 5.5.1.

4.2.7 Timed constraints

In real-time systems it is common to expect constraints related to time, such as deadlines and response times. There are a number of ways of specifying these using MARTE, based on the preferred approach (explicit or implicit clock reference). For the explicit clock approach, the **TimedConstraint** stereotype can be used. This is a specialization of two other MARTE concepts as shown in Figure 4.11.

The **TimedElement** parent is used to specify the reference clock (typically, the ideal clock), while the **NfpConstraint** parent allows us to specify whether the constraint is a **required**, **offered**, or **contract** type, based on the value of its **kind** attribute. The **interpretation** attribute of a timed constraint is typed by the enumeration, **TimeInterpretationKind**, and is used to specify whether the constraint refers to a **duration** or an **instant** value. (The **any** option is for those rare cases where the difference between the two is irrelevant.)

An example of the use of this stereotype can be seen in Figure 4.12. In this case, we are specifying that the duration between the receipt of message m by element a (timed instant observation @t1) and the receipt of message n by element b (timed instant observation @t2) is *required* to be no greater than 2 microseconds but less than 100 microseconds. In this case, we have created a simple

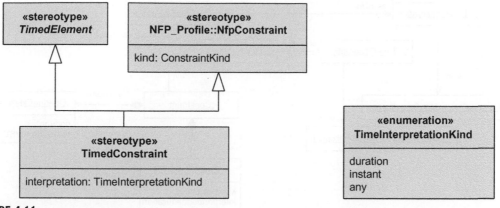

FIGURE 4.11

The **TimedConstraint** stereotype and the **TimeInterpretationKind** enumeration.

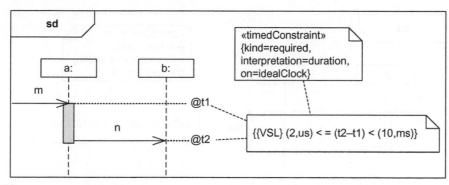

FIGURE 4.12

Example of using the **TimedConstraint** stereotype to specify a required time constraint.

UML constraint, which we then stereotyped using the **TimedConstraint** stereotype. As explained in Section 4.2.6.1, the time observations, @t1 and @t2, cannot be inserted directly in the constraint expression; instead, they are represented by their two associated time expressions named t1 and t2, respectively. The internal repository representation of the model elements involved in the constraint specification is depicted in Figure 4.13.

An alternative to the above approach is to represent the required duration using the UML **DurationObservation** concept is shown in Figure 4.14. In this case, the duration observation &d has an associated **Duration** element named d, whose **observation** attribute is set to point to the duration observation. This element is required so that its name can be used in the constraint expression. A constraint is then applied to the duration element, which is finally stereotyped as a **TimedConstraint**. Part of the internal repository structure corresponding to this construction is shown in Figure 4.15. The two **MessageOccurrenceSpecification** elements correspond to the start and end event occurrences of **DurationObservation&d**.

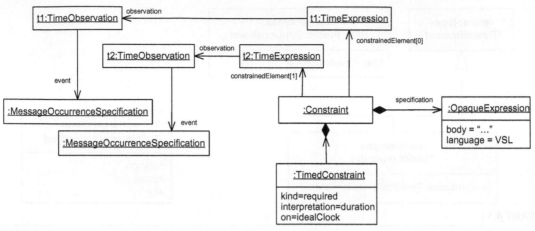

FIGURE 4.13

Fragment of the internal repository structure for the constraint specification in Figure 4.12.

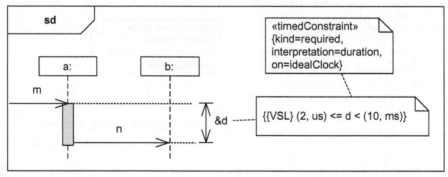

FIGURE 4.14

An alternative method to that of Figure 4.12 using a duration observation.

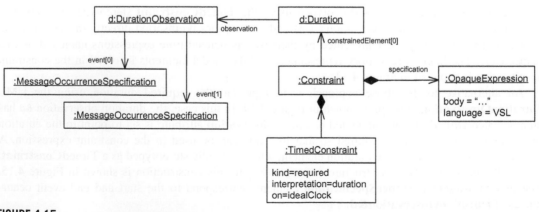

FIGURE 4.15

Fragment of the internal repository structure for the constraint specification in Figure 4.14.

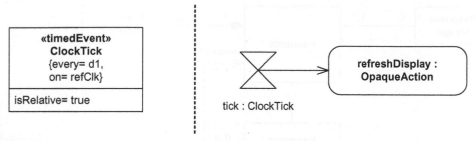

FIGURE 4.16

Example of using the **TimedEvent** stereotype to represent a repeating time event and its use in an activity diagram.

4.2.8 Modeling timers and timeouts

Timers are, in essence, clocks that are designed to detect the occurrence of a particular instant or set of instants and signal if and when they occur. If the explicit reference clock approach is used, it is possible to represent the *effect of a timer* via the MARTE **TimedEvent** stereotype. This is a kind of timed element, which means that it specifies an explicit reference clock. This stereotype can be applied to a basic UML **TimeEvent** model element, which is an event type that represents the occurrence of a particular time instant. This stereotype has two interesting attributes:

- **every** — This specifies the duration of the interval between two successive events of this type and is normally specified as a time expression associated with a duration observation, as explained in Section 4.2.6.2.
- **repetition** — This is an optional integer attribute that defines the number of times the event occurrence will be generated. If the event is not recurring, the value should be set to 1. If it repeats an unbounded number of times, then the attribute should be left undefined.

The example on the left side of the model fragment in Figure 4.16 shows a timed event type, ClockTick, which repeats every 50 milliseconds an unbounded number of times (**repetition** attribute left undefined). An application of this event type is shown in the activity diagram fragment on the right side of the figure.

However, the utility of this way of modeling timers is limited, since in UML the **TimeEvent** concept can only be used directly in two cases: to specify the triggers of state machine transitions or to specify the triggers of **AcceptEventAction**s in activities. One additional disadvantage of this method is that **TimeEvent** requires an explicit **TimeExpression** for specifying the time value, but this expression serves the same purpose as the **every** attribute of the **TimedEvent** stereotype. A more practical method for specifying timers and timeouts, based on the implicit clock reference approach, is described in Chapter 5.

Actually, both clocks and timers are examples of what MARTE refers to under the general notion of *resource*, a topic that is introduced in the following section.

4.3 Modeling resources

Resources play a major role in the MARTE view of the world and a large part of the specification is dedicated to describing the different manifestations of this key concept. However, in this chapter, we

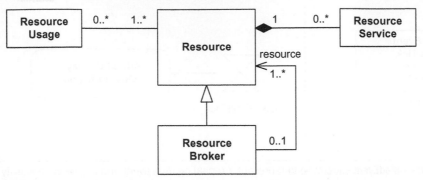

FIGURE 4.17

Simplified metamodel of the MARTE resource concept.

only focus on the *conceptual framework* that is shared by all its various specializations, which are described in this and subsequent chapters. This core framework is referred to as the Generic Resource Model (GRM) in the MARTE specification [5].

More detailed discussions on the structure, meaning, and usage of the specialized resource types can be found in subsequent chapters, particularly in Chapter 5, which deals with modeling applications using MARTE and Chapter 6, which addresses modeling of platforms.

4.3.1 Conceptual framework for representing resources

The basic conceptual model of resources in MARTE was briefly introduced in Section 1.5.2, but we provide a more general detailed explanation here. In essence, there are just a small number of core concepts involved (Figure 4.17):

- *Resource* — This is an abstract and generic concept that specifies an element *with some kind of physical underpinning* that participates in the realization of some software application. It may represent an actual *physical device*, such as a processor, a sensor, or a communications line. Alternatively, it can also represent a *logical device*, which is, in essence, an abstract rendering of some physical resource, such as an operating system thread or a message packet. Note that even logical devices have a physical foundation: an operating system thread is a kind of "virtual" processor ultimately realized (through a layer of software) by a real physical processor, and a message packet is an application-specific unit of memory implemented on top of some type of physical storage. It is this physical essence of resources that gives them their finiteness characteristic and which MARTE strives to represent.
- *Resource service* — As explained in Section 1.5.2, MARTE models resources as servers in a client-server relationship. Hence, resources are viewed as providers of one or more services, which, in most cases, are accessed via the interfaces of the resources. However, the concept of a service extends beyond just basic operation calls such as invoking an operating system API. For example, a CPU can be seen as a provider of "processing" services and a temperature sensor as a provider of temperature measurement services.
- *Resource broker* — A resource broker *may* exist as an intermediary between resource clients and resources. Its role is to enforce some type of *resource utilization policy* over a set of resources

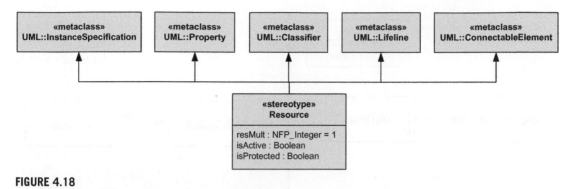

FIGURE 4.18

The **Resource** stereotype with its base classes.

in its domain.[9] Thus, rather than appropriating a resource directly, a client may need to ask the broker for the resource. A typical example of a broker is an operating system scheduler, which is responsible for allocating processor time to competing concurrent threads based on some scheduling policy.

- *Resource usage* — This concept captures the characteristics of a particular usage of one or more resources by some client or clients. These might include a list of the resources used, the respective amounts, and some service specific data such as execution time or energy consumed.

The conceptual model (i.e., metamodel) supporting these concepts is captured in the simple class diagram in Figure 4.17.[10] Note that the resource broker is just a special kind of resource, which means that it too can provide services (in fact, it is often the broker that provides the actual resource services while the resources themselves are passive entities).

The management of resources is very much resource specific. For example, management of processing resources is handled implicitly through a scheduler, whereas management of memory is often done by an explicit memory manager component. For this reason, there is no general MARTE stereotype for the concept of a resource broker or resource manager. Instead, there are specific stereotypes for the various kinds of resources, where appropriate.

4.3.2 Modeling resources

The generic resource concept is represented in MARTE by the general stereotype **Resource** (see Figure 4.18). This can be used directly to tag model elements, but MARTE provides a core set of specializations of this stereotype based on the nature and purpose of the resource. These include[11]:

- *Processing resources* (**ProcessingResource** stereotype), representing processors or, more generally, computers

---

[9] MARTE distinguishes between a resource broker and a *resource manager*, with the former responsible for resource usage and the latter for managing resources. These two functions are often combined in practice into a single unit. Hence, we will not refer to this distinction further.

[10] This is a much simplified version of the actual metamodel specified in the MARTE specification, with many details omitted in this introductory text.

[11] This is not an exhaustive list; other specialized resource types are also defined in MARTE.

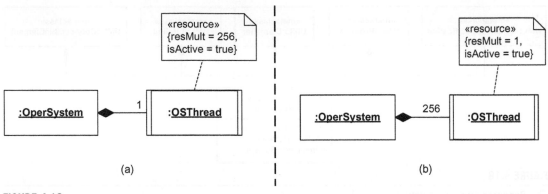

FIGURE 4.19

Two ways of representing collections of resources of the same type.

- *Storage resources* (**StorageResource** stereotype), for different kinds of memories
- *Communications resources* (**CommunicationMedia** and **CommunicationEndPoint** stereotypes), for communication facilities such as networks, busses, and so forth
- *Concurrency resources* (**ConcurrencyResource** stereotype), for elements such as operating system processes and threads (Figure 4.19 provides an example)
- *Mutual exclusions resources* (**MutualExclusionResource** stereotype) for devices that are used to synchronize the execution of concurrency resources (e.g., semaphores, mutexes, see Figure 4.21)
- *Device resources* (**DeviceResource** stereotype), for various specialized devices such as sensors and actuators
- *Timing resources* (**TimingResource** stereotype) for clocks and timers

Although these stereotypes can be used directly for relatively high-level modeling, such as technology agnostic system-level design, most of them are further refined by MARTE through more specialized stereotypes, which, as noted, are described in subsequent chapters.

The general **Resource** stereotype has three optional attributes, which are inherited by all its refined stereotypes:

- **resMult** is an integer that specifies how many instances of the resource are represented by the tagged model element. This can be used to represent collections of resources of the same type (see Figure 4.19a). However, in such cases, it is not possible to distinguish between individual instances of the resource. Conversely, modelers can leave this attribute at its default value of 1, if it is desired to model each instance separately, as in Figure 4.19b
- **isActive** is a Boolean attribute, which if **true** means that the resource is active in the same sense as a UML class can be active (in effect, a resource that executes independently of and concurrently with other entities)
- **isProtected** is another Boolean attribute, which indicates typically that access to the resource is guarded in some way, for example, by a resource broker

The resource concept can refer to either a type or an instance of a type. Rather than define a separate stereotype for the two cases, MARTE allows the same **Resource** stereotype (and its specialized stereotypes) to be applied to either one. Thus, it can be applied to elements that represent classifiers

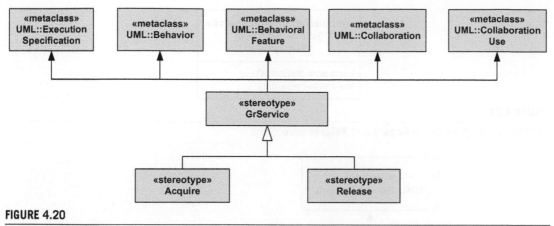

FIGURE 4.20

The **GrService** stereotype with its base classes and **Acquire** and **Release** refinements.

in general, including, notably, the UML **Class** and **Interface** concepts, or, alternatively, to model elements that represent instances of some type. UML has numerous ways of representing instances in a model, including:

- Object and link instances (represented by instances of the UML **InstanceSpecification** concept), as in Figure 4.19
- Lifelines in sequence and other types of interaction diagrams (instances of **UML::Lifeline**)
- Roles in collaborations (which are kinds of **UML::ConnectableElement**)
- Parts in internal class structures (also kinds of **UML::ConnectableElement**)
- Class attributes (kinds of **UML::Property**)

4.3.3 Modeling resource services

Resource services are represented via the generic **GrService** stereotype (see Figure 4.20). As such, this is typically too general to be of much use, so it is refined into two more useful stereotypes:

- **Acquire** representing services by which the corresponding resource is obtained
- **Release** representing a service by which a previously acquired resource is released

These stereotypes can be applied to any of the following UML model elements as indicated by Figure 4.20:

- A UML **Operation** or **Reception** (which are both kinds of **UML::BehavioralFeature**), as illustrated in Figure 4.21)
- Any kind of behavior (any specialization of the UML **Behavior** concept), such as a state machine or activity, that specifies a method that realizes an operation or a reception
- A collaboration representing an implementation of a method (**UML::Collaboration**)
- A usage of a collaboration representing an implementation of a method (**UML::CollaborationUse**)
- An execution occurrence block on a lifeline in a sequence diagram (**UML::ExecutionSpecification**)

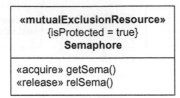

FIGURE 4.21

Example showing use of the **Acquire** and **Release** stereotypes.

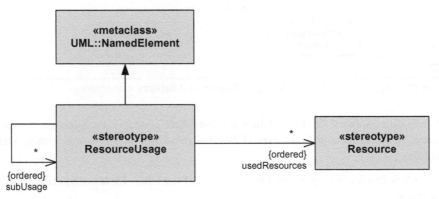

FIGURE 4.22

Definition of the **ResourceUsage** stereotype.

4.3.4 Modeling resource usages

As might be expected, resource usages can be specified using the **ResourceUsage** stereotype, which is an extension of the UML **NamedElement** abstract concept (see Figure 4.22). This allows the stereotype to be applied to a wide variety of different UML elements. An example of the application of this stereotype can be seen in Figure 1.8. This stereotype is useful in situations involving complex scenarios, in which multiple resources of different types are used. This is because this stereotype allows capturing the usage information associated with such a scenario in a single place as opposed to being scattered throughout the model. This makes it quite convenient for various types of model analyses, such as performance or schedulability analysis.

However, the characterization of resource usage is very much a function of the type of resource being used with hardly any commonality between the different characterizations. Therefore, MARTE provides a number of different resource-specific stereotypes for representing resource usage. These are described in subsequent chapters.

4.4 SUMMARY

Dealing with time and managing resources are first-order concerns in practically all cyber-physical systems and particularly in their software. The ability to accurately represent and specify the qualitative and quantitative characteristics related to time and resources is, therefore, a key feature of MARTE.

It supports three of the most common conceptualizations of time encountered in the real-time domain: logical, synchronous, and physical. For specifying time values, MARTE supports two different approaches, depending on the required degree of accuracy: the *explicit clock reference approach*, in which the sources of timing information and their characteristics are modeled explicitly and precisely, and the *implicit clock reference approach*, where timing information is based on central idealized clocks. However, in either case, it is possible to specify time values with a very high degree of precision.

In addition to modeling time and clocks with great precision, MARTE provides a rich set of capabilities for directly associating elements of behavior with time. This includes the ability to specify static temporal information, such as expected or required execution times of behavioral specifications, as well as to relate the unfolding of behaviors across time. The times of occurrence of specific events as well as intervals between occurrences can be captured precisely, so that they can be used for inspections or formal timing analyses of different types, possibly with the use of specialized analysis software.

For modeling resources, MARTE utilizes a simple yet comprehensive conceptual framework, based on the client-server paradigm. This is particularly well suited for engineering analyses that try to determine whether the available resources are sufficient to meet (client) demand or to estimate the amount of resources that might be required for an application. This basic framework is used for the definition of a wide variety of different resource types encountered in the real-time domain.

References

[1] André C, Mallet F, de Simone R. Modeling time(s). In: Engels G, et al. editors. Proceedings of the tenth ACM/IEEE Conference on Model Driven Engineering Languages and Systems (MODELS 2007). Springer. p. 559–73.
[2] Berry G, Gonthier G. The ESTEREL synchronous programming language: design, semantics, implementation. Sci Comp Programm 1992;19:87–152.
[3] Mallet F. Logical time @ work for the modeling and analysis of embedded systems. LAP Lambert Academic Publishing; 2011.
[4] Object Management Group (OMG), the, clause 9 ("time modeling") in UML profile for marte: modeling and analysis of real-time embedded systems, version 1.1, OMG document number formal/2011-06-02; 2011.
[5] Object Management Group (OMG), the, clause 10 ("Generic Resource Modeling (GRM)") in UML profile for MARTE: modeling and analysis of real-time embedded systems, version 1.1, OMG document number formal/2011-06-02; 2011.

Modeling Real-Time Systems with MARTE

PART

III

Modeling Software Applications

CHAPTER CONTENTS

5.1 INTRODUCTION

Applications are the ultimate objective of the software development process, which transforms a relatively general computing device into a specialized purpose-built machine. Hence, we show it at the top element in our framework (Figure 5.1). However, as argued previously, in practice there is almost always interplay between the elements in this framework, such that dependencies exist in both top-down and bottom-up directions. This favors an iterative development process, as our understanding of the ramifications of such dependencies gradually increases with experience.

In this chapter we describe ways in which MARTE can be used to enable more precise modeling of characteristic phenomena encountered in many real-time software applications but which are, typically, not adequately served by general-purpose modeling languages, including UML. Section 5.2 lists and describes the domain-specific application characteristics explicitly targeted by MARTE. These are then used as a basis for structuring the rest of the chapter. Section 5.3 examines the core concepts and design principles behind the approach chosen for application modeling in MARTE and

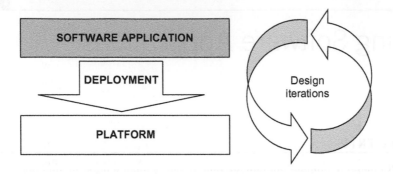

FIGURE 5.1

The design of real-time software applications.

also provides some general methodological guidelines. Sections 5.4 through 5.6 cover the essential aspects of application modeling, corresponding to traditional techniques used in real-time systems development, dealing with issues of concurrency, timeliness, and the asynchrony. Section 5.7 briefly introduces a MARTE-based method for tackling the problem of the interplay between real-time applications and platforms by making this dependence explicit. This approach is elaborated further in Chapter 6.

For readers seeking a deeper view, most of the MARTE stereotypes and concepts discussed in this chapter are specified in the Time Modeling section (clause 9) of the MARTE specification, the Generic Resource Model (GRM) section (clause 10), the Software Resource Modeling (SRM) portion of the Detailed Resource Modeling (DRM) section (clause 14.1), the High-Level Application Modeling (HLAM) section (clause 13), and the Model Library appendix (Annex D).

5.2 Distinguishing characteristics of "real-time" applications

MARTE provides numerous concepts for modeling phenomena typically encountered in real-time and embedded systems software applications. There is a widespread misconception that this is a very narrow domain, dealing with highly specialized concerns such as microsecond response times, hardware interfacing, efficient scheduling schemes, etc. However, as explained in Chapter 1, the scope encompassed by MARTE is much broader than the terms "real-time" or "embedded" might first suggest. *It covers the full range of software-intensive systems that interact with and have an effect on the physical world*. These are so-called cyber-physical systems. Systems in this domain are characterized by some combination of the following idiosyncratic characteristics, which are less commonly encountered in other types of software systems:

- *Concurrency*. Most real-time applications perform multiple temporally overlapping computations. This is usually a direct consequence of the concurrency in the environment in which the applications operate and which the systems are intended to influence in some way.[1] An

---

[1] This distinguishes it from concurrency that is introduced purely for reasons of efficiency, such as the fine-grained algorithm parallelization used in high-performance computing.

unfortunate and well-known consequence of this parallelism is that the concurrent executions can interfere with each other due to functional conflicts or contention for shared resources. Unfortunately, since the human mind is not particularly adept at reasoning about concurrent causal streams, concurrency adds significant complexity to the design of software applications and is the source of many design and implementation errors. A number of common mechanisms, such as concurrent tasks and mutual exclusion devices, have been devised over the years to help designers cope with these issues. MARTE supports this by providing facilities for direct and precise modeling of such mechanisms. This aspect is covered in Section 5.4.

- *Timeliness.* This is, of course, the most obvious and often most challenging characteristic of real-time systems: the need to produce a timely response to a stimulus stemming from the environment. Timeliness is often misinterpreted as implying the need to respond "as fast as possible." However, there are many situations where a response that is premature is as inappropriate as a response that is late. (As someone once noted: "real-time does not necessarily mean real fast.") It simply means "on time," whatever that signifies in a given application context (e.g., a program for weather prediction might take hours to complete its calculations and yet still be on time). Nevertheless, the principal challenge in most cases is to perform computations, some of which can be quite complex, at a rate that allows the software to keep pace with its environment. A particular requirement from the applications perspective is the ability to express timing constraints, such as deadlines and end-to-end processing times. MARTE provides a rich and highly customizable model of time as well as a catalog of different time-related mechanisms, such as clocks and timers. In addition, it includes capabilities to precisely express temporal constraints at different levels of abstraction. General methods for modeling time and time values using MARTE were covered in Section 4.1. In this chapter, in Section 5.5, we describe how these and other MARTE facilities can be used in the specific case of designing real-time applications.
- *Asynchrony and interaction with physical components.* In many real-time applications it is not always possible to predict when the interactions between the software application and its environment will occur. However, regardless of when they occur, the software has to be ready to respond, often resulting in the creation of new concurrent execution streams. Situations in which asynchronous events affect currently running execution streams requiring them to dynamically adapt to the new circumstances can be particularly problematic. Standard UML provides a rich set of modeling concepts and formalisms for representing asynchronous behavior. MARTE supplements these with the ability to more precisely characterize the sources and nature of asynchronous events and related mechanisms, such as interrupts and interrupts handlers. Like concurrency, problems of asynchrony in real-time software are the result of interactions with the physical world. Software interfaces to this world through various hardware devices and communication channels (which are also kinds of hardware devices) that are accessible to its computational machinery. Many of these devices are quite sophisticated and involve complex interaction protocols. MARTE provides modeling features that allow precise specifications of the interfaces between software and hardware including devices that differ from the general input–output machinery. This includes devices that provide monitoring and control of continuous phenomena, which present a unique challenge to the inherently discrete nature of software programs. MARTE supports well-known methods for dealing with this type of system, such as cyclical tasks whose execution rates are adjusted to the rate of change of the continuous

phenomena they control. The topics of modeling asynchrony and interfacing to hardware using MARTE are covered in Section 5.6.

- *Resource limitations.* In the real-time world it is often inappropriate to ignore the fact that computation takes time, that it consumes energy, and that it requires adequate CPU speed, memory capacity, and communications bandwidth (e.g., bus, network, web). For example, the need to maximize battery life and to limit memory consumption are major design concerns in the design of applications for modern mobile devices. Consequently, application designers need a means for specifying these characteristics and associated limitations, which generally translate into requirements for platform resources. Methods of dealing with resource limitations using MARTE are introduced in Section 5.7 and discussed further in greater detail in Chapter 6, which deals with platform modeling.

5.3 Application modeling foundations

The conceptual framework of MARTE is based on the general notions of time and resources introduced in Chapter 4. For the specific task of modeling real-time applications, the core concept of a resource is elaborated further through the notion of a software resource, which serves as a basis for a variety of different manifestations required in application modeling. For example, the general concept of a memory resource can be specialized into software-specific logical forms such as buffers, packets, or messages. Similarly, a basic communications resource can be refined into logical concepts such as channels and virtual circuits.

5.3.1 Software resources

A *software resource* is a logical concept that is obtained by viewing the base hardware resource notion as something that is more purpose oriented at the application level. In MARTE, software resources are represented by the **SwResource** stereotype, which is a refinement of the general **Resource** stereotype (Figure 5.2). The core **SwResource** stereotype is refined further to represent various specialized resource types, such as concurrent tasks, mutual exclusion devices, memory buffers, communication channels, etc. Analogously, the general concept of a resource service described in Section 4.3.3 and represented by the stereotype **GrService**, is refined via the concept of a *software access service* (the **SwAccessService** stereotype). However, in practice this particular stereotype is used infrequently. Instead, services are usually modeled either via the denotational attributes of **SwResource**, as explained in Section 5.3.2, or by using the **Acquire** and **Release** stereotypes described in Section 4.3.3.

Software resources are typically created dynamically by some program. It is worth reminding ourselves that, like all resources in MARTE, even software resources are ultimately constructed out of hardware. For example, an operating system process acts as a kind of virtual processor with its own CPU and memory, which, in the end, requires real physical processors and real physical memory. However, this physical underpinning is hidden behind layers of software whose purpose is to provide a more abstract or "logical", view of the hardware. This not only provides a more convenient view of the resource, but also enables portability of the application across different hardware platforms.

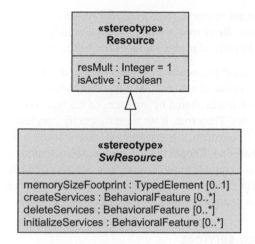

FIGURE 5.2

The **SwResource** stereotype.

The **SwResource** stereotype is intended as an abstract stereotype, which means that, like an abstract class, it cannot be applied directly. Instead, one of its refinements has to be used, based on what kind of element is being represented. However, all these refinements inherit the following commonly used attributes from their parent[2]:

- **resMult** is inherited from the general resource **Resource** stereotype, and specifies the multiplicity of the resource being modeled. This can be used either to model the capacity of a resource (e.g., a counting semaphore would have a capacity greater than 1) or to specify the number of resources when the model element is used to represent a collection of resources.
- **isActive**, also inherited from the general concept, is used to denote resources capable of autonomous behavior. This is used, for example, to model concurrent tasks.
- **memorySizeFootprint** is a denotational[3] attribute that identifies which specific feature of the underlying base model element contains information on the amount of memory required or consumed by this software resource. It is useful when analyzing memory requirements of applications. However, it is an optional attribute and can be omitted if not required.
- **createServices**, **deleteServices**, and **initializeServices**, are three denotational attributes of type **UML::BehavioralFeature**, which are described in the next section. These too are optional. They can be useful when analyzing execution scenarios. For example, the invocation of a create service operation indicates that some entity is being created, which may be useful information for an analysis tool, such as a model checker, which tracks the order in which resources are created and destroyed. These features are discussed in more detail in Section 5.3.2 below.

---

[2]As per the convention adopted in this book, only the most commonly used subset of attributes is covered in the text and shown in Figure 5.2. Readers interested in the complete specification should refer to the standard itself [2].

[3]Recall that a *denotational* stereotype attribute is used to *point* to a feature (attribute or behavioral feature) in its underlying base class and does not actually represent the feature itself (see Section 2.3.7).

In general, the base software resource stereotype, **SwResource**, can be applied to the same kinds of UML concepts as its parent **Resource** stereotype (see Section 4.2.2), depending on the nature of the concept being modeled. In particular, this includes the following:

- **Classifier** — As might be expected, when a classifier such as a UML **Class** or **Interface** is tagged as a software resource, the usual intent is to capture a type of resource. Recall from Section 2.4.2 that types typically capture the features shared by instances of the type, but they do not specify the actual values of these characteristics. Therefore, if we need to specify concrete values for resource attributes, we have to do it using UML elements that represent instances in some way, as described below.
- **InstanceSpecification**, **Lifeline**, **Property**, or **ConnectableElement** — Each of these kinds of model elements is used to represent an instance (i.e., usage) of a resource type in an object diagram, an interaction diagram, an attribute in a classifier definition, a role in a collaboration, or a part in a structured class decomposition.

5.3.2 Software resource services

For the general software resource concept, MARTE provides for explicit modeling of a common set of services, using the following denotational attributes of the **SwResource** stereotype:

- One or more resource *creation* services (**createServices**), that is, services used to create instances of a particular resource. Note that this type of service is often not defined as a feature of the resource itself (since the resource instance may not yet exist) but as a feature of a corresponding resource broker. The result of a successful invocation of a creation service is a new properly initialized instance of the resource with a unique identity.
- One or more *initialization* services (**initializeServices**), used to jumpstart the execution of a newly created software resource. In some systems this functionality is integrated with the creation service.
- One or more *destruction* services (**deleteServices**), which are used to terminate the associated software resource and return whatever internal resources it used (e.g., memory, identifier) back to the appropriate system resource pools.

As explained earlier, these modeling capabilities are used primarily for analyzing models representing systems in execution. For example, a memory leak analyzer will need to know the order in which memory is being requested and released. To do that, it has to know which application model operations acquire memory (i.e., creation services) and which ones release it (i.e., destruction services).

Consider the simple example in Figure 5.3. The class diagram in Figure 5.3a shows three classes. One of these, MemoryManager, is stereotyped as a **MemoryBroker**, which is a particular kind of MARTE **SwResource**. It represents a class whose instances are responsible for allocating heap memory to its clients. MemoryManager has two operations, new() and rel(), which are invoked to acquire and release blocks of heap memory. To ensure that the special semantics of these functions are recognizable (e.g., by a memory usage analysis program), the **Acquire** stereotype is applied to the new() operation and the **Release** stereotype to the rel() operation (see Section 4.3.3 for a description of these stereotypes). In this particular example, the Server class (an active object) performs some kind of special function, the details of which are omitted, which requires the use of a 512 byte block of memory. Its operation is initiated by a start signal from an instance of the ServerMaster class and continues until it is instructed to finish by a stop signal from the master. At that point, it releases the memory it obtained earlier. A particular instantiation of this application is shown in the collaboration diagram

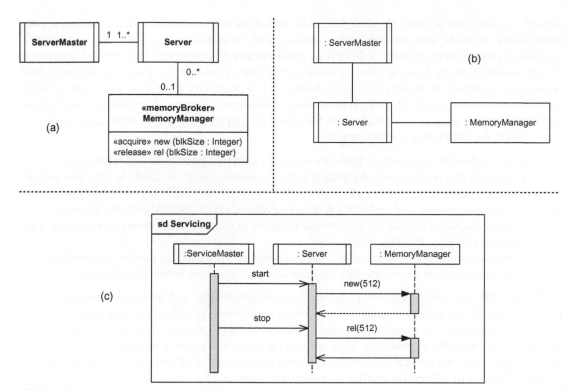

FIGURE 5.3

Example showing the use of designated resource services.

fragment in Figure 5.3b. Finally, the full interactions scenario just described is represented by the sequence diagram in Figure 5.3c. Note that this model could be statically analyzed by an automatic program or by a human inspector checking for memory leaks, by tracking the acquisition and release of memory blocks.

A semantically equivalent alternative to using the **createService** and **deleteService** attributes of **MemoryBroker** is to apply the **Acquire** and **Release** resource service stereotypes directly to elements in the model that represent invocations of the new() and rel() operations, respectively. An example of this approach is shown in Figure 5.18 in which the stereotypes are applied to execution occurrence elements.

5.4 **Dealing with concurrency**

The standard and most widely supported solution for dealing with concurrency is *multitasking*,[4] the capacity to execute multiple separate program streams (tasks) in parallel. It is common for such

---

[4]We use this term in a general sense to cover not only simple shared-processor multitasking, but also multiprogramming and distributed programming.

systems to share one or more physical processors as well as other resources, such as memory, communications channels, and, possibly, other devices. This, of course, requires that the execution of concurrent tasks be appropriately *ordered* (i.e., *synchronized*), to ensure that uncontrolled accesses to shared resources do not lead the system into an invalid state. Furthermore, if some of the concurrent tasks are cooperating in support of shared objectives, it is necessary to provide them with a means to *communicate* with each other. To support these capabilities, a range of specialized mechanisms and corresponding programming techniques have been developed. In MARTE, these mechanisms are grouped into the following basic categories:

- *Concurrent threads of execution.* These are resources used to support concurrent program executions. In this book, we use the generic terms "*concurrent task*" or "*task*" to refer to a unit of concurrent execution.
- *Synchronization (or, mutual exclusion) devices and related access control policies.* These are specialized resources that are used to manage the order in which shared resources are accessed by concurrent tasks (i.e., task synchronization).
- *Inter-task communications mechanisms.* These mechanisms are used for passing information but, in some cases, such as the rendezvous, they can also provide a synchronization function.

While UML has some support for representing concurrent tasks and inter-task communications, these are usually not refined enough for most real-time software specifications and even less so for any kind of qualitative or quantitative analysis. Hence, MARTE provides facilities that are built on top of these basic UML capabilities. They are general enough to cover a wide spectrum of variants of these basic mechanisms that occur in the real-time domain, and, if desired, they can be specialized further by additional refinement profiles as described in Chapter 12.

5.4.1 Modeling concurrent tasks

The constant need for ever-faster program execution has resulted in the development of complex multiprocessor chips. However, a major dilemma at present is how to best exploit this capability, so that the ability to represent and reason about concurrency in software has become paramount in many application domains.

Concurrent execution is supported in a variety of ways in software. In some cases, it is built into the programming language, as in Ada and Java, while in others (e.g., C/C+ +), support for concurrency is provided through specialized program libraries that may be supported by an underlying run-time system, which is often part of the operating system. In a way, these two approaches reflect two different viewpoints of the same system. For example, we can choose to view a program monitoring changes in temperature of some system as a concurrent software application running within an operating system task, or as an operating system task running some temperature-monitoring application. We refer to these two viewpoints as the *application viewpoint* and the *platform viewpoint*, respectively. Although this may seem like an overly pedantic and not particularly meaningful distinction akin to the "zebra conundrum,"[5] the models corresponding to these two viewpoints are likely to be quite different, as explained below. Fortunately, MARTE supports both perspectives. The platform

---

[5] That is. are zebras black animals with white stripes, or white animals with black stripes?

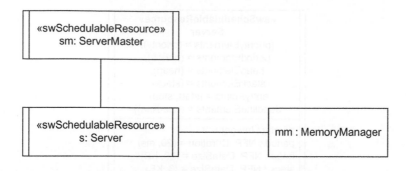

FIGURE 5.4

Example showing the use of the **SwSchedulableResource** stereotype to denote concurrent tasks.

viewpoint is particularly relevant if the application we are designing is software that is intended as a platform for other software, such as an application framework or operating system.

5.4.1.1 Modeling of concurrent tasks from the application viewpoint

From an application designer's perspective, we are rarely interested in explicitly representing things like schedulers or other resources used by the underlying multitasking implementation. Instead, our primary concern is to (1) identify those elements of the application model that represent concurrent tasks and (2) specify application-meaningful data concerning their concurrency properties, such as priority and deadlines.

The primary concept for representing concurrent tasks in MARTE is the relatively general **SwSchedulableResource** stereotype. Hence, we use it to tag elements that represent tasks in the system. It is derived indirectly from the even more general software resource concept (**SwResource**) described in Section 5.3.1.[6] By its nature, a schedulable resource is an active resource, which means that it should only be applied to model elements that can represent active entities in the UML sense (i.e., entities with their **isActive** attribute set to true[7]), such as active classes or instances of active classes. An example of its usage is shown in the collaboration diagram fragment in Figure 5.4.

Note that the **SwSchedulableResource** stereotype is also used for the platform viewpoint, but the stereotype attributes used for that viewpoint are mostly separate from those used in the application viewpoint. The attributes that are meaningful primarily from an application viewpoint include:

- **type**[8] — This is an optional attribute that is mostly used to specify certain real-time characteristics of tasks for analysis purposes. It specifies the occurrence pattern for executions of this task and is typed by the MARTE library type **ArrivalPattern** (see Appendix B.4).
- **schedparams** — This is an optional attribute for capturing any parameters, such as priority, which are required for scheduling a task. It is typed by the MARTE library type, **SchedParameters**,

---

[6] Actually, it is derived from an intervening stereotype **SwConcurrentResource**, which is a direct refinement of **SwResource**. However, in line with the introductory nature of this text, we do not discuss **SwConcurrentResource** further in this text.

[7] MARTE does not enforce such a constraint, but the authors recommend it as standard practice.

[8] This is a rather unfortunate choice of name for an attribute, since the term "type" usually has a different connotation in computer science.

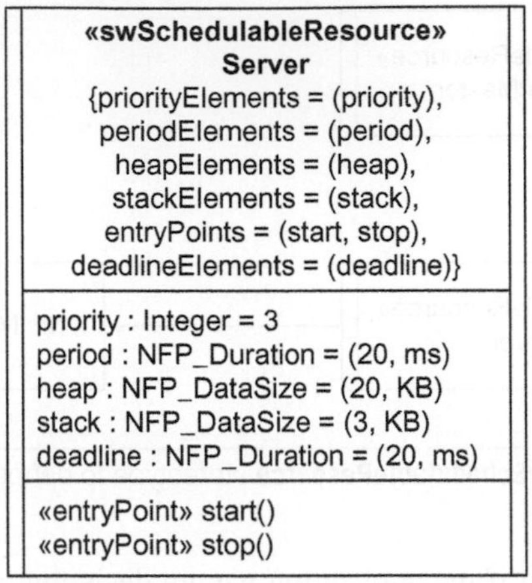

```
┌──────────────────────────────────────────┐
│           «swSchedulableResource»         │
│                   Server                  │
│        {priorityElements = (priority),    │
│          periodElements = (period),       │
│            heapElements = (heap),         │
│           stackElements = (stack),        │
│          entryPoints = (start, stop),     │
│        deadlineElements = (deadline)}     │
├──────────────────────────────────────────┤
│ priority : Integer = 3                    │
│ period : NFP_Duration = (20, ms)          │
│ heap : NFP_DataSize = (20, KB)            │
│ stack : NFP_DataSize = (3, KB)            │
│ deadline : NFP_Duration = (20, ms)        │
├──────────────────────────────────────────┤
│ «entryPoint» start()                      │
│ «entryPoint» stop()                       │
└──────────────────────────────────────────┘
```

FIGURE 5.5

Example of an application viewpoint model of a task.

which is a VSL "choice" type (see Appendix A.3.1.3) that supports a variety of standard scheduling policies (see Section 5.4.1.3).

- **periodElements** — This is an optional denotational attribute, which is meaningful only for tasks that execute periodically. It points to the attribute(s) of the underlying class that specify the period length and, possibly, other characteristics.

- **entryPoints** — This is a denotational attribute pointing to a list of model elements that specify the *entry points* of the resource. An entry point is usually either a UML operation, or a behavior that represents a resource service. If this attribute is used, then the denoted model elements must be typed by the **EntryPoint** stereotype (explained below).

- **deadlineElements** — This is an optional denotational attribute pointing to the attribute that contains deadline data. Clearly, this is only useful for tasks where deadlines exist.

- **priorityElements** — This is another denotational optional attribute that is used in case of priority-based multitasking systems.

- **heapSizeElements** — This is an optional denotational attribute that points to the underlying class attribute that contains information about the size of memory heap required by this task.

- **stackSizeElements** — This is an optional attribute similar to the one above, except that it relates to the stack space required by this task.

Figure 5.5 provides an example of a specification for a priority-based scheduling scheme for the Server task from Figure 5.4, which requires 20 KB of heap and a 3 KB stack. It is a cyclical task with a period of 20 milliseconds and a deadline equal to its period. Its priority level is 3.

This example also shows use of the **EntryPoint** stereotype for the start() and stop() operations, which have been flagged as entry points via the **entryPoints** stereotype attribute. This stereotype has two attributes:

- **isReentrant** — This is an optional Boolean attribute, which, if true, means that the entry point operation is reentrant.

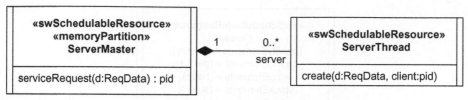

FIGURE 5.6

Modeling a process with its own address space and multiple threads (application viewpoint).

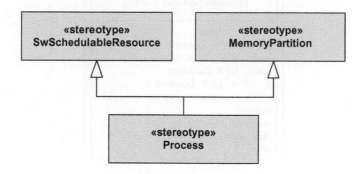

FIGURE 5.7

Extending MARTE with a custom **Process** stereotype.

- **routine** — This is a denotational attribute pointing to an operation that contains the actual code of the entry point; this is almost always a pointer to the same operation that is tagged by the **EntryPoint** stereotype, as illustrated by the example in Figure 5.10

Note that, in the application viewpoint, we are normally specifying resource *requirements* (i.e., the required quality of service; QoS). In the platform viewpoint, on the other hand, we typically specify the *offered* QoS.

A particular kind of concurrent task found in many operating systems is a *process*. In contrast to a simple concurrent thread, which can share memory with other threads, upon creation a process is allocated a dedicated address space. Furthermore, a process is often the creator and owner of threads that share its address space. An example of how such an entity can be represented using MARTE stereotypes is shown in Figure 5.6. In this example, ServerMaster represents a process with its own address space indicated by the use of the **MemoryPartition** stereotype in addition to the **SwSchedulableResource** stereotype. Whenever this process receives a service request (i.e., a call to the **serviceRequest**() operation), it creates a new thread in its address space (an instance of ServerThread) to handle the request concurrently.

If a more explicit representation of a process is desired, this can be achieved by defining a new custom stereotype in situations such as this as illustrated in Figure 5.7.

5.4.1.2 Modeling of concurrent tasks from the platform viewpoint

Unlike the applications view, in this case we are generally less interested in the purpose of a task. For instance, in the applications view in Figure 5.4, we distinguished between the ServerMaster and Server

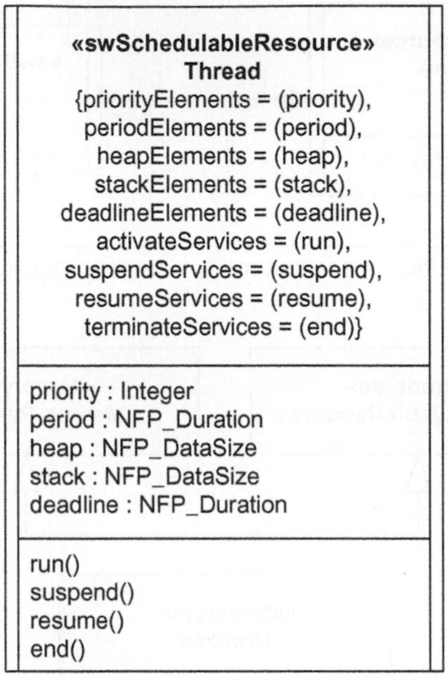

```
┌─────────────────────────────────────┐
│         «swSchedulableResource»      │
│                Thread                │
│        {priorityElements = (priority),│
│          periodElements = (period),  │
│           heapElements = (heap),     │
│           stackElements = (stack),   │
│        deadlineElements = (deadline),│
│            activateServices = (run), │
│        suspendServices = (suspend),  │
│         resumeServices = (resume),   │
│          terminateServices = (end)}  │
├─────────────────────────────────────┤
│  priority : Integer                  │
│  period : NFP_Duration               │
│  heap : NFP_DataSize                 │
│  stack : NFP_DataSize                │
│  deadline : NFP_Duration             │
├─────────────────────────────────────┤
│  run()                               │
│  suspend()                           │
│  resume()                            │
│  end()                               │
└─────────────────────────────────────┘
```

FIGURE 5.8

A platform view of a concurrent task.

tasks, but in the platform view (e.g., an operating system designer's view) all tasks tend to be viewed uniformly as tasks, regardless of the application they are carrying. They are all simply treated as instances of a common type (or types if there are multiple task types in the system), even though they may individually have different application-specific values for their characteristics. Figure 5.8 illustrates one such common task type (Thread) that could realize either of the application tasks in Figure 5.5. This is a specification that might be encountered in a model of some operating system application.

Note that some of the same attributes used in the application view appear in this platform view as well. These are, in fact, the multitasking attributes that the application cares about. However, this rendering adds further attributes that are only relevant to the platform viewpoint:

- **activateServices** — This is an optional denotational attribute identifying the operations of the underlying class that are used to start the initial execution of the task. Such a service is usually invoked when the application task is created. In our example, this function is realized by the **run()** operation, which might be invoked by the dispatcher component of the operating system.
- **suspendServices** — This optional denotational attribute points to operations that are used to suspend the execution of a running task.
- **resumeServices** — This optional denotational attribute indicates the operations that reverse the effects of the suspend services.
- **terminateServices** — This optional denotational attribute points to the operations used to completely and finally cease execution of a running or suspended task.

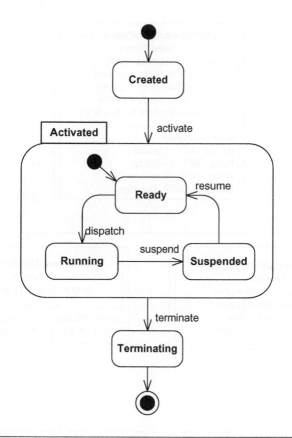

FIGURE 5.9

State machine model of a basic task dispatching procedure.

- **timeSliceElements** — This optional denotational attribute is used in case of time-slice-based scheduling. It points to items that specify the characteristics (e.g., duration) of the time slice allocated to this task.

The task execution model supported by this viewpoint is relatively simple and is represented by the implied state machine diagram in Figure 5.9. Of course, more sophisticated models exist, in which case it may be necessary to refine the **SwSchedulableResource** by adding additional service types.

Since it is often useful to model such elements both ways and since they share many common attributes, one useful pragmatic technique is to create a shared superclass for the two viewpoints as shown in Figure 5.10. This approach takes advantage of the generalization–specialization mechanism of UML to avoid duplication of definitions, while still maintaining separation between the two alternative viewpoints.

These different views of concurrent tasks occur either in different models or in different model fragments. Since both views represent the same entity, it may be desired to unify them by indicating that they are one and the same. This can be accomplished by using the MARTE **Allocate** stereotype

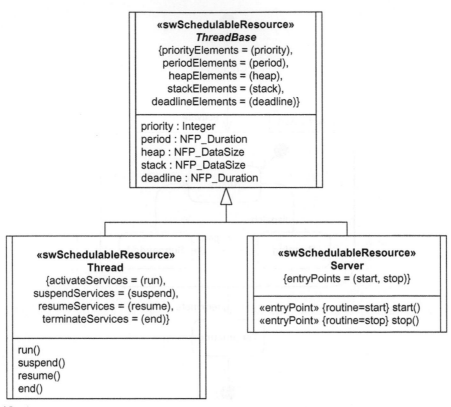

A pragmatic approach to supporting both the application and platform viewpoints of tasks.

as shown in Figure 5.11. More details on how to use this stereotype for this and other purposes are provided in Chapter 7.

5.4.1.3 Modeling scheduling policies

Scheduling policies are algorithms for allocating CPU resources to concurrent tasks deployed on (i.e., allocated to) a processor (i.e., computing resource) or a shared pool of processors. A rich variety of such policies has been developed over time for real-time systems, based on the nature of applications [1]. For example, in order to ensure timely response to certain critical events, a number of systems require *priority-based* scheduling schemes. Some of these even allow preemption, that is, the suspension of execution of lower-priority tasks by ones with higher priority. One concern with such policies is to avoid "starvation" of lower-priority tasks by a persistent demand from higher priority tasks. In general, the choice of scheduling policy depends on a number of factors, including first and foremost on the nature of the application and the relative importance of meeting its deadlines. Therefore, choosing or defining a suitable scheduling policy for a given real-time system can be a very complex problem. A number of *schedulability analysis* methods have been devised to assist with this problem, some of which are directly supported by MARTE (see Chapter 10).

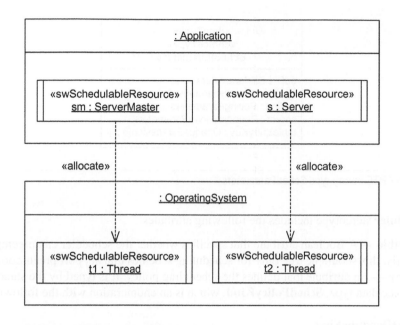

FIGURE 5.11

Unifying the application and platform views of tasks.

Standard MARTE defines modeling of the following basic set of common scheduling policies[9]:

- Earliest deadline first (EDF) scheduling
- First-in first-out (FIFO) scheduling
- Fixed priority scheduling
- Least laxity first scheduling
- Round robin scheduling
- Time table-driven scheduling

If necessary, it is possible to extend this list with new custom policies.

In MARTE, the system-scheduling policy is specified as an attribute of the *scheduler*, a specially designated model element that represents the system scheduler. The corresponding stereotype is **Scheduler**. Since this is a refinement of the general **Resource** stereotype (see Section 4.2.2), it can be applied to any model element that can represent a resource (e.g., a class, an object instance, or an attribute of a class). Perhaps the simplest way to capture this *in an application model* is to define a single object instance that represents the system scheduler and provide it with the necessary parameter values corresponding to the chosen scheduling policy (see Figure 5.14).

---

[9]Details for most of these different scheduling policies can be found in the Burns and Wellings reference on real-time systems [1] as well as in the MARTE standard itself [2].

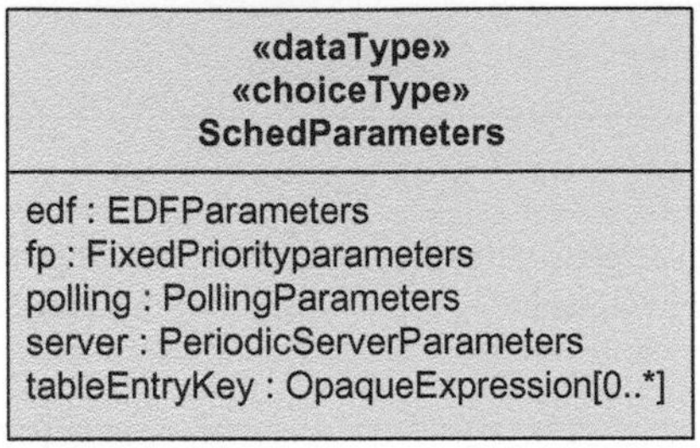

```
                     «dataType»
                    «choiceType»
                   SchedParameters

          edf : EDFParameters
          fp : FixedPriorityparameters
          polling : PollingParameters
          server : PeriodicServerParameters
          tableEntryKey : OpaqueExpression[0..*]
```

FIGURE 5.12

The standard MARTE library type **SchedParameters**.

The **Scheduler** stereotype includes the following attributes:

- **isPreemptible** — A Boolean attribute that specifies whether the scheduler can preempt executing tasks; clearly, this should be true only for scheduling schemes that support preemption.
- **schedPolicy** — An attribute that defines the scheduling policy. It is typed by the standard MARTE library choice data type, **SchedPolicyKind**, which is an enumeration with the following literal values:
  - **EarliestDeadlineFirst**
  - **FIFO**
  - **FixedPriority**
  - **LeastLaxityFirst**
  - **RoundRobin**
  - **TimeTableDriven**
  - **Undef** (for cases where the policy is left undefined)
  - **Other** (for cases where a custom policy is used)

The scheduling parameter values of *individual tasks* are defined via the **schedparams** attribute of the **SwSchedulableResource** stereotype (see Section 5.4.1.1). As noted, this attribute is typed by a "choice" type, **SchedParameters**, which means that it can be one of a predefined set of types. The definition of this library type is provided in Figure 5.12.

The following scheduling parameter types are defined in the MARTE library:

- **EDFParameters**
- **FixedPriorityParameters**
- **PeriodicServerParameters** (a refinement of **FixedPriorityParameters**)
- **PollingParameters** (a refinement of **FixedPriorityParameters**)

The library definitions of the **EDFParameters** and **FixedPriorityParameters** data types are given in Figure 5.13. Note that they have no shared attributes because the two scheduling policies share nothing in common.

The detailed specifications and explanations of the remaining data types can be found in clause 10 of the MARTE specification [2]. Clearly, the choice of parameter type should match the chosen system scheduling policy. Figure 5.14 shows an example with two model fragments: the left-hand fragment depicts an object instance representing an EDF scheduler, while the right-hand fragment

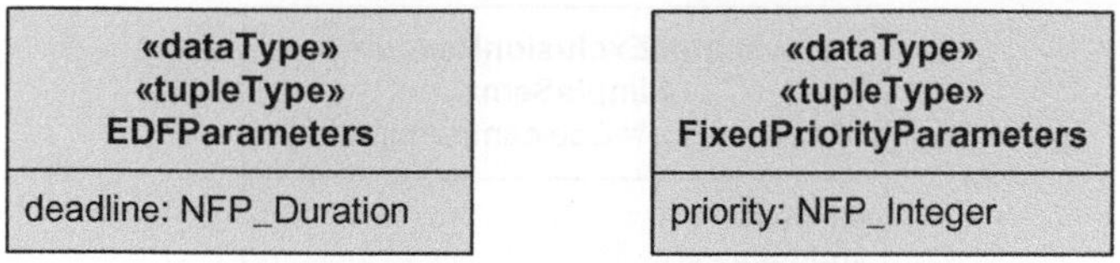

«dataType» «tupleType» EDFParameters	«dataType» «tupleType» FixedPriorityParameters
deadline: NFP_Duration	priority: NFP_Integer

FIGURE 5.13

The standard MARTE library types **EDFParameters** and **FixedPriorityParameters**.

«scheduler» sysScheduler : {schedPolicy= EarliestDeadlineFirst, isPreemptible= true}	«swSchedulableResource» SensorTask {schedparams::edf::deadline = (5, ms)}	«swSchedulableResource» DisplayTask {schedparams::edf::deadline = (50, ms)}

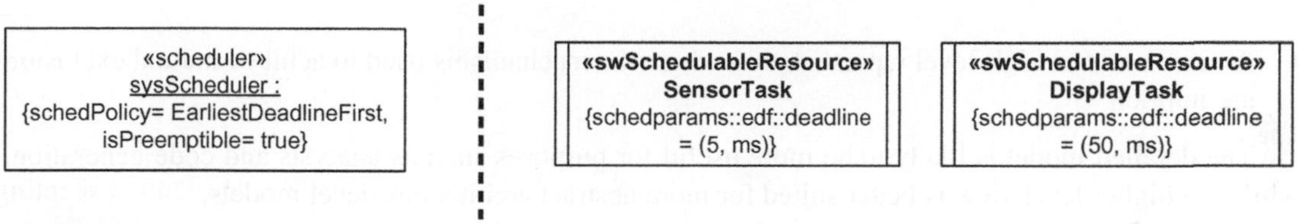

FIGURE 5.14

An EDF scheduler and two concurrent tasks with different deadlines.

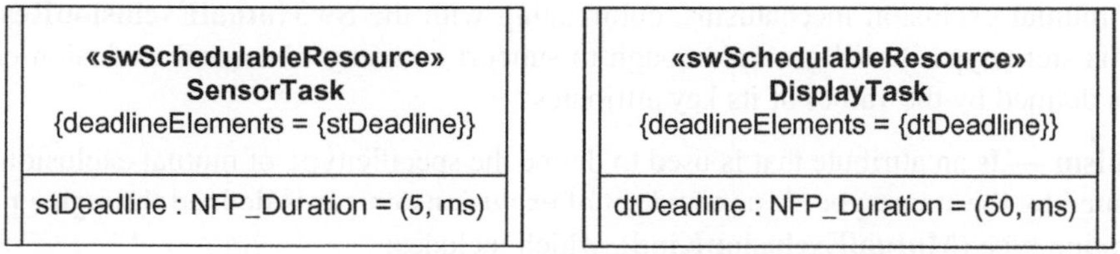

«swSchedulableResource» SensorTask {deadlineElements = {stDeadline}}	«swSchedulableResource» DisplayTask {deadlineElements = {dtDeadline}}
stDeadline : NFP_Duration = (5, ms)	dtDeadline : NFP_Duration = (50, ms)

FIGURE 5.15

An alternative method for specifying the deadlines for **SensorTask** and **DisplayTask** in Figure 5.14.

shows two task types in the same system, SensorTask and DisplayTask, with deadlines set at 5 and 50 milliseconds, respectively.

Note that, instead of using the **EDFParameters** type to specify the deadline, the **deadlineElements** attribute of the **SwSchedulableResource** stereotype could have been used, as shown in Figure 5.5.

A similar approach can be used for the **priority** parameter for fixed priority policies by using the **SwSchedulableResource::priorityElements** attribute instead. As a practical recommendation, if the application-level element definition has the right scheduling-relevant attributes defined, then the approach in Figure 5.15 should be used since it is slightly simpler and it avoids duplication of information.

5.4.2 Modeling synchronization mechanisms

To deal with concurrency conflicts to shared resources, MARTE provides two possibilities, targeting different levels of abstraction:

- A detailed resource-based view, for cases where the specifics of the mutual exclusion mechanisms need to be spelled out, or

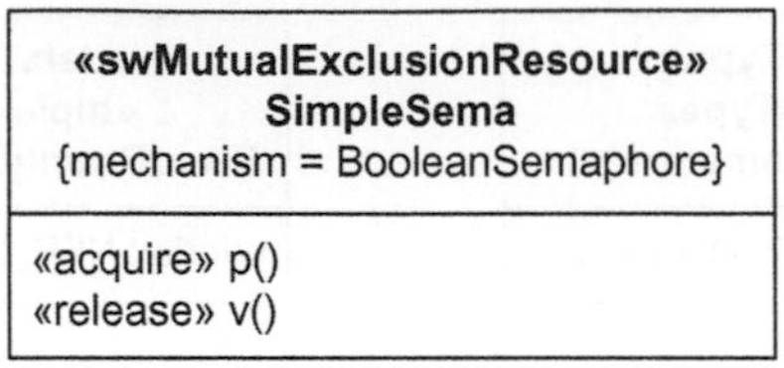

```
┌─────────────────────────────────────────┐
│       «swMutualExclusionResource»         │
│              SimpleSema                    │
│     {mechanism = BooleanSemaphore}        │
├─────────────────────────────────────────┤
│  «acquire» p()                            │
│  «release» v()                            │
└─────────────────────────────────────────┘
```

FIGURE 5.16

Example showing modeling of a basic binary semaphore.

- A more abstract high-level representation where the mechanisms used to achieve mutual exclusion are implicit

The detailed model is likely to be more useful for purposes such as analysis and code generation, while the higher level view is better suited for more abstract architecture-level models.

5.4.2.1 A resource-based model of mutual exclusion

In this case, the devices (i.e., resources) used to achieve mutual exclusion are rendered explicitly. To this end, the general **Resource** stereotype is refined in several steps to capture some general characteristics of mutual exclusion mechanisms, culminating with the **SwMutualExclusionResource** stereotype. This stereotype is still general enough to support a variety of mutual exclusion devices and methods, as defined by the values of its key attributes:

- **mechanism** — Is an attribute that is used to define the specific type of mutual exclusion device represented by the stereotype. A standard set of exclusion devices is defined through a predefined enumeration type (**MutualExclusionKind**), which includes:
  - **BooleanSemaphore** for the most primitive semaphores that allow only a single access to the protected resource before they block
  - **CountSemaphore** for counting semaphores that protect multiple identical resources (see the discussion on the **resMult** attribute below)
  - **Mutex** is quite similar to a Boolean semaphore, although there may be subtle differences between them in some operating systems (such as the feature that a mutex can only be released by the task that currently holds it)
  - **Other** is a general catch-all for other types of mutual exclusion devices.
- **resMult** — Is inherited from Resource (see Section 4.2.2). In the case of mutual exclusion resources, this attribute can be used to represent the maximum number of simultaneous concurrent accesses that are allowed by the mutual exclusion resource before it blocks further requests (i.e., the number of identical shared resources it protects).
- **waitingQueuePolicy** — Is used to specify queuing discipline for handling incoming acquire requests. Associated with this attribute is an extendable predefined enumeration type (**QueuePolicyKind**) that specifies the standard valid choices: **FIFO**, **LIFO**, **Priority**, **Undef**, and **Other**. Note that, in case of **Priority** queuing, it is possible to provide additional detail, as described below.
- **waitingQueueCapacity** — Is an optional attribute that can be used for implementations where there is a limit on the size of the waiting queue. Most implementations do not impose limits.

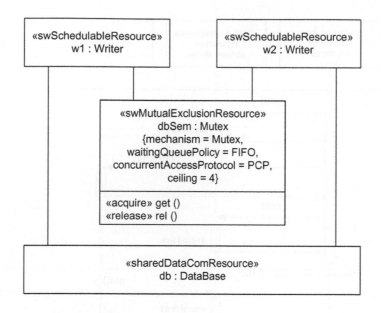

FIGURE 5.17

Collaboration diagram fragment showing use of a mutex for accessing a shared database.

- **concurrentAccessProtocol** — Is used to identify the specific protocol used by the mutual exclusion resource. A predefined set of common protocols are provided through an enumeration type (**ConcurrentAcccesProtocolKind**):
  - **PIP** for priority inheritance protocols
  - **PCP** for priority ceiling protocols; note that in this case, it is possible to specify the actual priority ceiling value through the additional attribute **ceiling** (an integer)
  - **NoPreemption** is for protocols that do not allow preemption by another task, regardless of priority, until the resource is released
  - **Other**

The use of this stereotype to model a basic binary semaphore class is shown in Figure 5.16. Note the use of the general **Acquire** and **Release** stereotypes, described in Section 4.2.3, to identify operations that are used to request access to the semaphore (p()) and to release the semaphore (v()), respectively.

An example of a more complex mutex type device that uses a priority ceiling protocol is shown in the collaboration diagram in Figure 5.17. The dbSem mutex serves to protect the database (db) shared by the two concurrent tasks w1 and w2, both of which write to the database.

A corresponding sequence diagram is shown in Figure 5.18. Recall that the parallel operator (par) in UML sequence diagrams represents all possible interleavings of the contained interaction fragments. This means that, in some cases, there could be conflicting resource accesses requests when a get() operation is invoked by one writer while the resource is busy serving the other. We capture this possibility here by including a gap on the lifelines between the reception of the get() operation call by the dbSem mutex and the actual start of operation execution.

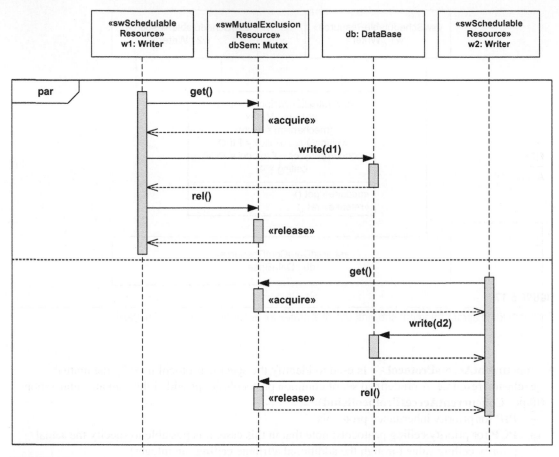

FIGURE 5.18

Sequence diagram corresponding to the collaboration shown in Figure 5.17.

5.4.2.2 A higher-level model of mutual exclusion

An alternative to the above method of representing mutual exclusion is simply to declare an access control policy on the device that needs to be protected. In this case, the mutual exclusion resource is not modeled explicitly but only implied. This is done using the concept of a *protected passive unit*, represented by the stereotype **PpUnit**. This stereotype includes an optional **concPolicy** attribute, which can take on one of the following values:

- **sequential** — This means that there is no access control so that concurrency conflicts can occur.
- **guarded** — Involves mutual exclusion such that only a single concurrent access is allowed while others are blocked until their turn comes.
- **concurrent** — Represents units that support multiple concurrent accesses with no blocking and no possibility of conflicts.

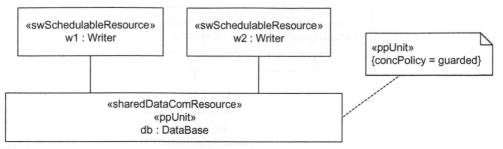

FIGURE 5.19

A more abstract model of the system in Figure 5.17 using the implicit mutual exclusion approach.

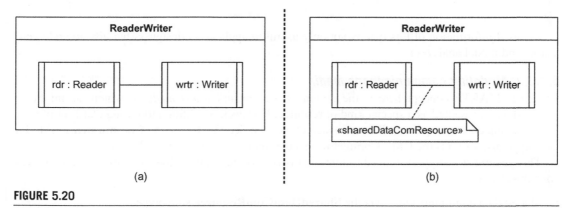

FIGURE 5.20

Parts communicating through a connector based on (a) an undefined mechanism and (b) via shared data using the MARTE stereotype **SharedDataComResource**.

For example, for the system in Figure 5.17, a more abstract representation would omit the explicit mutual exclusion device and simply model that database as a protected unit with a guarded concurrency policy, as shown in Figure 5.19.

5.4.3 Modeling task communications mechanisms

Synchronization deals with *ordering of the execution* of concurrent tasks, whereas communications has to do with *transfer of information* between concurrent tasks, or *inter-task communications*.

Consider the model fragment in Figure 5.20a, showing the internal structure of a composite class in which two parts are joined by a connector. The connector represents a communications link through which the two can interact. But this communication can be realized in a number of different ways, including shared memory, synchronous operation call, or asynchronous messaging. If we need to be more precise about this point, we need to supply additional information as shown in Figure 5.20b. In this case, we are stating that the communication path represented by a connector is realized by a communications resource shared by the two tasks, such as a shared memory space.

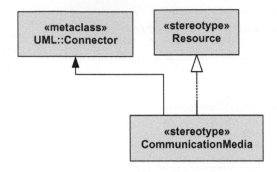

FIGURE 5.21

The **CommunicationMedia** stereotype definition.[17]

Detailed information of this type is not only useful to application designers but also to code generators and model analyzers.

5.4.3.1 Modeling communications media

The basic MARTE concept here is the notion of a *communications medium*, which, as might be expected, is represented as a special kind of resource. However, in addition to the standard set of base classes extended by the general **Resource** stereotype (see Section 4.2.2), the **CommunicationMedia** stereotype also extends the UML **Connector** concept (metaclass) as shown in Figure 5.21.

This general stereotype is refined to represent two basic communications of realizing communications in software:

- Shared data communications, via the **SharedDataComResource** stereotype
- Message-based communications, via the **MessageComResource** stereotype

From an applications viewpoint, we generally prefer to abstract away the implementation details of these mechanisms, viewing them primarily from a client perspective as service providers. Thus, in Figure 5.20, the communication service of the underlying operating system is not represented explicitly, but is merely implied by the connector "service" that it provides to applications (note that a single service may realize many such connectors).

5.4.3.2 Modeling shared data communications

Shared data repositories that can be used to exchange information between software entities are identified by applying the **SharedDataComResource** stereotype. This stereotype has two attributes for identifying appropriate access services:

- **readServices** — This is an optional denotational attribute that identifies one or more operations in the underlying UML model element that is used to read data stored in the shared repository.
- **writeServices** — This is an optional denotational attribute that identifies one or more operations in the underlying UML model element that is used to write data into the shared repository.

---

[17] Some details of the actual metamodel are omitted for clarity.

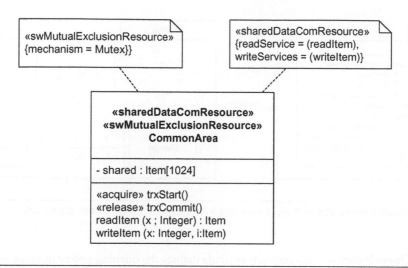

FIGURE 5.22

A class representing a protected shared data area.

Figure 5.22 shows an example of a UML class that represents such a communications facility. Note that, in this particular case, it happens to be a protected shared data repository, which supports a transaction-like mechanism through its trxStart() and trxCommit() operations.

5.4.3.3 Modeling message-based communications

Message-based communications involves placing information generated by the source element into a message block, which is then delivered to the destination element or elements. What distinguishes this mode of communications from shared data is that, at least conceptually, it involves movement of data from one location to another. Messages can be used to convey either synchronous or asynchronous communications. Note that this is not determined by the communications medium, but by the application's choice of UML communication primitives: asynchronous signals or synchronous operation calls.

For representing message-based communications media, MARTE provides the **MessageCom Resource** stereotype. This stereotype includes the following major attributes:

- **mechanism** — This defines the type of communications supported by the medium. It is typed by the predefined enumeration type **MessageResourceKind**, which defines the following literal values:
  - **MessageQueue** for representing mechanisms that store and forward messages; note that the term "queue" here does not necessarily imply a first-in-first-out policy; other queuing policies may also be covered by this option, as defined by the additional **msgQueuePolicy** attribute (see below)
  - **Pipe** for UNIX-like streaming data flows between sender and receiver(s)
  - **Blackboard** for basic single-buffer communications (e.g., in support of synchronous communications)
  - **Undef** for cases where the type of messaging is left undefined
  - **Other** for custom application-specific mechanisms

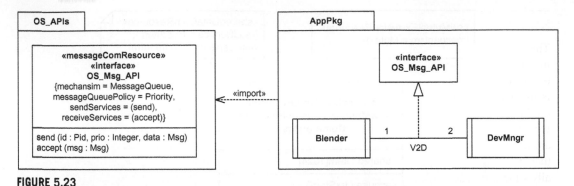

FIGURE 5.23

Using the **MessageComResource** stereotype to define a message-based communications link.

- **messageQueuePolicy** — This optional attribute defines the queuing policy in cases where the **mechanism** attribute, described above, is set to the value **MessageQueue**. It can be one of the following literal values:
  - **FIFO**
  - **LIFO**
  - **Priority**
  - **Undef** for cases where the policy is undefined
  - **Other** for custom application-specific policies
- **sendServices** — Is an optional denotational attribute pointing to one or more operations that are used by clients to create and dispatch messages.
- **receiveServices** — Is an optional denotational attribute pointing to one or more operations that a client of the resource used to register that it is ready to receive messages.

Figure 5.23 provides an example of how a message-based communications medium can be modeled. This particular application consists of a Blender task that takes inputs from two device manager (DevMngr) tasks and merges them in some way. Communication between these tasks is achieved by means of a priority-based asynchronous messaging approach. Messages are sent by invoking the send operation of the underlying operating system and received by invoking the blocking accept operation. The application programming interface (API) of the operating system messaging service is defined by the OS_Msg_API interface. This interface is stereotyped as a message communication resource, with the appropriate attribute settings. To indicate that the association between the two classes, V2D, supports the OS_Msg_API interface, a realization relationship is drawn from the association to the interface.[10] Based on our assumption about the transitivity of classifier stereotype applications to instances,[11] all links that are typed by this association will also be based on the messaging model defined by the interface.

---

[10]For those who are uncomfortable with the idea that an association can "realize" an interface in UML, one option is to define the association as an association class, which then realizes the interface. However, it is not really necessary, since UML does allow a simple association to realize an interface (although the precise meaning of that is not defined).
[11]See Section 2.4.2 describing this convention.

5.5 **Dealing with timeliness**

The general aspects of how MARTE represents time and related mechanisms are described in detail in Chapter 4. However, the focus there was mostly on the *explicit clock reference* approach, in which time-related information was expressed with respect to an explicit reference clock. This approach is intended primarily for modeling distributed systems, where multiple independent time references might exist. In this chapter we deal with the more lightweight *implicit clock reference* approach, which is *based on a single, often implicit, clock*, whose imperfections (drift, jitter, accuracy, etc.) are deemed negligible. This is a common assumption in many real-time software applications. Since there is no need to bother with reference clocks and their properties, this implicit approach is generally simpler to use than the alternative.

From an *application modeling perspective*, recall that the following are basic time-related capabilities supported by MARTE for the implicit approach:

- Modeling timing mechanisms such as *clocks* and *timers*
- The ability to associate time with behavior, including the ability to specify *timing constraints* that represent either timing *requirements*, such as deadlines, or timing *properties* of modeled elements, such as execution durations

5.5.1 **Modeling clocks and timers via the implicit approach**

Timing devices in the implicit clock approach are based on the general resource model described in Section 4.2. Specifically, two time-related resource stereotypes are provided:

- **ClockResource** — For representing clocks and clock instances
- **TimerResource** — For modeling *interval* timers[12]

As specializations (subclasses) of the general **Resource** stereotype, both of these can be applied either to classifiers or to various model elements that represent instances of classes, such as attributes, parts in structured classes, roles in collaborations, and lifelines in interactions.

Note that there is no explicit support for absolute (i.e.," time of day") timers. But, these can be represented using the **ClockResource** stereotype, which can generate an asynchronous message at the appropriate time. Figure 5.24 depicts a clock resource that issues a time message at noon.[13]

The **TimerResource** stereotype used for modeling interval timers has two generally useful attributes:

- **duration** — This is used for specifying the duration of the timed interval, expressed as **NFP_Duration.**
- **isPeriodic** — This is a Boolean attribute that, if true, indicates that this is a recurring timer.

Figure 5.25 shows an example of a class, PerTimer, which represents a periodic timer that sends out a timer signal every 50 milliseconds.

---

[12] There is also a stereotype, **SwTimerResource**, in MARTE, which is a refinement of **TimerResource**, which redefines **duration** as a denotational attribute. However, **TimerResource** is better suited to the methods recommended in this text because it supports more explicit expression of durations based on MARTE NFP types.

[13] The procedure for associating values with event occurrences is described in detail in Section 4.2.6.

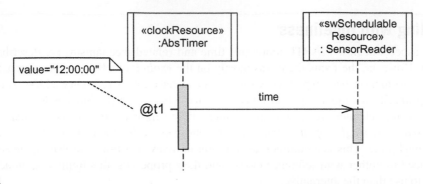

FIGURE 5.24

Using the **ClockResource** stereotype to model an absolute time-of-day timer.

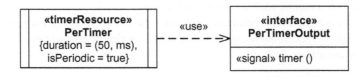

FIGURE 5.25

A periodic timer.

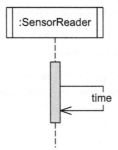

FIGURE 5.26

Common method of modeling effects of clocks and timers (not recommended).

Including an explicit entity that represents a timing mechanism such as a clock or timer, which generates signals, is often a preferred alternative to the widespread modeling convention of representing these effects as messages to self, as depicted in Figure 5.26. The problem with this approach is that it is not only technically inaccurate, but also does not provide a convenient means for specifying timing information.

Figure 5.27 illustrates the use of **TimerResource** to represent a periodic timer that is created by another task after which it sends a timer signal every 50 milliseconds back to its creator.

Note that in these examples the time message is not marked in any special way to signify that it represents the occurrence of a timeout event. It is simply assumed that an asynchronous signal generated by a clock or timer resource represents a timeout.

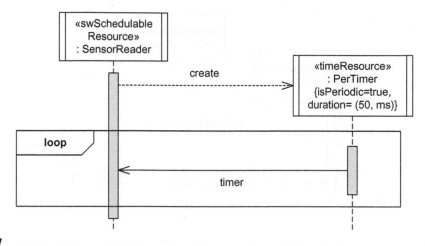

FIGURE 5.27

Modeling timers using **TimerResource**.

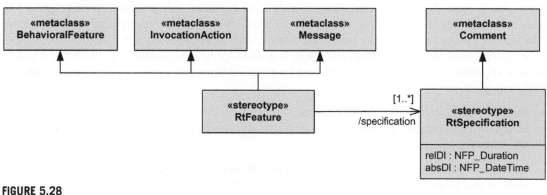

FIGURE 5.28

The **RtFeature** and **RtSpecification** stereotype definitions (simplified).

A special provision exists in MARTE for representing *watchdog timers*, that is, timers that are used to detect and prevent livelocks and deadlocks in software. In MARTE, watchdog timers are modeled as a source of interrupts (which is how it they are implemented in most real-time operating systems). The modeling of interrupts and related facilities is described later in Section 5.6.1.

5.5.2 Associating time with services and service invocations [Advanced]

It is often necessary to specify timing information, such as deadlines, when *invoking services*. Two related stereotypes are used for this purpose: **RtFeature** and **RtSpecification**. A slightly simplified specification of the definition of these stereotypes is given in Figure 5.28.

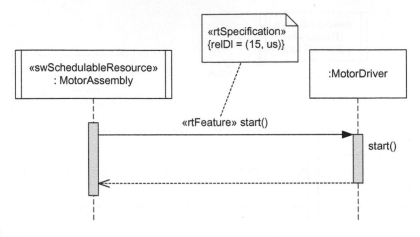

FIGURE 5.29

Use of the **RtFeature** and **RtSpecification** stereotypes.

This is a rather unusual pair of stereotypes that are intended to be used jointly. The **RtFeature** stereotype is applied to an invocation action such as an operation call or asynchronous signal send (e.g., in an activity diagram) or a message in an interaction diagram representing such an action. Alternatively, it can be applied to a behavioral feature, such as an operation or a reception declaration. Its complementary stereotype, **RtSpecification**, is used to specify the *deadline by which the response must be received* (i.e., required QoS). This can be specified using two optional and, usually, mutually exclusive attributes:

- **relDl** — This specifies the relative deadline, starting from the instant the invocation was initiated.
- **absDl** — This specifies the absolute time of day (i.e., calendar time) when the response has to arrive back at the invoker end.

What is unique about this arrangement is that the **RtSpecification** stereotype has to be attached to a comment that is itself associated with the invocation action, message, or behavioral feature. Unless the tool provides direct support for specifying it, this requires typically the following series of steps:

1. Identify the target invocation action (or behavioral feature) model element and add a new UML Comment element to it (via the comment's **annotatedElement** attribute).
2. Attach an **RtSpecification** stereotype to the newly created comment and enter the appropriate values for its attributes (e.g., **relDl**).
3. Attach an **RtFeature** stereotype to the selected base model element (invocation action or behavioral feature).
4. Set the **specification** attribute of the newly added **RtFeature** stereotype to point to the **RtSpecification** stereotype created in step 2. Since this is a derived attribute, this should be done automatically by the tool, in principle (but not necessarily in practice).

An example of the use of this pair of stereotypes is depicted in Figure 5.29. The message representing the call to the start() operation has an attached **RtSpecification**, requiring that the operation be completed within 15 microseconds.

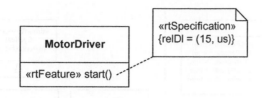

An alternative use of the **RtFeature** and **RtSpecification** stereotypes.

If the required deadline is to apply to all invocations of this feature, then the stereotype **RtFeature** should be applied directly to the behavioral feature declaration as shown in Figure 5.30.

5.5.3 Modeling cyclical behaviors

Many real-time and embedded applications involve concurrent tasks that are executed cyclically with fixed periods. In particular, this is a common method of dealing with continually changing phenomena in the physical world, including analog (continuous) quantities. For example, to monitor the air pressure in a tank, we would create a task that wakes up periodically and reads the value of an associated pressure sensor. The duration of the period between successive runs is dependent on the highest possible rate of change of the associated physical phenomenon. Since different phenomena have different rates of change, different concurrent tasks will have different periods. Note that, in some cases, different instances of a given type of concurrent task may have different periods specified. In those situations, information about the duration of the period has to be specified on an instance rather than on a type basis.

There are at least three basic design patterns for implementing these types of cyclical behaviors:

1. Through a simple application-level routine that is triggered by a clock interrupt, which then explicitly invokes the appropriate behavioral routines in a predefined order (described in Section 5.5.3.1)
2. Using simple concurrent tasks that are awakened by periodic (cyclical) timers provided through a system timing facility (Section 5.5.3.2)
3. Using *cyclical* concurrent tasks whose execution is controlled by a system scheduler (Section 5.5.3.3)

5.5.3.1 Cyclically executed routines

This method does not require any special concurrency management mechanisms such as threads and schedulers, but simply a means for specifying the timing information. The basic **TimerResource** stereotype, described in see Section 5.5.1, is usually adequate for this purpose. Two possible ways of realizing this are illustrated in Figure 5.31 (other similar techniques are also possible).

In the first case (Figure 5.31a), the individual routines are modeled as operations of an overall system, each cyclical routine tagged individually as a kind of timer resource with appropriate period values specified. In the second case (Figure 5.31b), the routines are all specializations of a common parent behavior class (Cyclical). Each specialization implements its specific function.[14]

---

[14]Not shown in these diagrams is the behavior that invokes these routines.

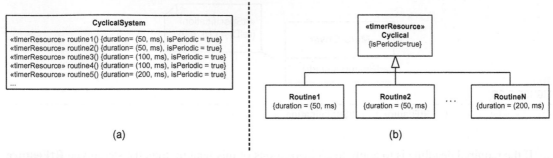

(a)

(b)

FIGURE 5.31

Two ways of modeling cyclically executed routines.

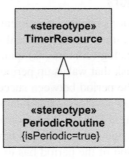

FIGURE 5.32

Creating a specialized alias stereotype for cyclical routines.

Of course, the elements tagged as **TimerResources** are not actually timers in the traditional sense. Instead, the attributes of the stereotype are used to indicate that these are cyclical behaviors with specified periods. If this is a source of confusion, then it is recommended to create an alias by defining a new specialization of the **TimerResource** stereotype with a more appropriate name as shown in Figure 5.32.

5.5.3.2 Using timers for cyclical tasks

This method involves the use of concurrent tasks (e.g., identified by the **SwSchedulableResource** stereotype) and corresponding periodic timers as described in Section 5.5.1. Each task is awakened by its corresponding timer (it is possible for tasks with the same period to share the same timer), performs its function, and then yields control of the processor until it is activated again by the next timeout signal. If the underlying system does not support recurrent (periodic) timers, then, as the last action prior to yielding control, the tasks need to explicitly initiate a new timer that will generate the next timeout signal. Because of queuing and scheduling delays incurred in dispatching of tasks, this pattern is only suitable for soft real-time applications.

5.5.3.3 Cyclical scheduled tasks

This is perhaps the most widely used method of implementing time-triggered software systems and it is directly supported by many custom and standard real-time operating systems. In this case, the

```
┌─────────────────────────────────────────┐
│          «swSchedulableResource»         │
│              «timerResource»             │
│                   Task1                  │
│    {duration = (50, ms), isPeriodic = true}│
└─────────────────────────────────────────┘
```

FIGURE 5.33

Using **TimerResource** to model cyclical concurrent tasks.

responsibilities for timing and task scheduling are left to the system (see Section 5.4.1.3). All that is needed at the application level is to specify the timing properties of the individual tasks, as shown in the example in Figure 5.33.

Note that an approach similar to that used in Figure 5.31b can also be used here to take advantage of any commonality that may exist between the concurrent tasks. Also, if there is concern with the potentially confusing name of the **TimerResource** stereotype, an alias stereotype can be created as illustrated in Figure 5.32.

5.6 Dealing with asynchrony and hardware interfacing

Asynchronous events are quite common in the environment of many real-time software systems and are an unavoidable aspect of the physical world with which the software interacts. The difficulty they create is that, though they occur at unpredictable times, they may need to be handled on a priority basis. This can result in interruption and temporary suspension or even termination of ongoing activities. Unfortunately, this typically requires complex "housekeeping" actions to be performed by the interrupted applications, such as capturing and restoring the current state or releasing acquired resources.

At higher levels of abstraction, asynchronous events can be handled by discrete behavioral formalisms such as UML state machines, which were designed explicitly for capturing event-driven behaviors. However, for applications that are not explicitly based on this formalism as well as for cases where there is need for a more detailed representation of the underlying mechanism, this approach is either inadequate or inappropriate. For this reason, MARTE provides additional specialized facilities for modeling various forms of asynchrony typically found in real-time systems. In this context, asynchrony may be manifested in any of the following basic forms:

- Interrupts, raised by either hardware or software
- Alarms and signals, which are raised by software when some type of exceptional condition is detected
- Asynchronous messages generated by concurrent tasks
- Timeout signals

The modeling of timeouts was described in Section 5.5.1 for the implicit clock reference approach, and in Section 4.2.8, for the explicit clock reference approach. For basic asynchronous messages generated by concurrent tasks, the standard UML Signal and Reception concepts can be used, or, in case of interactions (e.g., sequence diagrams), the standard asynchronous message construct can be used, as illustrated in Figure 5.34.

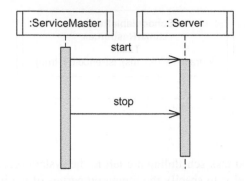

FIGURE 5.34

Using the standard UML asynchronous message construct to model asynchrony.

5.6.1 Modeling interrupt sources and interrupt handling

MARTE explicitly supports the modeling of *sources of interrupts* via the **InterruptResource** stereotype. This is a subtype of the more general **SwResource** stereotype described in Section 5.3.1. As with all resources in MARTE, this stereotype can be used to tag various kinds of classifiers, object instance specifications, connectable elements, lifelines, and properties. This stereotype is also useful when modeling platforms (Chapter 6).

An example of how this stereotype can be used when modeling applications is shown in the class model fragment in Figure 5.35. In this case, we distinguish between the actual device that generates the interrupt, PressureOverloadDetector, and its software handler component, POHandler. (Although not mandatory, note that both are rendered as active objects, to emphasize their asynchronous natures.) The association between the handler and the actual device is achieved via the **EntryPoint** stereotype, which is a specialization of the UML Abstraction concept. This stereotype has an optional additional attribute, **routine**, which denotes the software operation that handles the interrupt (in this case, the handleIRQ() operation of the handler). Finally, we show the asynchronous signal that is raised by the interrupt handler, POdetected, via a standard UML uses relationship. Note that it is stereotyped with the MARTE **Alarm** stereotype, which can be used (among other things), to explicitly represent interrupt signals.

A simpler and more abstract representation of this same system involves abstracting away the actual physical device that generates the interrupt, and implying its presence by denoting the handler as the source of interrupts, as depicted in Figure 5.36.

In its full definition, **InterruptResource** has many different attributes, but the following are the most useful for application modeling:

- **kind** — Identifies the type of interrupt, as defined by the literals of the MARTE **InterruptKind** enumeration:
  - **HardwareInterrupt** — For hardware generated interrupts
  - **ProcessorDetectedException** — For representing a special kind of hardware interrupt detected by the CPU, such as attempts to divide by zero, numerical overflows, etc.
  - **ProgrammedException** — For software generated interrupts, such as breakpoints

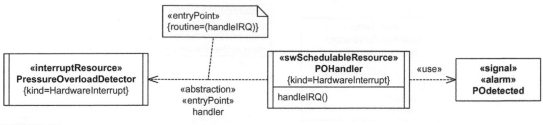

FIGURE 5.35

Modeling an interrupt source and corresponding handler.

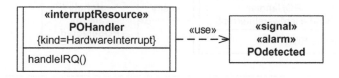

FIGURE 5.36

Modeling an interrupt source and corresponding handler as a single unit.

- **activateServices** — This is an optional denotational attribute pointing to a set of operations that are used to attach an interrupt handler to a particular interrupt level (note, however, that the concept of service activation is more general, so that this is merely a recommendation on how to use this attribute).
- **suspendServices** — This is an optional denotational attribute pointing to a set of operations that temporarily disable (i.e., mask out) interrupts from an interrupt resource.
- **resumeServices** — This is an optional denotational attribute pointing to a set of operations that re-enable (i.e., unmask) a temporarily disabled interrupt resource.

The use of these attributes can be seen in Figure 5.37, which is an expanded version of the system in Figure 5.36. Note the use of a generic interrupt handler interface in this case as a means of capturing the common characteristics of all interrupt handlers.

A common source of interrupts in most real-time systems is the watchdog timer, a device that needs to be reset before it expires, or the system raises a hard interrupt, which is usually interpreted as a signal to reset the system because it is assumed that either a deadlock or a livelock has occurred. Watchdog timers can be modeled explicitly using the MARTE **Alarm** stereotype as shown in Figure 5.38.

The **Alarm** stereotype is actually a specialization of the **InterruptResource** stereotype (which is why it has a **kind** attribute), with two additional attributes:

- **isWatchdog** — Is a Boolean attribute that is set to true when representing a watchdog timer.
- **timers** — Is an optional denotational attribute that points to a model element representing a timer (in this example, this attribute points to the WatchdogTimer class itself, which is also stereotyped as a **TimerResource**, with a period of 100 milliseconds).

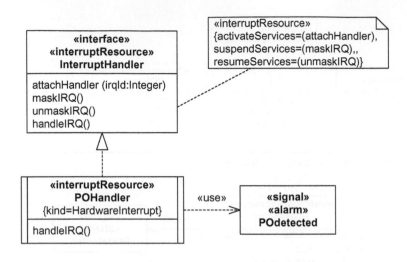

FIGURE 5.37

A more detailed model of an interrupt resource with key operations identified.

A signal is also defined, watchdogTimer, which is tagged with the **Alarm** stereotype to indicate that this is the signal that is raised if the watchdog timer is not reset on time.[15]

5.6.2 Modeling signal-based notifications

A number of real-time operating systems provide a higher-level software-based asynchronous mechanism for signaling the occurrence of asynchronous events. In a sense, it is the software equivalent of an interrupt mechanism. MARTE provides two core stereotypes for modeling these types of mechanisms:

- The **Alarm** stereotype, described in Section 5.6.1
- The **NotificationResource** stereotype and its related enumeration types

In contrast to the **Alarm** stereotype, which is used to represent interrupt-like mechanisms (in fact, **Alarm** is a specialization of the **InterruptResource** stereotype), that simply generate signals and dispatch them asynchronously to targeted concurrent tasks, **NotificationResource** provides a synchronization facility for its client tasks. Specifically, a notification resource will detect the occurrence of particular type of asynchronous event and buffer it until a client task is ready to consume it. Consequently, such occurrences will not be lost. Conversely, if an expected event has not yet occurred when the client task is ready to receive it, the task will be suspended until the event does occur.

---

[15] The use of this stereotype to represent both a resource and a signal that is generated by the resource is somewhat unusual, since these are two semantically different concepts. It would have been more appropriate if a distinct "alarm signal" stereotype had been defined, since it is not quite right to treat a signal as a kind of resource.

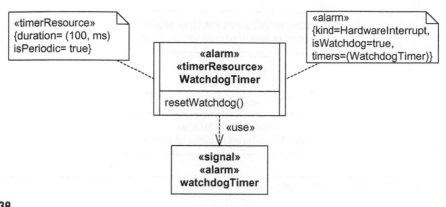

FIGURE 5.38

Modeling a watchdog timer.

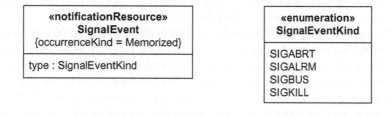

FIGURE 5.39

An example of a notification resource.

The **occurrence** attribute of the **NotificationResource** stereotype defines how successive notifications are to be treated. This is an enumeration that provides the following possibilities:

- **Memorized**, which means that successive notification occurrences are maintained in a buffer until processed.
- **Bounded**, which means that a previously unhandled occurrence is overwritten with the arrival of a new one, but a count of unhandled ones is maintained.
- **Memoryless**, which means that no record is maintained of any previous unhandled event occurrences.

The usual application of **NotificationResource** is to use it to tag a class that represents an asynchronous event, as illustrated in Figure 5.39.

5.7 Dealing with resource limitations (Specifying platform requirements)

As explained in Section 5.2, real-time software design may have to account for resource limitations of the underlying platform (memory, CPU speed, reliability, etc.). Of course, we would prefer to design the application independently of any particular platform, not only to simplify design, but also to allow

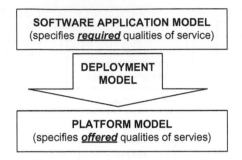

FIGURE 5.40

QoS specifications for applications and platforms.

the application to be deployed on a variety of different platforms. This is the so-called principle of *platform independence.* However, as mentioned earlier, *platform independence should not be interpreted as platform ignorance,* particularly in real-time and embedded software, since technological limitations and idiosyncrasies can greatly affect design.

One way of supporting platform independence is to explicitly specify, in a platform-independent way, the assumptions that a particular application has about the capabilities of the underlying platform. This decouples the application from any specific type of platform, while still explicitly recognizing potential technological and other physical constraints. For example, we may specify that our application requires a processor with a speed rating of 5 MIPs and a memory capacity of 500 MB. This does not constrain us to any particular platform, but identifies the range of possible acceptable platforms.

To support this pragmatic approach to platform-independent application design, we require the ability for application models to include *explicit specification of the qualities of service that the underlying platform must support.* This can be achieved in MARTE by expressing such requirements as special kinds of constraints based on the **NfpConstraint** stereotype described in Section 3.6.

In case of software applications, **kind** should always be set to the literal value **required**. Conversely, for platform models, the kind should normally be set to **offered**[16] (Figure 5.40).

Figure 5.41 illustrates this method of specifying application resource requirements: the action DB, which reads from some data base, is required to execute within 10 milliseconds from when it starts. This information can then be used to select a platform with a CPU that has the appropriate performance characteristics. *Note that the* **NfpConstraint** *stereotype is applied to the* **TimedProcessing** *stereotype rather than to the read action, because* **duration** *is an attribute of the* **TimedProcessing** *stereotype.*

This way of specifying application resource requirements (and their required qualities of service) can be used for all kinds of platform-related application requirements. It has the advantage that the **kind** attribute of the **NfpConstraint** clearly identifies which constraints represent platform requirements. Therefore, if used consistently throughout the application model, it can make it relatively easy

---

[16]Note that, in case of software platform models (e.g., an operating system model), both a required and an offered constraint may be used, since software platforms are simply applications that require their own platforms.

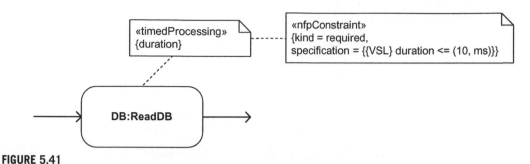

FIGURE 5.41

Specifying the required worst-case value for a read operation using **NFP_Constraint**.

to spot and collect the full set of platform requirements of the application. However, in Section 6.5.4, we describe a different method of specifying an application's platform requirements.

5.8 SUMMARY

The design of real-time software is distinguished from other types of software primarily because it is required to react appropriately to events in the real physical world. The difficulty lies not only in providing a timely response to such happenings but also coping with the immense diversity, concurrency, and general unpredictability of that world. In this chapter, we have categorized the design challenges that characterize most real-time systems as follows:

- Coping with concurrency
- The need for timely response
- Interacting with the physical world and its complexities through specialized hardware equipment
- Coping with resource limitations of the underlying platform

Over time, a number of standard solutions and design patterns have evolved for dealing with these challenges, such as multitasking mechanisms, mutual exclusion mechanisms, interrupts, inter-task communication facilities, and so on. In this chapter, we explained how the various MARTE concepts and facilities allow direct and precise modeling of these solutions.

References

[1] Burns A, Wellings A. Real-time systems and programming languages (fourth edition): Ada 2005, real-time java, and c/real-time POSIX, Addison Wesley Longman; 2009.
[2] Object Management Group, The, A UML profile for MARTE: Modeling and Analysis of Real-Time and Embedded Systems, version 1.1, OMG document no. formal/2011-06-02; 2011.

Modeling Platforms

6

CHAPTER CONTENTS

6.1 INTRODUCTION

In this chapter, we examine the modeling of platforms using MARTE. This is obviously a meaningful thing to do if we are responsible for designing such platforms, whether they are hardware or software. However, in this book we are primarily interested in modeling platforms for the specific purpose of *determining the impact that the characteristics of the platform can have on a software application.* Consequently, we consider platforms not from the perspective of platform designers but, instead, *from an application designer's viewpoint.*

Unfortunately, in cyber-physical systems and in real-time and embedded systems in particular, it is not always possible to view the platform as a monolithic "black box" represented simply by its interface (API) and its observable *quality of service* (QoS) characteristics. In many situations and particularly in case of physically distributed systems, a more refined view of the platform is necessary, exposing a network of interconnected platform components each with its specific characteristics. In

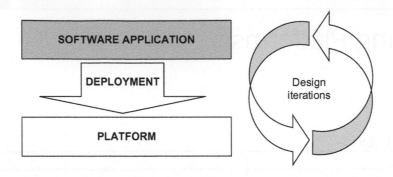

FIGURE 6.1

The relationship between applications and platforms in design.

such situations, different elements of the application are allocated (deployed) to different platform parts whose individual QoS characteristics can have a significant impact on the QoS of the application as a whole.

This brings up a number of important design issues, such as, what is the best way to deploy an application given a particular platform? Or, perhaps more crucially, can a given platform provide the necessary facilities required to support a given application? A suitable model of the platform can be of great help in answering such critical questions.

In those circumstances overall system design may even involve multiple iterations in which different trade-offs between application and platform configurations are proposed and evaluated before a final decision is reached (see Figure 6.1).

6.2 What is a platform?

The term "platform" is most often associated with computing hardware. While hardware is clearly the ultimate platform, in most cases some intervening software lies between the application and the hardware. That is, most modern software, including real-time software, requires one or more layers of software to isolate it from the full complexity of the hardware and also to help increase its portability across different types of hardware. This software includes things such as device drivers, operating systems, and, with increasing frequency, various domain-specific application frameworks. Hence, for our purposes, we define a *platform* as *the full complement of hardware and software that underlies and supports an application.*

Note that this definition is both relative and recursive: any software elements of an application platform will require their own platform, and so on down to the raw hardware, as illustrated in Figure 6.2.[1] Thus, how the terms application and platform are interpreted depends on the vantage point in this hierarchy.

---

[1]This is, of course, a simplified representation; for example, many operating systems depend on a more basic software layer that shields them to a certain extent from the hardware.

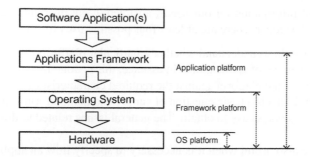

FIGURE 6.2

The platform concept refined.

Of course, a software layer supporting an application is an application in its own right, with its own underlying platform. This means that, if our objective is to use MARTE to design elements of a software platform, all of the modeling techniques discussed in the Chapter 5 on software application modeling with MARTE apply. However, as noted above, we are interested here in modeling platforms from an application designer's viewpoint.

Regardless of whether we are dealing with pure hardware or some combination of hardware and software, the concepts used to describe platforms in MARTE are all rooted in the basic notions of *resource* and *resource service* introduced in Section 4.3. That is, applications are viewed as *users* (i.e., clients) of platform resources and services, whereas platforms are *providers* of resources (i.e., servers) and their services. This is the core conceptual framework for how MARTE represents the relationship between applications and platforms.

6.3 Why model platforms?

It is reasonable to ask: Why should we bother modeling platforms in the first place? After all, isn't the notion of "platform independence" a core principle behind OMG's MDA® initiative [2] and, more generally, an ideal we should be striving for in any case? Clearly, platform independence yields important benefits—it allows applications to be ported transparently across different platforms and it helps reduce the conceptual load on application designers by unburdening them of the often intricate platform concerns during design.

However, while it is indeed a sound objective, *platform independence must not be confused with platform ignorance.* Much as it might be undesirable, the influence of platform characteristics on software applications is unavoidable: from the speed of the CPU, to the amount and characteristics of the memory, to context switching overheads, to power consumption properties. In a very meaningful sense, we can say that platforms provide the "raw material" out of which software applications are constructed. Consequently, the performance and other characteristics of a running application are a function of the characteristics of the platform that supports it. This is particularly true for real-time applications, which typically have stringent demands for performance, response time, availability, reliability, safety, and other "ilities." Thus, it may not always be meaningful to discuss the quality of an application independently of the characteristics of the platform on which it runs.

Needless to say, to understand the influence of the platform, we need to know about the platform and its characteristics. As might be expected, models can help us here. A platform model can provide just the right amount of information for our needs, abstracting out everything else that is of no concern to the application developer. There are at least four possible uses for such models:

- Platform models can help us understand whether a particular platform can support a particular application or set of applications. In essence, this is done by comparing the offered characteristics (QoS) of the platform against the required characteristics of the application. As noted in Section 1.5.2, this is a basic question of supply and demand. Unfortunately, the answer to this question is not always easy to obtain. The general issues related to this are discussed in Chapter 9.
- Platform models are also useful when it is necessary to specify how an application is to be deployed on a platform. If the platform is just a single processor, this is a relatively trivial exercise. But, if the platform is a multiprocessor or a physically distributed system, a model of the platform is essential. This information can be used in several different ways. It can be used by automatic code generators to ensure that the appropriate executable code is generated, or it may be used to validate a proposed deployment specification before it is committed to ensure that the platform can properly support the application. Finally, it can also be used to produce the artifacts required for software installation, such as deployment descriptors used for service-oriented architectures and similar systems. Deployment is discussed in more detail in Chapter 7.
- In some cases, platform models can serve as specifications for platform designs. The most obvious example is that of software applications such as frameworks or operating systems, which serve as platforms for higher level applications. However, such platform models can also be used as "blueprints" for hardware design in situations where custom hardware is required. For that purpose, MARTE has a very rich set of modeling concepts, particularly for specifying the elements of hardware platforms, including both their logical and their physical aspects (e.g., component layout information, physical dimensions, etc.).
- Last but not least, as explained in Section 6.5.4, a platform model can also be used to specify precisely and unambiguously the minimal characteristics that an application requires from its platform—in a platform independent way.

6.4 MARTE approach to modeling platforms

As noted in Section 4.3, platform modeling in MARTE is based on the two fundamental notions: resources and resource services. In the context of platform modeling, these are grouped into the following general categories:

1. *Processing resources* — Active entities that can execute software programs (e.g., virtual machines, physical processors, application-specific integrated circuits or ASICs).
2. *Storage resources* — Logical or physical devices for storing information, (e.g., files, disks, semiconductor, and other memories).
3. *Communications resources* — Facilities for transfer of information between system components (e.g., sockets, virtual circuits, networks, hardware busses).
4. *Concurrency resources* — Mechanisms, such as operating system tasks and schedulers, used for handling concurrency.

5. *Mutual exclusion resources* — Mechanisms for synchronizing the activities of concurrent active entities (e.g., semaphores, monitors, critical regions).
6. *Hardware device resources* — Devices for interacting with the physical world (servomotors, sensors, printers, etc.) as well as ancillary equipment such as power supplies and cooling systems.
7. *Timing resources* — Devices dedicated to timekeeping, such as clocks and timers.

Depending on the problem on hand, MARTE supports modeling platforms at three different levels of abstraction[2]:

1. A mostly abstract *system level* in which resources are represented primarily in terms of their purpose and functionality (e.g., communications, processing, storage), but stripped of most implementation details, such as whether they are realized by software or hardware.
2. A more *detailed logical* level, in which a clear distinction is made between software and hardware resources.
3. A purely *physical* level, intended primarily for hardware designers with its facilities to capture the concrete *material* properties of platform components, including characteristics such as board layouts, chip dimensions, energy dissipation characteristics, etc.

In this chapter, we concentrate primarily on the first two levels. A very brief description of the physical level approach is provided in Section 6.4.8, but readers interested in using MARTE for hardware design should consult the standard itself [3].

6.4.1 Platform modeling—core concepts

Practically all MARTE concepts for modeling platforms are derived from the foundational **Resource** stereotype described in Section 4.3.2. This concept is refined in various ways, depending on the desired abstraction level and type of resource. For the more abstract, system-level platform models, MARTE provides a corresponding refinement of this core stereotype for each of the resource categories listed in the preceding section. Alternatively, for more refined platform modeling, the **Resource** stereotype is first partitioned into two distinct *abstract* stereotypes:

- **SwResource** is for software-based resources, such as virtual machines, operating system processes, files, and so forth.
- **HwResource** is for physical hardware resources/

The **SwResource** stereotype, its attributes, and corresponding services are described in detail in Section 5.3.1.

The **HwResource** stereotype is an abstract stereotype that is the root of all MARTE stereotypes that represent hardware resources. It adds the following potentially useful attribute:

- **description** — A string that is used to document some useful information about the resource, such as its product code (e.g., the sensor elements in Figure 6.23).

Neither **SwResource** nor **HwResource** are intended to be used directly in models. Instead, they are both specialized further based on the type of resource as discussed in the following sections.

---

[2]For a discussion on how to choose the appropriate level of abstraction for a given situation refer to Section 6.5.2.

6.4.2 Modeling processing resources

The general notion of a processing resource has a variety of manifestations. The most obvious are computers themselves, although the same generalization also applies to just the actual data processing element of a computer such as the CPU. It can also be used to characterize various ASICs and other programmable devices. In the software domain, the concept can be applied to virtual machines and processor partitions.

6.4.2.1 Modeling processing resources: system level

For modeling these processing resources at the highest system level, where we are unconcerned with whether the computing resource is hardware or software, MARTE provides the very general **ComputingResource** stereotype. It deals with such devices as monolithic entities, with no concern about the details of memories, CPUs, busses, and so forth.

From an application designer's perspective perhaps the most interesting attribute of this stereotype is the following:

- **speedFactor** — An optional attribute of type **NFP_Real** that specifies the ratio of the computing speeds of the processor resource relative to some implicit or explicit reference. Thus, a value of 1 means that the computing speed of the resource is the same as that of the reference resource.

Note that the **resMult** attribute, inherited from the general **Resource** stereotype, can be used to model multiprocessors at this level, if need be. For example, Figure 6.3, depicts a class representing a processor with four cores and a performance ratio of 3.5 relative to some reference.

6.4.2.2 Modeling processing resources: hardware

For modeling a hardware processing device, MARTE provides a joint specialization of the general **ComputingResource** and the **HwResource** stereotypes called **HwComputingResource**. Its primary and almost only distinction from its abstract-level parent is that it can explicitly designate a specific hardware device. An example of this is depicted in Figure 6.4 representing a hardware processor of a particular brand (**ZX432**).

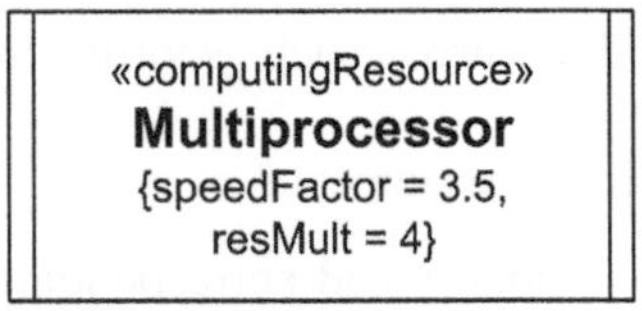

«computingResource»
Multiprocessor
{speedFactor = 3.5,
resMult = 4}

FIGURE 6.3

A high-level model of a four-core multiprocessor.

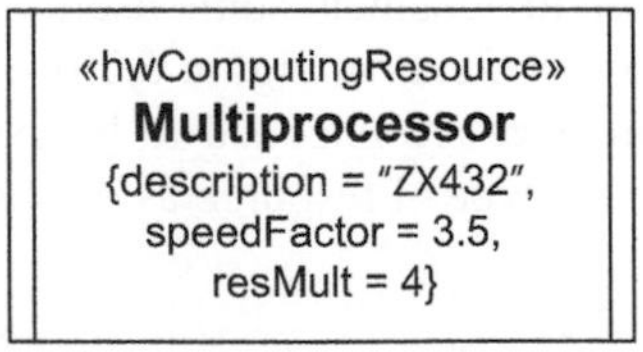

«hwComputingResource»
Multiprocessor
{description = "ZX432",
speedFactor = 3.5,
resMult = 4}

FIGURE 6.4

A logical model of a hardware multiprocessor with an explicit processor type specification.

Note that it is even possible to model computing resources at a more refined level. MARTE identifies three different types of hardware processing devices:

- **HwProcessor** is primarily intended to represent the processing component of a traditional stored program computer. It provides numerous attributes that can be used to specify various characteristics of processors, such as the type of its caches and memory management units, its instruction set architecture (RISC or CISC), etc. Of these we single out the following attributes that appear most useful for the kind of platform modeling we are focused on here:
  - **mips** is a positive number that specifies the MIPS rating of the processor.
  - **nbCores** is a positive integer that specifies the number of processor cores (for multiprocessors).
- **HwASIC** is for representing ASICs.
- **HwPLD** is for capturing various programmable devices.

6.4.2.3 Modeling processing resources: software

No custom stereotype is provided for modeling software-based processing resources in MARTE. If required, the general **ComputingResource** stereotype can be used or, alternatively, a custom stereotype (probably a subclass of **ComputingResource**) can be defined. Figure 6.5 shows a Java virtual machine modeled as a logical processor.

6.4.3 Modeling storage resources

Today, computer memories come in many flavors and appear in many different contexts: RAM and (P)ROM main memories, fast dynamic cache memories connected to processors, detachable persistent semiconductor memories and disk drives, etc. As with other types of platform resources, MARTE provides significant variety in modeling memories of different kinds and at different abstraction levels.

6.4.3.1 Modeling storage resources: system level

At the most abstract level, MARTE represents memory via the relatively basic **StorageResource** stereotype, a refinement of the general **Resource** stereotype (Section 4.2.2). In addition to the attributes of its parent, this stereotype has only one additional optional attribute:

- **elementSize**, which is an integer that specifies the size of the basic memory unit in bits (e.g., a byte-based memory would have a value of 8 for this attribute).

Note that this stereotype does not have an attribute that specifies the total amount of storage space of the resource. However, this can be specified via the **resMult** attribute inherited from the **Resource** stereotype. For example, the storage resource in the example in Figure 6.20 has a basic unit (word) that is 32 bits long while its total capacity is 1,000,000 such words (i.e., approximately 4 MB).

```
«computingResource»
     JavaVM
```

FIGURE 6.5

A Java virtual machine represented as a logical processor.

Although this is a reasonable approach, readers are warned that it is not standardized so that there is no guarantee that it will be interpreted as intended by MARTE-compliant tools.

It should be noted, however, that this stereotype does not distinguish between persistent and volatile store, which is an important difference in many cases. Consequently, it is often necessary to refine the model and use some of the more precise hardware-specific concepts explained below.

6.4.3.2 Modeling storage resources: hardware

The basic stereotype for modeling hardware storage resources is **HwMemory**, a refinement of both the **HwResource** stereotype (see Section 6.4.1) and the general **StorageResource** stereotype described above. It includes the following useful attributes:

- **memorySize** expressed as an instance of the **NFP_DataSize** standard library data type. As a reminder, **NFP_DataSize** is a tuple, defined in the standard MARTE library, usually consisting of an integer value and a unit (one of: **bit**, **Byte**, **KB**, **MB**, or **GB**)
- **throughput** defines the maximum speed of information transfer to and from the storage resource; this parameter may be important, particularly when it comes to slower hardware-based memories such as disks. This characteristic is specified as an instance of the **NFP_DataTxRate** standard library data type. Similar to the **NFP_DataSize** type, it comprises an integer value followed by a unit (one of **b/s** (i.e., bits per second), **Kb/s**, or **Mb/s**).

Although this stereotype is more refined that **StorageResource**, it may not always be precise enough, since it also cannot distinguish between different types of devices. To that end, MARTE refines **HwMemory** further into the following four subtype stereotypes based on the kind of storage in question:

- **HwCache**
- **HwRAM**
- **HwROM**
- **HwDrive**

Each of these has a variety of additional optional characteristics that can be used to provide a relatively detailed model of the memory. More information on these can be found in the MARTE standard [3]. For our purposes it is deemed sufficient to be able to differentiate these four basic categories, without going into further details.

Examples of the use of some of these stereotypes are given in Figures 6.12 and 6.23.

In addition to these concepts, MARTE also supports the explicit modeling of memory management (MMU) units (via the **HwMMU** stereotype) and direct memory access (DMA) controllers (using the **HwDMA** stereotype).

6.4.3.3 Modeling storage resources: software

The software view of memory is rarely as refined as the hardware view. Software-based memory resources such as heaps, stacks, buffers, and so forth can usually be modeled via the basic **StorageResource** stereotype, since they are all usually constructed from the same basic memory pool owned by the platform. In other words, from the platform perspective it is all just one big chunk of memory, its differentiation is based on use which is an application-level concern.

On the application side, however, it may still be necessary to specify explicitly the memory requirements expected of the platform, particularly if the acceptable platform pattern is used for that

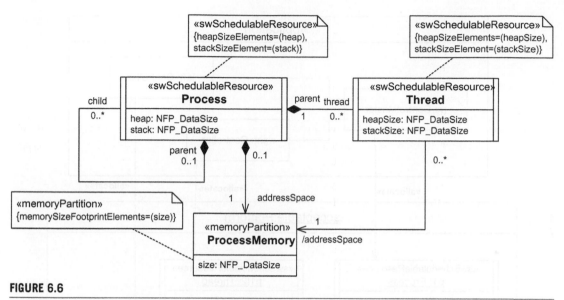

FIGURE 6.6

A model of a POSIX-like process with internal threads and a shared address space.

purpose (see Section 6.5.4). One MARTE concept that may[3] come in handy in these situations is the notion of a **MemoryPartition**. This is a specialization of the abstract **SwResource** stereotype (see Section 5.3.1), and is intended to model a virtual address space, such as that associated with a process in some operating systems. Its most useful attribute is:

- **memoryFootprintSizeElements**, which is a denotational attribute that identifies which of the attributes of the base class contains information on the size of the memory partition.

Figure 6.6 depicts a model of a POSIX-like concurrent process class that may have internal threads that all share the same memory partition. Note the use of the denotational-style stereotype attributes to identify which attributes of their respective classes contain information about required memory sizes. An alternative to this model would have been to avoid the memory partition element and simply tag the process element as both a schedulable resource and a memory partition. The problem with this, however, is that it is no longer clear that the process and its threads share the same address space.

This type of structure can be used in models using the "acceptable platform" pattern, described in Section 6.5.4, to capture the specific memory requirements of a concurrent application. A fragment of such an acceptable platform model based on the above class specification is depicted in Figure 6.7 along with its application.

At first glance, it may seem rather cumbersome to construct a complete platform model just so that we can specify memory constraints, especially when compared to simply attaching the memory

---

[3]Whether it is needed or not depends on the desired level of detail of platform model.

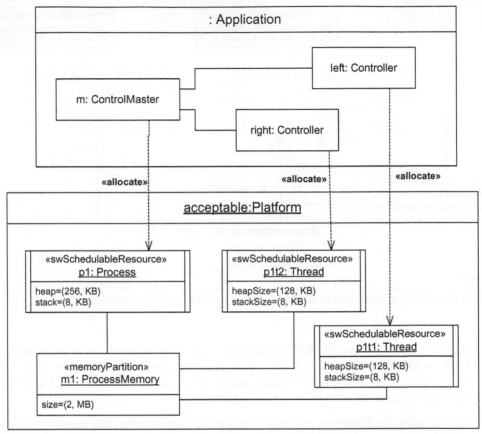

FIGURE 6.7

A fragment of an acceptable platform model for a concurrent application with explicit memory requirements.

information directly to the application model. However, note that there may be elements in the platform model that do not even appear in the application model, such as the memory partition element m1:ProcessorMemory. A different approach might have been to include the memory partition in the application model, but that would clutter the model, mixing application logic and technology-specific elements. Combining application models with platform models into a single unified model would have the negative consequence that it would make it much more difficult to explore different combinations and allocations of applications and platforms. (This issue is discussed in more detail in Chapter 7.)

When modeling software platforms, it may also be necessary to represent the software elements that are responsible for managing and allocating memory resources to other software components; i.e., *memory managers*. In MARTE, a memory manager is represented by a refinement of the general **SwResource** stereotype (see Section 5.3.1) called **MemoryBroker**. This stereotype includes the following useful attribute:

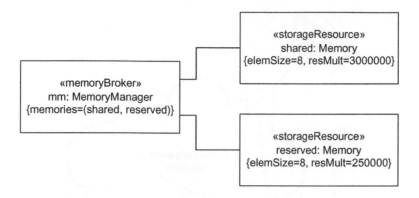

FIGURE 6.8

A memory manager model as represented with MARTE concepts.

- **memories** — This is an optional denotational attribute, which points to one or more model elements that represent blocks of memory and which must be tagged by the **StorageResource** stereotype or one of its subtypes.

An example of a memory manager element (**mm:MemoryManager**) in a fragment of a software platform model is given in the collaboration diagram in Figure 6.8. This manager supports two separate memory blocks, one, shared, for general use (approximately 3MB) and another, reserved, allocated for special system use (approximately 250 KB).

6.4.4 Modeling communications resources

MARTE reduces the complex world of communications facilities and services to just two core concepts: *communication media* and *communication end points* (see Figure 6.9). Information is sent out through a source end point and relayed by the medium to the destination end point. The end points are the interfaces between a communications facility user and the medium. This simple model is then refined in various ways to support more detailed modeling of both hardware and software communication mechanisms. Information is generally assumed to flow through the end points and media in discrete frames (packets or messages).

In most application models, the actual facilities that support communications are implied rather than explicitly rendered. This is because we are usually much more interested in what they accomplish (i.e., couplings between application elements) rather than the details of the communication facility itself. In UML, for instance, we use simple linear representations for associations, links, or connectors, as shown in Figure 6.10a, to indicate where communications between application elements are required. However, we rarely show the communications mechanisms that realize that functionality directly in the application model (as in Figure 6.10b). This is because that would effectively hide the important application-level couplings that the communications facility achieves. Thus, unless our application happens to be an implementation of some communications facility, these types of elements usually belong only in platform models.

Nevertheless, we may on occasion use some of these MARTE stereotypes in application-level models, in situations where we want to say something about the properties of the communication channels involved.

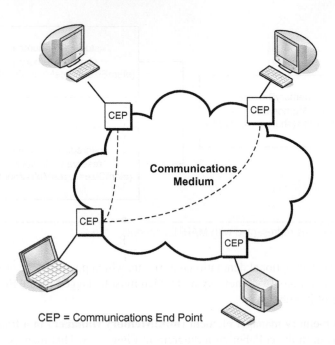

CEP = Communications End Point

FIGURE 6.9

The MARTE model of communications.

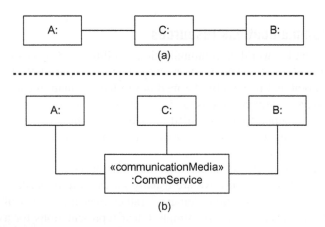

(b)

FIGURE 6.10

The effects of explicit rendering of communication facilities in an application model.

6.4.4.1 Modeling communications resources: system level

At the most abstract level, the simple core model is realized through two specializations of the standard MARTE **Resource** stereotype (see Section 4.3.2): **CommunicationEndPoint** and **CommunicationMedia**. As with all kinds of resources, the stereotypes can be applied to standard elements such as classes, interfaces, instances, etc. Note, however, that the **CommunicationMedia** stereotype and its specializations can *also* be applied to instances of UML Connector—for obvious reasons.

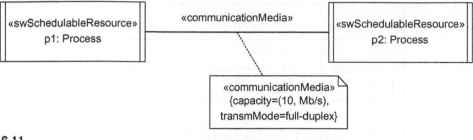

FIGURE 6.11

A connector between two processes representing a channel with a capacity of 10 MB/s.

The most useful attributes of the **CommunicationsMedia** stereotype are the following:

- **capacity** — This is an optional attribute used to specify the maximum possible transmission rate of the medium. It is an instance of the standard MARTE library type, **NFP_DataTxRate**. This data type includes a **Real** value and a unit. The unit can be one of the following enumeration literals: **b/s**, **Kb/s**, or **Mb/s**.
- **elementSize** — This is an optional integer attribute specifying the size of the information frames that are transmitted through the medium (NB: the standard does not prescribe any specific unit of measure for this, but a useful convention is to use it to specify the maximum packet size in bytes).
- **transmMode** — This is an optional attribute specifying the mode of transmission; its value can be one of the following enumeration literals defined by the standard MARTE library type **TransModeKind**: **simplex**, **half-duplex**, or **full-duplex**.

Also, this stereotype inherits the **resMult** integer attribute from the general **Resource** parent, which can be used to capture the number of channels that the medium is able to provide (note that this interpretation of the **resMult** attribute is non-standard).

An example of the use of this stereotype to model a channel connecting two operating system processes is given in the structure diagram fragment in Figure 6.11. This type of model fragment might appear in an acceptable platform specification, indicating the required capacity for a connection between two concurrent processes.

The **CommunicationEndPoint** stereotype has only one optional attribute:

- **packetSize**, which generally should match to the **elementSize** attribute of the **CommunicationMedia** stereotype.

6.4.4.2 Modeling communications resources: hardware

MARTE provides a set of concepts for modeling of hardware communications facilities that can be used to define very detailed models of computing hardware. Many of these are intended for actual hardware design specifications and are, thus, of little interest to software application designers and developers. Consequently, we focus only on the following primary stereotypes:

- **HwMedia** is for hardware-based communications media. This is a generic stereotype derived from **HwResource** that does not specify precisely what kind of interconnection topology is involved. It adds one attribute:
    - **bandwidth** is an attribute of type **NFP_DataTxRate**, which specifies the bandwidth of the communication medium.

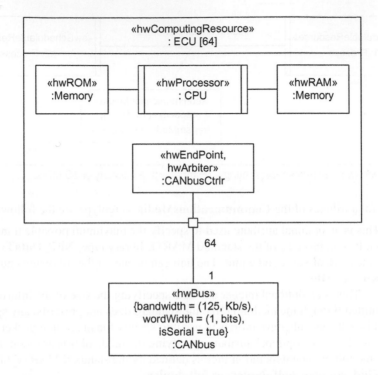

FIGURE 6.12

Example hardware platform model with 64 ECUs interconnected by a CAN bus.

- **HwBus** is a specialization of the **HwMedia** stereotype intended for capturing bus-type communication media, comprising a single network component (e.g., an Ethernet cable or a twisted pair) to which multiple communication end points can be attached. This stereotype adds the following attributes:
  - **addressWidth** is an attribute of type **NFP_DataSize** specifying the number of bits used for storing address information sent through the bus.
  - **wordWidth** is an attribute of type **NFP_DataSize**, which specifies the width of the data sent through the bus, expressed in bits.
  - **isSerial** is a Boolean attribute that distinguishes a serial bus (if true) from a parallel bus (if false).
- **HwEndPoint** is a hardware communication end point.
- **HwArbiter** is a kind of resource broker that is used to control (arbitrate) access to the communication medium in cases where there are redundant resources.

An example of the use of these stereotypes is shown in the structure diagram fragment in Figure 6.12 depicting a system comprising 64 Electronic Control Units (ECUs) communicating over a single CAN bus. The latter is an international standard[4] (ISO 11898-1:2003) for a multimaster serial bus that is frequently used in the automotive and other technical domains. Since it is a serial bus, based

---

[4]http://www.iso.org/iso/iso_catalogue/catalogue_tc/catalogue_detail.htm?csnumber=33422.

on a twisted-pair technology, the word width is just a single bit and the **isSerial** attribute is set to true. The CAN bus does not have a single arbiter; instead, each connection end point (an element of type CANbusCtrlr) also acts as an arbiter.

6.4.4.3 Modeling communication resources: software

This view pertains exclusively to the modeling of *software elements* that perform a communications function, such as various inter-process communication (IPC) mechanisms (e.g., sockets). Although hardware is invariably involved in the realization of such facilities, software communications can sometimes be realized without the use of any communications hardware (e.g., shared memory communications).

In this view, MARTE refines the general concept of a communications medium into two basic types: shared memory and message-based media.[5] Message-based facilities work by physically moving data from one location to another, which normally involves some data copying. In contrast, shared memory communication means simply that a writer deposits data in a location where readers can access it. Because there is no copying of data, it tends to be more efficient, but it does require that the readers and writers share the same address space (which, of course, can lead to concurrency conflicts unless special care is taken to avoid them). Note that this logical view does not necessarily imply a particular implementation; it is quite possible that a message-based system may actually be implemented using shared memory where the situation permits.

The two key stereotypes for modeling software-based communications facilities are **SharedDataComResource** and **MessageComResource**. They are both refinements of the general **CommunicationMedia** stereotype (see Section 6.4.4.1), which is, in turn, a specialization of the abstract software resource stereotype (**SwResource**). Hence, they should *never* be used to model hardware communications facilities.

The **SharedDataComResource** stereotype represents a chunk of shared memory, so that it may sometimes be used in conjunction with the software **StorageResource** stereotype as shown in Figure 6.13.

The **MessageComResource** stereotype has the following major characteristics (all of which are optional):

- **mechanism** — Specifies the kind of mechanism used for messaging. The following enumeration literal values are defined for this attribute:
  - **Blackboard** — For systems where the medium can buffer at most one outstanding message (outstanding because the medium is blocked due to the preceding transmission)
  - **MessageQueue** — for cases where multiple outstanding messages are buffered
  - **Pipe** — for POSIX-like pipe mechanisms, which allow data between memory partitions
  - **Undef** — for cases where it is useful to make clear explicitly that this attribute is not defined
  - **Other** — for possible user-defined values
- **waitingQueuePolicy** — for the case when **mechanism = MessageQueue** this attribute specifies the queuing discipline and can be one of the following values:
  - **FIFO**

---

[5]In the software domain, MARTE conflates the end point and media concepts so that the two are not differentiated. This means that the same two stereotypes (**SharedDataComResource** and **MessageComResource**) can be used to model both end points and media.

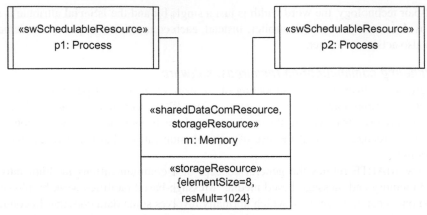

FIGURE 6.13

Example of shared memory communications between processes.

- **LIFO**
- **Priority**
- **Undef**
- **Other**
- **waitingQueueCapacity** — an integer value that specifies the number of buffers available for outstanding messages

Message-based communications media covers a very broad range of communications facilities. Among others, it is useful for modeling both point-to-point channels as well as networks, such as LANs, WANs, and even the full or partial Internet, as shown in Figure 6.14. (In this example, we have chosen to model explicit communication end points using the UML port concept. However, this design choice is optional and should be used only for models that make use of ports.) MARTE also includes a facility for explicit modeling complex repetitive structures, such as might be found in high-performance computing systems (annex E in the MARTE spec [3]).

When specifying the deployment of software communications facilities to underlying platforms, it is useful to keep in mind that there is often no simple one-to-one correlation between a logical connection as it appears in an application model and the underlying implementation. Modern communications media often multiplex multiple connections over a single physical link. Conversely, a single logical channel may be realized by a chain of distinct physical connections. Thus, it is quite possible to have a one-to-many, a many-to-one, or a many-to-many assignment between application communication channels and platform communication elements.

6.4.5 Modeling concurrency resources

Concurrency resources in MARTE are distinguished from other types of resources used for platform modeling in the sense that they represent a purely software-based concept: the notion of an independently executing software program sharing a hardware computing environment with other such programs. This concept has many names and many variations, such as Ada tasks, Java threads, and various operating system threads and processes.

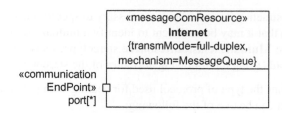

FIGURE 6.14

The Internet as a message-based communications resource.

In Section 5.4 we adopted the convention to refer to all these variants using the common term *concurrent task*, or more simply, *task*. We also explained there that a task can be viewed from two different viewpoints: the application viewpoint and the platform viewpoint. Finally, we described that the stereotype, **SwSchedulableResource**, can be used for either viewpoint, but using a different set of attributes for each. Naturally, when modeling platforms, we are interested in the platform viewpoint. The details of how this can be done can be found in Section 5.4.1. In addition, an example of a relatively detailed platform viewpoint representation of a UNIX process with multiple threads is provided in Figure 6.6.

If a more abstract representation of tasks is desired for our platform model, unburdened by the fine-grain detail represented by the various attributes of the **SwSchedulableResource** stereotype, the more abstract **SchedulableResource** stereotype can be used instead.

When modeling the concurrency mechanisms of platforms, in addition to modeling tasks, we may also want to explicitly represent the actual schedulers. These can sometimes be quite complex in larger systems. Schedulers serve as brokers who control access to one or more computing resources.[6] For details on modeling of schedulers, refer to Section 5.4.1.3. Figure 6.20 shows a simple model of an operating system consisting of a collection of thread instances (thrds:OSThread) and their corresponding fixed-priority scheduler (schd:OSScheduler). (Note the use of the **host** attribute of the **SwSchedulableResource** stereotype and the **schedulableResources** attribute of the **Scheduler** stereotype to connect the two model elements to each other.)

6.4.6 Modeling synchronization resources

This section covers the modeling of various software and hardware devices used for protecting against conflicting concurrent accesses to shared resources. It does not include, however, algorithmic solutions to concurrency conflict issues such as Dekker's algorithm or the run-to-completion model of execution.

6.4.6.1 Modeling synchronization resources: system level

The basic facility for modeling mutual exclusion resources in their most abstract form is the **MutualExclusionResource** stereotype, a direct specialization of the abstract **Resource** stereotype (see Section 4.3.2) and, therefore, can be applied to any base class associated with its parent.

---

[6]In fact, the MARTE model of schedulers is somewhat more general and can be applied to scheduling for other types of resources, such as communication channels. However, this broader application of the scheduler concept is outside the scope of this book. More information on this can be gleaned from the MARTE spec [3].

At higher levels of abstraction it is usually not necessary to specify the details of the actual mutual exclusion mechanism, so that it may be sufficient to identify a mutual exclusion platform device simply by tagging it with the **MutualExclusionResource** stereotype. Nevertheless, if desired, it is possible to provide more details using the following attributes of the stereotype:

- **protectKind** — Defines the type of protocol used for dealing with potentially conflicting concurrent accesses; it can be one of the following:
    - **NoPreemption** — Used for situations where an acquired device remains locked until the protected resource until the current user relinquishes it, regardless of priorities.
    - **PriorityCeiling** — In this case, a set priority is temporarily assigned to a client that is accessing the resource regardless of the priority of the accessing task; this strategy allows a low-priority task to temporarily block out higher priority tasks (note that, if this value is used, then the **ceiling** attribute described below must be set to the appropriate value[7]).
    - **PriorityInheritance** — This represents the basic priority inheritance protocol in which the priority of the current client accessing the resource is temporarily raised to match the highest priority of any tasks that are requesting access to the resource (note that this is the default value of the **protectKind** attribute, so that, if a different protocol is desired it should be assigned explicitly).
    - **StackBased** — This is a protocol similar to priority ceiling in intent but applicable to systems that are not based on explicit priorities.
    - **Undef** — Used if it is desired to leave the access protocol unspecified.
    - **Other** — Used for cases where the protocol is not one of the ones listed above; if so, the name of the protocol can be specified via the **otherProtectProtocol** attribute described below.
- **ceiling** — An integer-valued attribute that defines the ceiling value in case of the priority ceiling protocol (if some other value is used for the **protectKind** attribute, this attribute is not meaningful and should be omitted).
- **otherProtectProtocol** — Used only if the **protectKind** attribute is set to the value **Other**.

6.4.6.2 Modeling synchronization resources: hardware

MARTE does not provide a specialized concept for modeling mutual exclusion devices at the hardware level. Instead, modelers have the option to represent them as hardware devices (using the **HwDevice** stereotype) that are also tagged with the general **MutualExclusionResource** stereotype as illustrated in Figure 6.15. Alternatively, a new stereotype can be defined that is a refinement of both of these, as shown in Figure 6.16.

6.4.6.3 Modeling synchronization resources: software

The modeling of basic mutual exclusion resources such as semaphores and mutexes in software platforms, using the **SwMutualExclusionResource** stereotype, is described in detail in Section 5.4.2. Note that this stereotype uses its own approach to modeling the details of access protocols based on its own specialized attributes. Consequently, when using this stereotype, the access protocol attributes inherited from the **MutualExclusionResource** stereotype should *not* be used as they could either duplicate information or, even worse, be in conflict.

---

[7]These and other protocols were all devised to protect against priority inversion, whereby a higher priority task has to wait for a lower priority task to complete. More information on this topic and the various protocols can be found in [1].

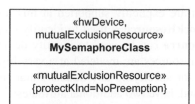

FIGURE 6.15

Representing a hardware semaphore using combined stereotypes.

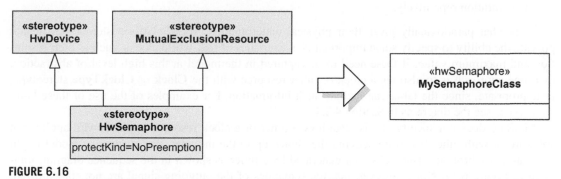

FIGURE 6.16

Defining a new stereotype for modeling hardware semaphore devices.

6.4.7 Modeling hardware devices and interrupt sources

Many dynamic systems interact with their environment through a variety of specialized hardware devices, such as motors, sensors, scanners/readers, etc. Asynchronous inputs from such devices are often manifested as interrupts. Needless to say, in MARTE, all of these concepts are rooted in the basic **Resource** abstraction described in Section 4.3.2. Devices that can generate interrupts are, invariably, active devices, which means that their **Resource::isActive** attribute must be set to true.

Clocks and timers form a special category of platform devices. Their modeling from an *application* viewpoint is covered in Section 5.5.1. In that domain, they are treated as abstract devices, quite distinct from any physical machinery that implements them. From a *platform* perspective, on the other hand, clocks and timers are treated as resources implying a more physically oriented interpretation. Hence, there is a separate set of stereotypes for representing such devices in platform models.

6.4.7.1 Modeling hardware devices: system level

At the highest level of abstraction, most kinds of special devices are treated as *device resources* (stereotype **DeviceResource**), which MARTE treats as a special case of a *processing resource.* Other than the general attributes that it inherits from **Resource**, this stereotype has no other major attributes. Of the inherited ones, the attribute that seems most relevant is **isActive**, which should be set for devices that can generate asynchronous inputs in the form of interrupts.

The only special devices that are explicitly supported at this level by MARTE are those dedicated to time. The stereotype **ClockResource** is used to identify clocks, which mark the linear progression of time, and **TimerResource** can be used to identify devices that measure time *intervals*, such as watchdog timers. Clock resources are modeled at a very high level of abstraction and, consequently, there is no provision for specifying any details about the clock, such as its resolution. **TimerResources**, on the other hand, have two additional attributes:

- **duration** — An optional attribute typed by the standard MARTE library type **NFP_Duration** (see Section 3.3.1), which specifies the time interval measured by this timer.
- **isPeriodic** — An optional Boolean attribute, which, if true, means that the timer will measure the same duration repetitively.

Somewhat paradoxically given their physical underpinnings, these platform stereotypes do not provide the ability to specify some important characteristics of real-world clocks, such as their resolution and maximum value. If these need to be captured in the model at this high level of abstraction, then one approach is to also tag a clock or timer resource with the **Clock** or **ClockType** stereotype, as appropriate, since the latter can include such information. For examples of the use of these latter stereotypes see the diagrams in Section 4.2.4.

MARTE does not specify at this level how a timer or a clock resource interacts with application software or with other hardware, leaving the choice up to the modeler. For instance, a model might show an asynchronous "timeout" signal generated by a timer as shown in the sequence diagram fragment in Figure 6.17. Note, however, that the semantics of the outgoing signal are not standardized, which means that there is no guarantee that such a signal will always be recognized as representing a timeout notification.

If more refined models of specialized devices are required, then either the more detailed stereotypes described in the following sections should be utilized, or a new specialized stereotype of **DeviceResource** or the timing stereotypes can be defined.

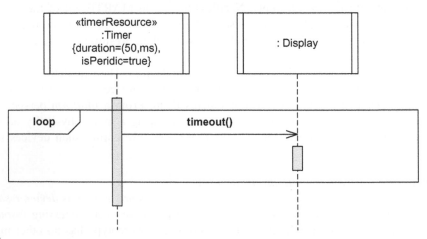

FIGURE 6.17

Modeling a timer resource and its output.

6.4.7.2 Modeling hardware devices: hardware

For more detailed device modeling of hardware devices MARTE defines several stereotypes, all of which are refinements of the basic hardware resource stereotype **HwResource** (see Section 6.4.1). Their primary distinction relative to the more abstract view of devices at the higher level is that they clearly identify that the tagged model element represents hardware. The following stereotypes are defined at this level:

- **HwDevice** — This is a specialization of both **HwResource** and the more general **DeviceResource** described above; this is probably the most useful stereotype for identifying specialized devices. An example o f its application is given in Figure 6.23. If more detail is required, it can either be provided in the **description** attribute inherited from **HwResource**, or a new custom stereotype can be defined as a refinement of this one, as shown in Figure 6.16.
- **HwClock** — This is used to model active *hardware* devices that maintain and provide *discrete* time-of-day information; such devices do not normally generate asynchronous signals, but may do so, in some cases, where an alarm needs to be raised that a particular time of day has transpired.
- **HwTimer** — This is typically used to model hardware-based timers such as watchdog timers.[8]

6.4.7.3 Modeling hardware devices: software

The software view of special devices is typically manifested through interrupts, whose job is to translate an external hardware event into something that is meaningful to software. It could be a message, an alarm, or a change in value of some variables. This function is performed by interrupt handlers, which are described in Section 5.6.1.

Similarly, the handling of clocks and timers (including watchdog timers) is described in Section 5.6.

6.4.8 Modeling concepts for physical platform modeling

As noted at the beginning of this chapter, the focus of this text is on the application view of platforms, including hardware platforms. This view generally does not deal with issues such as specific details of electronic components, board layouts, power supplies, and various other aspects that generally do not directly impact software design. However, for the benefit of those who may need to model such aspects, we note here that MARTE does provide for modeling this as well. For instance, the definition of the **HwComponent** stereotype, which is a specialization of **HwResource** and a part of a general "hardware layout" subprofile, includes the following attributes:

- **dimensions: NFP_Length [0..3]** identifies the physical dimensions (breadth, width, height) of an electronic component.
- **position: Interval <NFP_Natural> [0..2]** is used to specify physical position (Cartesian coordinates) within the containing physical component (e.g., a circuit board).
- **nbPins: NFP_Natural [0..1]** is the number of pins on the component.
- **weight: NFP_Weight** is the weight of the component.
- **price: NFP_Price** is the cost of the component.
- **staticConsumption: NFP_Power** is the power consumption in standby mode.
- **staticDissipation: NFP_Power** is energy dissipation.

---

[8]For an application-oriented method of modeling watchdog timers, see Section 5.6.1.

There is even a facility for modeling the physical arrangement of components for boards laid over with regular patterns of components, such as memory boards (Annex E: Repetitive Structure Modeling (RSM) in the MARTE spec. [3]).

6.5 Platform modeling guidelines

Software application developers often have a very superficial understanding of platforms. However, given the critical role that platforms play in system development and in order to take advantage of the full analysis capabilities of MARTE, it is often necessary to include platform models during development (refer to Section 6.3 for a more detailed discussion of this topic). Consequently, in this section, we provide some guidelines and usage tips on how to deal with some of the major design issues involved in modeling platforms.

6.5.1 Specifying offered quality of service using NFP_Constraint

In Section 5.7, we explained how constraints stereotype by **NFP_Constraint** can be used to specify the required QoS of application components. The same approach can be used for specifying the offered QoS of platform components. The only difference in this case is that the **kind** attribute of the constraint should be set to **offered**. However, this method may be redundant, since it can be generally assumed that the attribute values of platform elements represent the offered QoS—at least in cases where platforms are modeled from an application designer's viewpoint (as explained at the beginning of this chapter). For example, consider the class **Multiprocessor** shown in Figure 6.18a. In this case, the offered QoS values specified by the attributes of the **ComputingResource** stereotype, **speedFactor** and **result**, are defined directly with the stereotype. Figure 6.18b, on the other hand, shows how the **NFP_Constraint** stereotype can be used to specify the offered QoS. (Note that the constraint needs to be applied to the stereotype rather than to the actual platform element, since its body references the attributes of the stereotype and not the attributes of the **Multiprocessor** class.)

6.5.2 How detailed should a platform model be?

Needless to say, the more precise the platform model, the better our ability to correctly predict the impact of the actual platform on the qualities of a software application. However, from an application design perspective, there is typically not much value in developing a platform model that is more detailed than the application. The resolution of the platform model should be dictated by the needs of the analyses that are to be performed. For example, if all we are interested in is whether a platform provides sufficient memory to host our application, there is no need to go into details about how the memory on that platform is structured and managed.

In many cases in which only rough calculations are needed, the various software and hardware platform layers can be collapsed into simple "black boxes," such as the model shown in Figure 6.19.

A more complex model might be required if, for example, it is necessary to model the deployment of application-level tasks to operating system threads. In such cases, the platform model needs to include an explicit representation of concurrent threads (processes) and, possibly, a representation of a scheduler responsible for allocating processor time to the threads according to some scheduling

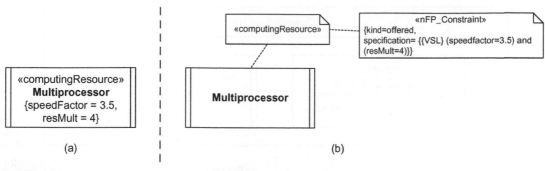

FIGURE 6.18

Defining offered QoS: (a) implicit method and (b) explicit using **NfpConstraint**.

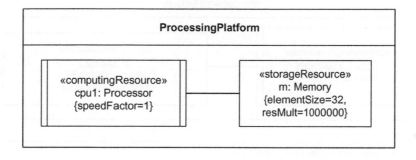

FIGURE 6.19

A very basic model of a hardware platform.

policy, as depicted by the instance of the OperatingSystem class in Figure 6.20. The overall platform model in this case also contains a representation of the underlying processing resource that supports the operating system platform, in this case an instance of the ProcessingPlatform class defined in Figure 6.19. The operating system instance is deployed on this lower level platform as indicated by the **Allocate** relationship (see Chapter 7 for a discussion of this concept). The combination of the operating system, the processor platform, and the deployment specification constitutes the complete model of the platform.

Clearly, even in this case, the processor platform is represented at a relatively high level of abstraction. An even more precise model might specify, for example, the type of cache or memory management unit attached to a processor, and whether the CPU is a RISC or CISC architecture, etc.

6.5.3 **Platforms: Class-based or instance-based models?**

Since one primary reason for modeling platforms is to determine whether they are capable of supporting an application, in most cases it is necessary to model them at the *instance level*, as opposed to the *class level*. A class is a generalization of all of its instances, that is, it captures what is common across all of its instances, abstracting out the particular. This type of information is rarely sufficient to answer the question about a platform's ability to support an application. For example, in

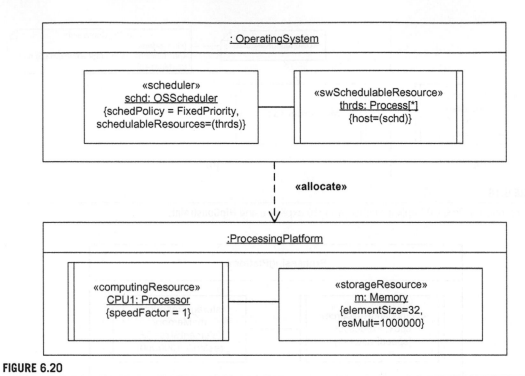

FIGURE 6.20

A basic model of a combined software–hardware platform.

determining whether the delay incurred through a set of identical routing nodes in a communications network is acceptable or not, we may need to know not only the precise number of nodes involved but also their interconnection topology. This type of information is often difficult and, in some cases, impossible to capture in a class diagram. Consider the example shown in Figure 6.21a and b: two collaboration diagrams showing two different networks composed of relay points (relay nodes) each of which is an instance of the same RelayNode class, and each of which introduces a transmission delay of 1 unit ($\Delta = 1$). Even though they have the same number of nodes, due to the differences in connection topologies, they incur different delays. Moreover, note that both of these networks share the same class diagram specification (Figure 6.21c). This clearly demonstrates that it is not always possible to compute this type of quantitative characteristics directly from a class-based model (it abstracts away the required information) and why it is usually necessary to model platforms at the instance level.

This is the reason why, in Figure 6.7, the application model and the acceptable platform model were represented by a collaboration and an instance model, respectively. The roles, instances, and connecters in these models all represent instances and their interconnection topologies. The main difference between using instance models and collaborations or structured classes for this purpose is that the latter two forms are a bit more flexible, since they abstract out object identities. This allows a given object to support multiple different roles in a collaboration (although this capability is not particularly relevant in case of platform modeling).

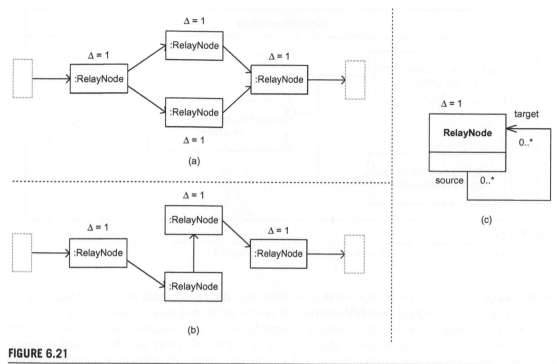

FIGURE 6.21

Class-based versus instance-based modeling.

This is also the reason why most of the MARTE resource modeling stereotypes apply to both class-level base concepts (e.g., UML Class) and instance-level concepts (e.g., parts and roles in structured classifiers). For example, in Figure 6.23 the **HwComputingResource** stereotype is applied to both the class ProcessorS and its instance p1:ProcessorS. Despite the fact that we have adopted the convention in this book (see Section 2.4.2) that, when a classifier is stereotyped, any instances typed by that classifier are also assumed to be implicitly tagged with that stereotype, there is still a need sometimes to stereotype instances separately, since different instances may require different values for their stereotype attributes.

6.5.4 The acceptable platform design pattern [Advanced]

It is often necessary to explicitly specify the platform requirements of a software application. For example, parts of the operating system class in the example in Figure 6.20 might need to specify certain minimal acceptable requirements that a platform must fulfill for the operating system to guarantee its advertised QoS. These requirements depend on the type of resource and vary widely in their natures and unit types.

In some cases, but not all, these platform requirements can be attached directly to the application model elements as discussed in Chapter 5. For example, the memory requirements of the operating system threads in Figure 6.20 could be specified using the **memorySizeFootprint** attribute of the

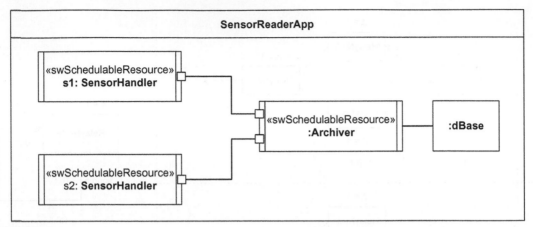

FIGURE 6.22

A simple distributed concurrent software application (Sensor-Reader).

SwResource stereotype (which requires that we stereotype the model element as a specialization of the concept, such as **SwSchedulableResource**). However, we do not have a similar predefined attribute should we want to specify the maximum acceptable context switching time of the scheduler and would require some other approach for that case (e.g., a constraint). Therefore, this method of specifying platform requirements has the drawback that it mixes a variety of different techniques, making it difficult to identify and summarize the necessary platform characteristics.

A method that is sometimes better suited for specifying the platform QoS requirements of applications is to use the so-called *acceptable platform* design pattern [4]. In this case, an application's platform requirements are specified through a separate model that represents a hypothetical platform, whose components have characteristics that are sufficient (i.e., acceptable) for the application to perform according to its specification. Application components are then deployed to the appropriate platform components that capture their requirements.

Consider for example, the distributed fault-tolerant software application in Figure 6.22, which reads data from a hardware sensor, processes that data, and then stores the results of the processing in an archival database. To protect against sensor and processor failures duplicate sensors are used, each one attached to a different physical processor. Concurrent SensorHandler tasks are used to interface to the sensors and perform the input data processing. They forward their outputs to a separate Archiver task, which persists them in a database. Note that the hardware devices are not included in the model, since they are not part of the software.[9]

Furthermore, assume that the data from the sensors arrives at a maximum rate of 1 Kb/s. This information is subject to some complex signal processing by the sensor handlers. To keep pace with the data and perform the complex computations necessary for the application, the CPU hosting the handler must be capable of at least 5 MIPS and have a minimum of 100 KB of fast memory. The

---

[9]This may be because the model is used to generate code, in which case it is typically necessary to keep the hardware and software elements separate.

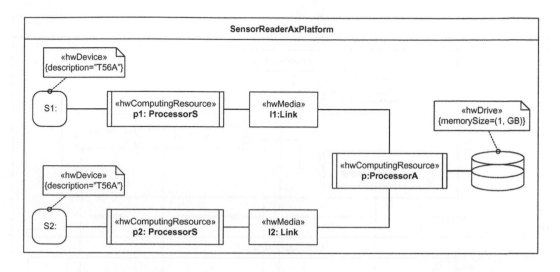

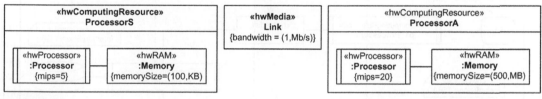

FIGURE 6.23

Model of the acceptable platform for the Sensor Reader application.

output produced by a sensor handler arrives at the Archiver task at a maximum rate of 1 Mb/s. Given the high volume of data that needs to be processed, the processor required by the Archiver task must have a CPU rated at 20 MIPS and have at least 500 MB of main memory. The persistent memory (e.g., disk) must be capable of storing a minimum of 1 GB of data.

All of these application requirements can be captured in the form of a platform model as shown in Figure 6.23. The platform is modeled by a structured class, SensorReaderAxPlatform whose various parts represent the necessary platform elements *and their required characteristics*. For example, processor p1, an instance of the ProcessorS class, is shown as attached to a hardware device S1, whose characteristics are captured by a part tagged with the **HwDevice** stereotype, which includes information on the type of device (T56A). Similarly, it is connected to the processor hosting the Archiver task through an instance of a communications channel of type Link. The nature of the processor and link are identified by their respective stereotypes, **HwComputingResource** and **HwMedia**. The desired properties of these hardware elements are captured via their respective classes, each of which is tagged with the appropriate stereotype. The stereotype attributes are assigned default values corresponding to the desired characteristics.

To get a complete specification of the application, we need both the application model and its associated platform requirements. This can be achieved with a collaboration model (SensorReaderFull), which includes a part representing an instance of the software application class and a part

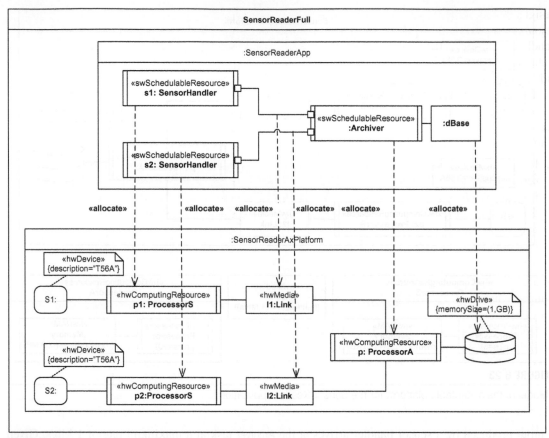

FIGURE 6.24

Complete Sensor-Reader application model including a specification of its platform requirements (acceptable platform).

representing an instance of the acceptable platform of the application (Figure 6.24).[10] In addition, also included is a specification of how the application elements are deployed to the elements of the platform using the standard MARTE **Allocate** concept.

But, if we use the acceptable platform pattern, does this not violate the well-established concept of platform independence? Actually it does not. In fact, to the contrary, the acceptable platform pattern actually facilitates platform independence. As stated in several places in this book: *platform independence does not mean platform ignorance.* In the sensor reader example above, there were strict responsiveness constraints imposed by external factors, which have to be respected if the software application is to meet its specification. Ignoring them completely or putting them off for consideration until after the software application design is completed can easily lead to inadequate

---

[10]It is worth reminding readers that the graphical form of allocating application elements to platform elements mapping does not scale very well in practical situations. A more pragmatic method is to specify the assignment by other means (e.g., drag and drop between tables), but this depends on the capabilities of the available tools.

designs that might be too slow or too expensive (e.g., because they require significant and expensive resources), or simply infeasible. For instance, when selecting a processing algorithm for the sensor handler, it may be necessary to consider design trade-offs based on capabilities of current hardware technologies as well as their cost. In modern mobile devices, for example, it is often critical to provide algorithms that are not only fast but that also conserve battery power.

The acceptable platform is a means to make explicit any assumptions about platform capabilities made during application design, *but without being specific to any particular platform*. In effect, the acceptable platform is an explicit statement of the *contractual obligation* that must be satisfied by any platform intended to support its corresponding application. It serves three important purposes:

1. It separates the application model from its platform requirements model, thereby achieving separation of concerns (which is one of the primary advantages of platform independence).
2. It provides a facility for validating all assumptions about the platform made during application design, since they are not only specified explicitly but are also conveniently grouped in one convenient model, and
3. It can help determine whether a given platform will be capable of running the application successfully.

The latter function is achieved by comparing the characteristics of the candidate platform against the requirements specified in the acceptable platform. If a given platform has characteristics that are equal to or exceed the corresponding characteristics specified by the acceptable platform model, then it may be capable of executing the application under consideration. However, this does not necessarily hold if the same platform is slated to run more than one application at the same time, since then the applications will contend for the same resources (at least for the CPU, if nothing else). Consequently, meeting the acceptable platform requirements is only a necessary (but not sufficient) condition for determining the suitability of a particular platform for a given application. Additional analyses are required in cases where a platform is shared by multiple applications. Some of these are covered in Chapters 9–11.

Because the acceptable platform pattern maintains distinct platform and application models, it is possible to consider them separately, although not fully independently. The traceability between the two is captured in yet a third distinct model, such as the one in Figure 6.24, which shows the assignment of application elements to acceptable platform elements. Through these links it is possible to examine the consequences that a change in one model may have on the other, if any. For example, if we decide to introduce a new processing algorithm, it is relatively easy to determine if any hardware changes may be required to support it.

Another benefit of this important design pattern is that it can simplify the task of application deployment across different platforms, since it is sufficient to deploy the acceptable platform, which typically has far fewer elements than the application (due to sharing of platform resources such as CPU and memory between different parts of the application). Chapter 7 provides more details on how application deployment can be specified using MARTE.

6.6 SUMMARY

The design of cyber-physical systems and in particular their software components often requires taking into account the characteristics of the underlying platform, particularly its resources and their physical and logical limitations. The latter can often have a fundamental impact on the design of a real-time application. For example, if the CPU provided by the platform is slow, then the application may have to sacrifice the use of numerically complex and precise algorithms in favor of less precise but more efficient ones. Or, if power consumption is a concern (as it is in many modern mobile devices), the architecture of the application may need to be structured around specific power-saving modes of operation.

MARTE provides facilities for modeling platforms at different levels of detail. The highest and most abstract is the system level, where the focus is on functionality and general QoS characteristics of platform resources. At the next level more detail can be added and a distinction is made between hardware resources and software resources. Finally, MARTE also provides capabilities for representing hardware, covering even aspects such as layout and other physical characteristics. However, the latter are out of scope of this book and are mentioned only briefly in this chapter.

The MARTE concepts covered in this chapter deal with the following platform concepts at the both the system level and the two detailed levels (software and hardware):

- Processing resources (CPUs, etc.)
- Storage resources of various types
- Communications resources
- Concurrency management resources
- Task synchronization resources
- Hardware devices

Although it is possible to use MARTE for platform design, the primary focus in this book is representing platforms from the application designer's viewpoint, so that it becomes possible to determine how platform characteristics can affect the QoS of applications. This means that platforms are modeled only to the extent (i.e., level of detail) necessary to make those determinations. Thus, much detail that would be of interest to a platform designer, particularly one designing a hardware platform, is omitted here.

Following explanations of the various platform modeling concepts, the final part of the chapter (Section 6.5) includes a number of practical guidelines on how to make effective use of MARTE for the purpose of gauging the impact of platforms on applications. This included suggestions on determining how detailed a platform model should be, as well as a description of the "acceptable platform" pattern, which can be used to realize a practical form of "platform independence" for real-time system design.

References

[1] Burns A, Wellings A. Real-Time Systems and Programming Languages: Ada Real-Time Java and C/Real-Time POSIX, 4th edition : Addison-Wesley; 2009.

[2] Object Management Group, The, Model Driven Architecture Guide (MDA™), OMG document no. omg/03-06-01, 2003.

[3] Object Management Group, The, A UML Profile for MARTE: Modeling and Analysis of Real-Time and Embedded Systems, Version 1.1, OMG document no. formal/2011-06-02, 2011.

[4] Selic B. Accounting for Platform Effects in the Design of Real-Time Software Using Model-Based Methods. IBM Systems Journal 2008;Vol. 47(No. 2) , IBM.

Modeling Deployment

CHAPTER CONTENTS

7.1 INTRODUCTION

We use the term *deployment* to refer to the allocation of elements from the software application to those elements of the platform that are responsible for their realization (see Figure 7.1). MARTE provides a simple yet highly flexible construct for specifying deployment.

Readers familiar with standard UML may know that it already provides a basic model and representation of deployment through its *deployment diagrams*. This particular model was largely inspired by the JavaBeans™ approach to deployment, with its notions of "containers" and "deployment descriptors,"[1] However, this method is often either too specific or insufficiently precise to accurately represent the full variety of deployment relationships encountered in real-time systems (see Section 7.7 for a discussion of the limitations of the standard UML deployment model). Consequently, the MARTE approach to deployment is an *alternative* to the UML approach. To avoid confusion and conflicts, it is generally not advisable to mix the two in the same user model.[2]

7.2 The two primary use cases for deployment modeling

When specifying deployment of software applications to platforms, we are primarily interested in two common use cases:

1. Specifying the deployment of software artifacts
2. Specifying location of run-time entities

---

[1] http://www.oracle.com/technetwork/java/javase/tech/index-jsp-138795.html.

[2] This only applies to the way that deployment is modeled, but does not preclude the use of base concepts from the UML deployment model, such as **Artifact** or even **Node** (possibly refined using MARTE stereotypes).

155

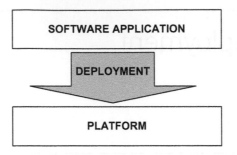

FIGURE 7.1

The role of deployment.

In standard UML, *artifacts* represent the concrete physical products that are used in or are the result of software development. This encompasses a wide variety of things including: source files, executable binaries, configuration descriptors, make files, etc. *Deployment of artifacts*, therefore, refers to specifying how the *information required at run time* (e.g., executables, routing tables, configuration data) is allocated across different parts of the platform. This form of deployment is primarily used to capture *where and how* the various units of the software application (i.e., its artifacts) are to be *loaded* on the platform.

Once the required artifacts are loaded and the software starts executing, diverse run-time entities, such as concurrent tasks, object instances, communication links, etc., will be created under program control. The number, location, and time of existence of such entities may be a function of dynamic circumstances in which the software is operating so that it cannot always be determined from the static deployment specification. For example, the number and frequency of telephone calls in a software-based telephony system will vary over time, requiring a corresponding dynamic creation and destruction of dedicated tasks and objects. In some systems it is even required that code and other artifacts move from one location to another, depending on current circumstances.

Information about the deployment and nature of run-time entities is also required *for analysis purposes*, such as performance or timing analyses, as discussed in Chapter 9.

7.3 The assign and allocate stereotypes

MARTE provides two very similar stereotypes for specifying allocation of software application elements to platform elements: **Assign** and **Allocate**. The **Allocate** stereotype was introduced in the initial release of MARTE, and was inspired by the **Allocate** concept defined in the SysML language. However, practical experience with it uncovered some undesirable side effects that are a consequence of how it was defined. Specifically, when the **Allocate** stereotype is used, it has the sometimes undesirable effect of modifying the allocated element. This creates problems if different allocation patterns are needed (e.g., when a given application needs to be deployed differently to different platforms, as discussed in Section 7.6). To get around this hurdle, in a later release of MARTE the **Assign** stereotype was introduced, with an almost identical definition and capabilities, but one that avoids the problems of **Allocate**.

In principle, both **Assign** and **Allocate** represent very general notions and can be used to associate any source model element with any target model element or elements. The semantics of this association are intentionally defined very broadly, so that it can be interpreted in many different ways and for different purposes. For example, it could be used to "assign" responsibility for designing some part of a system to a particular development team or to connect (i.e., allocate) a fragment of a behavior model with a corresponding fragment of a structural model responsible for realizing that behavior. *In this book, however, we focus exclusively on the use of these stereotypes for deployment purposes.* Furthermore, since this is an introductory-level text, we intentionally steer clear of some of the more sophisticated capabilities associated with these stereotypes. Readers interested in other applications of **Assign** and **Allocate** as well as their more advanced features, should refer to the MARTE and SysML specifications respectively [1,2].[3] A particularly interesting capability of the **Allocate** stereotype that is useful in more complex scenarios is the ability to be more precise about the semantics of the source and target ends of an allocation.

The MARTE definition of the **Assign** stereotype includes the following attributes, which are intended to provide additional information about the meaning of the allocation:

- **from** — This is an attribute that identifies the collection of source model elements (e.g., artifacts) that are being deployed.
- **to** — This is an attribute that identifies the collection of target model elements (e.g., platform elements) onto which the source elements are to be deployed.
- **kind** — This is an attribute of the type **AssignmentKind**. This is an enumeration type, with the following literal values:
  - **structural** — which means that both the source and target elements represent structural entities (e.g., an artifact being deployed on a particular processor node)
  - **behavioral** — which means that both the source and target elements represent behavioral entities (e.g., assigning a state machine behavior to an activity to represent the case where the activity realizes the state machine)
  - **hybrid** — which means a combination of the above two kinds, such as assigning a behavior to a structural component responsible for realizing it (e.g., assigning an activity to a concurrent task)
- **nature** — This is an attribute of the type **AssignmentNature**. This is an enumeration type with the following literal values:
  - **spatialDistribution** — which is used for specifying the location of the assigned elements (e.g., allocating active objects to corresponding operating system tasks)
  - **timeScheduling** — which is used to indicate that the assigned elements are distributed in time (i.e., scheduled) by the target elements (e.g., allocating multiple concurrent tasks to a CPU for multiplexed execution)
- **impliedConstraint** — This is an optional attribute containing a collection of constraints typed by the **NfpConstraint** stereotype, which can be used to explicitly specify required and offered quality of service (QoS) values (see Section 7.4).

In addition to the above, the **Assign** stereotype also provides an optional **body** attribute, which is of type **String** and can be used to specify any additional information that a modeler deems useful.

---

[3]However, despite sharing the same purpose and name, the definitions of the **Allocate** stereotype differ between the two profiles.

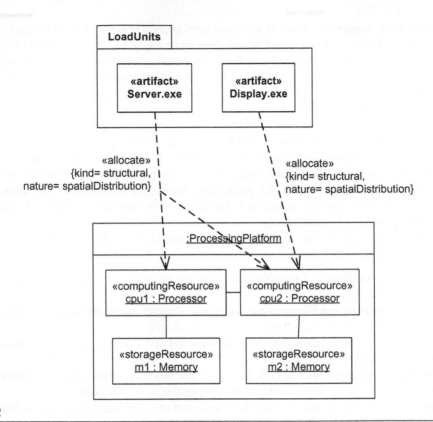

FIGURE 7.2

An simple deployment specification of two application artifacts.

The **Allocate** stereotype in MARTE has the same set of attributes, except for the **from** and **to** attributes, which are unnecessary since the source and targets of the deployment are specified by the base metaclass (**Abstraction**).[4] In addition, the **kind** and **nature** attributes are typed by **AllocationKind** and **AllocationNature**, respectively.

For the *artifact deployment* use case, the following combination of attribute values can be used:

- **kind = structural** (since we are deploying structural elements (artifacts) to components of the platform)
- **nature = spatialDistribution** (since we are specifying the location of artifacts)

An example of an artifact deployment specification is depicted in Figure 7.2. In this case, we have the artifact Server.exe, representing a binary executable file, deployed on two processors, cpu1 and cpu2, and a different binary executable artifact, Display.exe, deployed only on cpu2 (note the use of a single **Allocate** element with multiple destinations).

An equivalent deployment specification using the **Assign** stereotype is shown in Figure 7.3.

---

[4]In UML, **Abstraction** is a subclass **Dependency**, which is a kind of directed relationship with explicit source and target elements.

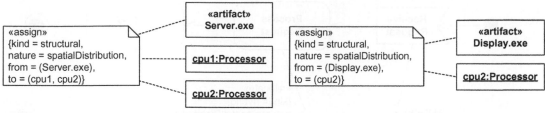

FIGURE 7.3

A deployment specification using the **Assign** stereotype equivalent to that shown in Figure 7.2.

	from	to	kind	nature
1	Server.exe	cpu1, cpu2	structural	spatialDistribution
2	Display.exe	cpu2	structural	spatialDistribution

FIGURE 7.4

Tabular representation of the deployment specification in Figure 7.3.

It should be noted, however, that, in practice, these graphical deployment specifications are rarely used, since that format does not scale very well when it comes to more complex real-world systems that involve a large number of deployable artifacts. Such diagrams quickly become cluttered and unreadable. Instead, a tabular form is much more suitable in such situations. An example of such a format is shown in Figure 7.4.

For the second type of use case, *run-time entity deployment*, the same attribute values can be used. However, additional possibilities may also make sense. For example, since many types of formal analyses require specifying dynamic execution scenarios, which could be expressed using activities, state machines, or interactions (e.g., sequence diagrams), it may be required to specify elements of these behavioral models to platform elements, as shown in Figure 7.5. Note that the **kind** attribute here is set to **hybrid**, to indicate that we are allocating behavior to structure.

7.4 Specifying required and provided QoS values via deployment

As mentioned earlier, it is possible to specify the required and provided QoS values in a deployment specification as an alternative to the approach described in Chapter 6, in which these values are stored with the model elements themselves. This is done using the **impliedConstraint** attribute of either the **Assign** or **Allocate** stereotype.

Figure 7.6 gives an example of this approach. It shows a binary executable, Server.exe, which is being deployed on an instance of the Processor class. Both elements are stereotyped as **computing-Resources**, which means that they have a **speedFactor** attribute (see Section 6.4.2.1). The deployment is specified using the **Allocate** stereotype, which includes a specification of the required and provided execution speeds, via the constraints, reqSpeed and offeredSpeed.

The advantage of this method is that the corresponding QoS values are directly linked to each other via the deployment specification, which simplifies analysis. Its disadvantage, however, is that

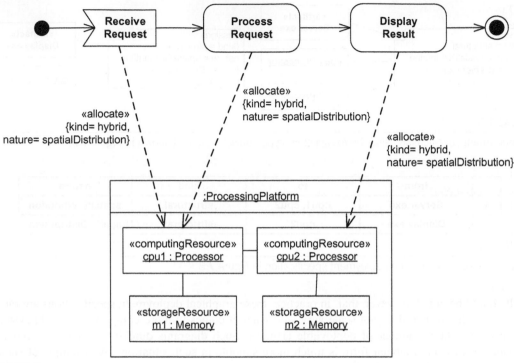

FIGURE 7.5

An example of a deployment specification of a behavioral element to a platform element.

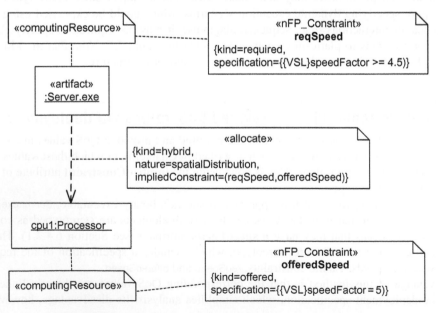

FIGURE 7.6

An example of using the allocate stereotype to specify required and offered QoS values.

the QoS values are not directly attached to their corresponding elements. Thus, if the same elements are reused in another model, these values need to be re-entered.

7.5 Granularity and meaning of deployment specifications

Neither **Assign** nor **Allocate** impose any restrictions on what kind of element is allocated to what other kind of element. This allows deployment to be modeled at any level of granularity. The choice is fully up to the modeler and is only constrained by the granularity of the application and platform models under consideration (which is chosen by the modeler). For example, one could conceivably allocate individual low-level actions of an activity to specific CPUs if desired. Alternatively, one could choose to represent the deployment of a complex component-based application across a complex distributed platform by just a single deployment relationship.

This raises the question of how to interpret such deployment specifications. In fact, except for the relatively informal qualifications captured via the **kind** and **nature** attributes, there is nothing in MARTE to indicate that an **Assign** or an **Allocate** actually specifies a deployment. Since there are no predefined constraints in MARTE that would formally restrict assignments to meaningful allocations, one could easily do something meaningless, such as allocating a device to a state. If stricter validation constraints are desired, then an extension of the MARTE profile can be defined that specializes the **Assign** and **Allocate** stereotypes and adds the desired constraints. Details on how the MARTE profile can be extended can be found in Chapter 12.

7.6 Capturing multiple deployment variants

There is often a need to specify different alternative deployments for a given software application. Since a deployment specification consists of assign elements, which are also part of the model, we

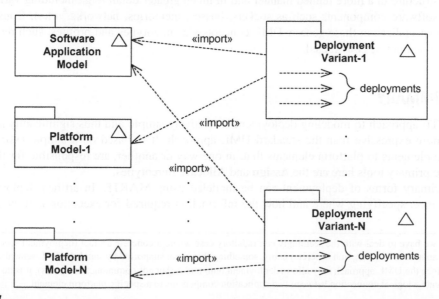

FIGURE 7.7

Realizing multiple deployment variants.

will need a separate model for each deployment variant. One efficient way of achieving this is to have the application and platform models in distinct reusable model fragments, along with multiple *deployment models*, one for each deployment variant (see Figure 7.7). A deployment model here is a model that imports (i.e., reuses) the application and platform model fragments and then simply adds the desired deployment relationships between them. This type of arrangement provides maximal flexibility to experiment with different combinations of application and platform models and different deployment strategies, without necessarily changing or cloning these models.

7.7 Limitations of the UML approach to modeling deployment [Advanced]

The UML view of deployment is built around two primary concepts: *deployment targets*, which are somewhat comparable to MARTE platforms, and *artifacts* as described in Section 7.2. A *deployment* captures the fact that an artifact has been deployed to a target, as specified by some kind of *deployment specification* (e.g., a JavaBeans-like *deployment descriptor*). There is some ambiguity about whether a deployment represents an abstract notion (i.e., the fact that some artifact is deployed on some target) or a concrete one (an actual data item of some kind). Note that, in this approach, deployments are owned by corresponding deployment targets and, in turn, deployments own deployment specifications. This suggests that a deployment is a concrete element, since a deployment specification is a kind of artifact.[5] In that case, the result is a very specific mechanism for specifying and realizing deployment.

Furthermore, the representation of deployment targets in the UML approach may not be discriminating enough for certain types of systems. For example, only two types of nodes are defined: *devices* (representing various types of hardware) and *execution environments* (representing computational devices). In Chapter 6 we have shown that it may be useful and even necessary to model their components and structure in a more refined manner and in much greater detail (e.g., including various hardware and software components such as sockets, busses, memories, networks,[6] etc.). Consequently, unless one specializes in these generic UML concepts via stereotypes and profiles, such refined platform models cannot be constructed.

7.8 SUMMARY

The MARTE approach to modeling deployment is relatively simple and thus significantly more flexible and more expressive than the standard UML approach. It is based on a simple assignment of application elements to platform elements that, in one way or another, are responsible for their realization. The primary tools here are the **Assign** and **Allocate** stereotypes.

Two primary forms of deployment can be modeled using MARTE. In artifact deployment, we are, in essence, specifying where and how the information required for execution is to be allocated.

---

[5]Otherwise, we have to deal with the seemingly contradictory case where a concrete artifact (deployment specification) is "owned" by an abstraction (i.e., non concrete) entity, something that is not supported by standard UML semantics.

[6]Note that since the UML approach only allows deployment onto nodes (but not communication paths), it is not possible to directly allocate a logical connection between two application components to a specific platform element.

Alternatively, run-time entity deployment modeling is intended primarily for various kinds of analyses, such as performance and timing analyses.

References

[1] Object Management Group, The, Clause 11 in A UML Profile for MARTE: Modeling and Analysis of Real-Time and Embedded Systems, Version 1.1, OMG document no. formal/2011-06-02, 2011.
[2] Object Management Group, The, Clause 15 in OMG Systems Modeling Language(OMG SysML™), Version 1.3, OMG document no. formal/2012-06-01, 2012.

Modeling Cyber-Physical Systems: Combining MARTE with SysML

8

CHAPTER OUTLINE

8.1 INTRODUCTION

A modern *cyber-physical system* is a heterogeneous technical system consisting of a network of potentially diverse physical components controlled primarily by software. A central design tenet of this category of systems is that a system should be designed as a whole. This means that, even following decomposition into constituent parts (subsystems), it is necessary to constantly evaluate and, if necessary, adjust the relationships between the parts and the whole [7]. This is a departure from the more traditional strict divide-and-conquer engineering approach. It is primarily necessitated by the growing functional complexity of modern technological systems, which are typically much more functionally integrated than in the past. For instance, in the design of modern automobiles, more and more couplings are being introduced between previously independent systems, such as the linkage between the door-locking system and the braking system for improved safety. As a consequence, there is an often unavoidable interplay between the design of the parts and the global system design, where each can affect the other.

For embedded and real-time software design using model-based methods this means maintaining a connection between the models (or parts of models) representing the software and higher level system models (or parts of models). The connection between these models can be either a *refinement* relationship or a *peer* relationship. In the first case, a language such as SysML might be used to capture the high-level system architecture, while a combination of UML and MARTE could be used for capturing a more refined representation of parts realized with software and supporting computing hardware. In case of a peer relationship, the SysML and MARTE models are used at the same level of abstraction, either in the form of distinct but related models, or, in some cases, in a single model with

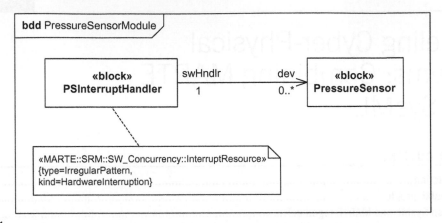

FIGURE 8.1

An example showing joint use of SysML and MARTE in a SysML block definition diagram (bdd).

both profiles applied simultaneously. Typically, SysML is used for specifying general system require-ments as well as for representing the mechanical and other physical components that interact directly with the software. The UML-MARTE combination is applied to modeling the software components, and, in particular, the information related to their real-time and embedded aspects. Figure 8.1 shows an example model fragment in which MARTE is applied to a SysML model. The PressureSensor block represents a hardware pressure sensor element while the PSInterruptHandler block is its corre-sponding interrupt handler software. To that end, the latter element has the **InterruptResource** ste-reotype from MARTE applied to it, which also provides additional information on the nature of the interrupt (via its **type** and **kind** attributes).

In designing complex cyber-physical systems, which combine software and hardware, there is clearly value in taking advantage of both SysML and MARTE. It is, therefore, important to under-stand how these two relate to each other and how to best take advantage of them in practical sit-uations. In this chapter, we first briefly explain the motivation for SysML, and then analyze its relationships to MARTE, i.e., where they overlap and where they complement each other. Finally, we identify the different ways in which the two can be combined in practice and describe some typical joint use cases. Throughout this chapter, it is assumed that readers are generally familiar with SysML. Those seeking an introduction should refer to either the textbook by Friedenthal et al. [3] or to the official language specification [9].

8.2 The SysML profile

Although systems engineers have been using models and various domain-specific modeling lan-guages for decades, the popularity of UML prompted the definition and standardization of a new modeling language designed specifically for systems engineers. This was the Systems Modeling Language, or SysML [9]. Although the language was developed within the Object Management Group (OMG), it was commissioned and endorsed by the International Council on Systems

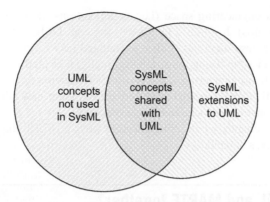

FIGURE 8.2

The relationship between SysML and UML concepts (not to scale).

Engineering (INCOSE), a global organization founded to support the dissemination of principles and practices of modern systems engineering.[1] Instead of defining a new language from scratch, SysML was defined as *a profile of UML*. This approach was taken for a number of reasons including:

- *The two languages share the same semantic foundation* (UML). This enables a relatively smooth transition between one language and the other. This is particularly useful when refining system-level components defined in SysML into corresponding software components specified in UML.
- The SysML language reuses most of the features of the UML language semantics and syntax (see Figure 8.2). This not only simplified the task of defining the language but also ensured that it was based on a field-proven modeling language.
- UML is supported by numerous commercial and open source tools, many of which are fully capable of also supporting UML profiles. This means that, to produce a SysML tool, it is sufficient in principle to provide just an incremental SysML add-on to an existing UML tool, such as Papyrus.[2] Furthermore, this also enables reuse of additional tools that were adapted to work in conjunction with UML tools, such as code generators and various model analysis tools.
- The UML language is relatively well known in the engineering community and is likely to continue to be used for a while. It is taught in many software engineering and computer science curricula throughout the world and is the subject of numerous textbooks and professional courses. Therefore, it was felt that basing SysML on UML would increase the likelihood of a faster and more widespread adoption of the language.
- In general, UML can serve as a "pivot" language, which can be used in conjunction with SysML as well as other UML profiles and even other languages that cover concerns or domains that are beyond SysML, but that may be of interest to systems engineers. MARTE is one such example, but other UML profiles, such as the testing profile [10], may also prove useful.

The relationship between UML and SysML is often depicted as shown in Figure 8.2. To make the language more manageable, SysML explicitly excludes certain UML diagram types that were deemed

---

[1] http://www.incose.org.
[2] http://www.eclipse.org/papyrus.

less useful in the systems engineering space (i.e., collaborations, deployment modeling, and communication overview diagrams). It reuses a number of the core UML diagrams (e.g., state machine, activity, sequence, and use case diagrams) either unchanged or with only slight modifications (i.e., a few minor extensions and simplifying constraints). Finally, it extends a subset of core UML concepts to either provide system-engineering variants of those concepts (e.g., the SysML *Block* concept as an extension of the UML *Class* concept) or to derive from them new concepts specific to systems engineering needs (e.g., Constraint Blocks and Requirements).

In the remainder of this chapter we describe different ways in which these languages can be combined, based on the objectives at hand.

8.3 Why use SysML and MARTE together?

There is a natural complementarity between SysML and MARTE, as illustrated by the simple example in Figure 8.1. First, there is complementarity of technology coverage: while SysML supports modeling of a whole spectrum of diverse engineering technologies (e.g., mechanical, electrical, and hydraulic), MARTE focuses primarily on real-time and embedded systems software and supporting platforms. In addition, the two can complement each other in terms of the level of abstraction they cover: the broader scope of SysML makes it a natural choice for representing systems at a higher technology-agnostic level, whereas UML and MARTE are better suited for finer grained modeling (e.g., the software aspects).

For historical reasons,[3] this complementarity was not fully exploited when the initial versions of the two profiles were specified, resulting in some conceptual overlaps. Both were concerned with representing physical entities and their quantitative characteristics and both were designed to support various kinds of engineering analyses, yet they provided different (albeit conceptually similar) solutions to these needs. Fortunately, this overlap was recognized and there is currently an ongoing effort within the OMG to align these two specifications [2].

The following is a brief summary of the areas in which SysML and MARTE either complement each other or overlap. These need to be considered whenever the two are to be combined.

1. *Value specification*. MARTE provides a rich formal language called VSL (see Appendix A) for specifying the concrete values of physical types (see Chapter 3) and related data. This language permits the use of complex expressions for computing values, including expressions that capture interdependencies between values of different model attributes. Needless to say, such a feature is invaluable in various engineering analyses. SysML, on the other hand, has no direct equivalent, but relies instead on other languages for this purpose. Of course, one obvious candidate for this is VSL, although using it with SysML requires a bit of extra effort as explained in the following paragraph.

2. *Support for physical types*. As noted above, both SysML and MARTE provide a library of predefined physical types. SysML defines its physical types using a simple pairing of standard "quantity kinds" (e.g., time, volume, mass, temperature or even electric current) and corresponding standard units (e.g., second, cubic meter, kilogram, degrees Celsius, volt). MARTE provides analogous facilities, including many equivalent physical types, but uses a

---

[3] The two languages were developed by different teams at approximately the same time.

different mechanism to define them (see Section 3.4). One interesting difference is that the physical types of MARTE include optional attributes to specify additional information about the data represented, such as the source of the data or its statistical properties. However, from a modeler's perspective, the primary difference is that the MARTE data types can *directly* take full advantage of the expressive power of VSL. To get the equivalent capability with SysML would require applying the VSL profile to the standard SysML model library, resulting in a new but non-standard version of that library.

3. *Time modeling.* SysML relies on the so-called Basic Time model of UML for representing the passage of time. As explained in Section 4.2, this model assumes the presence of an implicit centralized time source and, therefore, does not directly support a distributed time model with multiple independent time sources.[4] In contrast, MARTE provides very rich and flexible facilities for capturing a range of different conceptual models of time, including distributed time, and provides a direct means for relating time to modeled behavior. Furthermore, through VSL, MARTE provides a very powerful mechanism for specifying time values, constraints, and dependencies that has no equivalent in SysML.[5]

4. *Parametrics.* To support the specification of interdependencies between the values of different features in a model, SysML defines the concept of structured constraint blocks. For example, Newton's second law that relates force with mass and acceleration (F = m*a), can be expressed as a constraint that involves three parameters, force, mass, and acceleration, in a precisely defined functional relationship. A distinguishing feature of such constraint blocks is that they are non-directional, or, more precisely, *acausal*. This means that there is no concept of input and output parameters involved, in which a set of input values "causes" a set of output values. This more accurately reflects the physics of the real world than causal models, since there are no privileged parameters—any of them can change leading to a corresponding adjustment in the other parameters as dictated by the constraint. SysML makes this possible through its *parametrics* diagram type. This is a refinement of the structured classifier concept representing complex hierarchical networks of interconnected constraints, reminiscent of modeling languages such as Modelica [6]. But, SysML does not provide a dedicated language for specifying the constraints, allowing different user-selected languages to be used for this purpose. Of course, one obvious candidate here is VSL, as shown in the model fragment in Figure 8.3 (the constraint for NewtonsLaw).

   Note that VSL can also be used to capture complex relationships between attribute values by defining value expressions involving variables and features that correspond to the constraint equations. However, its textual syntax is not as expressive as the graphical rendering provided by SysML constraint blocks.

5. *Modeling of continuous phenomena.* UML was originally conceived for modeling software systems, which are inherently discrete. MARTE extends this with the ability to model certain

---

[4] It is, of course, possible to extend the Basic Time model by adding model components that represent distributed clock sources, which are skewed relative to the central clock, but this requires extra modeling effort and, not being standardized, the true semantics of such "modeled" clocks would not be recognized by external analysis or model transformation tools as such.
[5] There is actually an additional language facility in MARTE called the Clock Constraint Specification Language (CCSL), which allows the specification of complex conditional constraints that supports the logical time concept of MARTE. This advanced capability is described in [5].

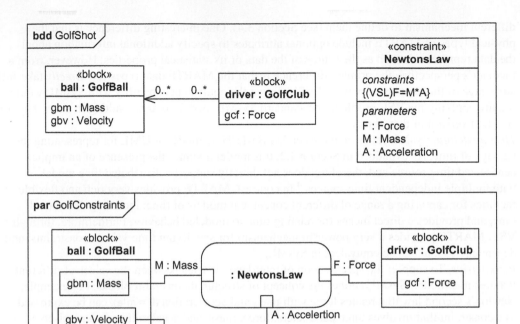

FIGURE 8.3

Example of joint use of VSL with SysML.

continuous physical phenomena, such as electrical current, energy consumption, fluid flow, and so forth. However, this is limited to representing them implicitly through data types of the appropriate kind (e.g., the library type **NFP_Energy**). In contrast, SysML, with its broader systems scope, provides facilities to model explicitly the mechanisms and processes involved in the transfer and manipulation of continuous flows, which fits well with the MARTE continuous model of time. For instance, it is possible to explicitly designate a flow type, such as electrical current, as *continuous* and then to specify that it flows through specific conduits and devices. It is also possible to specify that certain types of behaviors, such as activities, are continuous.

6. *Modeling of discrete flows.* The flow of continuous quantities is just one type of flow supported by SysML. It can also represent discrete flows, such as data and message streams, discrete electrical signals, etc. In fact, the SysML conceptual framework for modeling both is the same, differing only in whether the flows are designated as continuous or discrete. For its part, MARTE provides a special mechanism for explicit modeling of discrete data flows with its concept of a *flow port*.

This is intended almost exclusively for representing streams of *discrete* data, such as streaming video.[6]

7. *Requirements modeling.* SysML provides a unique model-based facility for capturing requirements and their relationships. Although it is possible to use this in lieu of a specialized requirements management tool and repository, it is really best used for capturing the *relationships* that exist between different requirements, between requirement and corresponding design artifacts, and between requirements and corresponding tests. A typical requirement captured in a SysML model would merely be a pointer to the actual requirement maintained in a dedicated requirements tool. However, its presence in the system model allows an effective mechanism for linking requirements to corresponding design elements of a model (and tests) with a level of granularity and control that could not be easily achieved by other means. Requirements modeling is a typical example of where MARTE and SysML complement each other (see the example below).

8. *Detailed modeling of computing platforms.* As described in Chapter 6, MARTE provides a comprehensive set of domain-specific concepts for modeling computing platforms that support software applications. Of course, SysML bocks could be used to model these as well, but these would not be recognized as first-class language concepts and, consequently, would not be readily recognized by external tools. Without that capability, the potential for automating functions related to code generation and model analysis would be greatly reduced.

9. *Allocation modeling.* Both MARTE and SysML provide a means to specify the allocation (i.e., deployment) of software application model elements onto platform-level model elements (see Chapter 7). In addition, as explained in Section 7.3, MARTE provides allocation concepts for specifying how source elements are deployed on target elements without introducing formal couplings between sources and targets. It also adds the ability to explicitly specify and match required and offered qualities of service.

8.4 Methods of combining SysML and MARTE

In essence, there are three basic ways in which SysML and MARTE can be combined:

- *Disjoint models.* In this case, each profile is applied to a different model, although the individual models all relate to the same system. However, the individual models are physically scattered and may even be owned by different kinds of tools. One common case of this type is where the models are at different levels of abstraction, as shown in Figure 8.4. Typically (but not exclusively), SysML is used to specify the more abstract system-level designs, while other languages, including a UML-MARTE combination, may be used for capturing the detailed technology-specific refinements of system level components. The related elements in the respective models may be coupled via external *traceability links* (represented by the dashed lines in Figure 8.4).[7] For example, element B

---

[6]SysML includes an almost identical flow port concept for modeling flows. However, the concept was deprecated in newer versions of the language. In these later versions flow ports are represented simply by standard ports that are typed by special data types designated as *flow specifications*. In this chapter, we consider both variants of SysML flow ports.

[7]Traceability links of this type can be realized using SysML, UML, or some other facility that has access to model elements in all the tools involved (in cases where the models are realized by different tools).

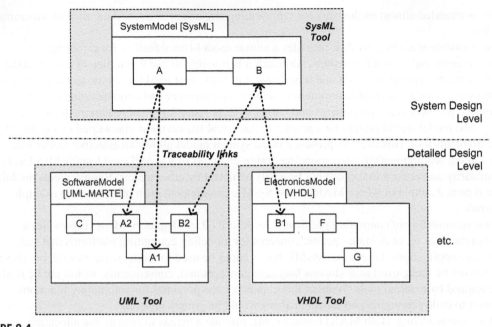

FIGURE 8.4

Joint use of SysML and UML-MARTE for models at different levels of abstraction.

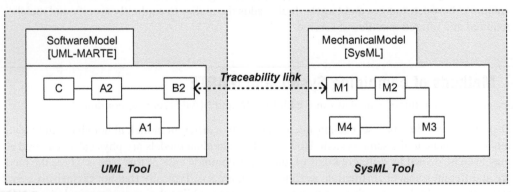

FIGURE 8.5

Joint use of SysML and UML-MARTE for peer-level models.

in the system-level model is decomposed into a software component (B2) in the detailed software model and a hardware component (B1) in the detailed electronics model.

Alternatively, the models may be at the same level of abstraction (i.e., "peer" models), but dealing with different parts of the system, as shown in Figure 8.5. Again, related elements in the different models may be linked via some external traceability mechanism. For instance, component B2 may be the software driver for the mechanical part represented by M1.

As a practical matter, even in the case of peer models, it may be better to link the related elements via the higher level model as opposed to linking them directly to each other. Thus, instead of directly linking elements B2 and M1 in the example in Figure 8.5, they could be linked via their joint higher level representation, such as element B in Figure 8.4. This indirect coupling strategy has several important advantages: (1) it makes it easier to identify when a change in a detailed design model has an impact on the overall system, (2) it reduces the number of different *kinds of couplings* between different kinds of models, and (3) it reuses any refinement traceability links that may have been defined. In fact, because it reuses refinement links, this approach typically requires fewer links compared to a peer-based linking approach, thereby simplifying traceability maintenance.

- *Partitioned model.* In this approach, both profiles are present within the same model, but each is applied to different parts of the model so that there are no overlapping elements. The situation is similar to that shown in Figure 8.5, except that all the "part" models are housed in the same tool and are encompassed within a single "master" model. This approach is possible because UML allows multiple profiles, such as SysML and MARTE, to be applied simultaneously to the same model. In this case it is possible to link the related parts in different models using standard UML relationship constructs (e.g., associations, dependencies, realizations, traces), or corresponding SysML constructs (allocate, trace, etc.) Or, if more specialized traces are needed, via some constructs defined in a special "traceability" profile.

- *Overlapping models.* This approach involves concurrent and overlapping use of SysML and MARTE on *the same model or set of models.* Overlapping means that some model elements may be tagged with both MARTE and SysML stereotypes, as shown in Figure 8.1. For example, we may want to overlay the MARTE performance modeling subprofile (see Chapter 11) on top of a SysML model to determine its performance characteristics. In cases of overlapping use, special care must be taken to avoid semantic conflicts, such as mixing SysML and MARTE physical types. In this approach, it is *helpful to define separate dedicated views, each focusing on a specific concern (or set of concerns) as prescribed by* [2]; for example a SysML-based view for the functional view of the system architecture, and a MARTE-based view for dealing with concerns related to real-time or embedded concerns (e.g., performance evaluation).

In the partitioned and overlapping cases, both profiles need to be applied to the same model. Note, however, that it is not necessary to always apply all parts of a profile to the entire model. UML allows a profile to be applied to individual submodels or packages within a model, which means that the scope of the profile (i.e., its stereotypes, constraints, etc.) is limited to just those submodels or packages. Furthermore, because MARTE has a highly modular structure, it is possible to apply only those MARTE modules (subprofiles) that are strictly necessary. For example, if we are only interested in using the VSL language, which is defined as a subprofile of MARTE (see Appendix A), in our SysML model, all we need to do is apply it to those model packages where VSL is to be used.

8.5 Common scenarios of joint use of SysML and MARTE

There are, of course, many possible ways of using these two profiles in combination. However, because this is an introductory user guide, we focus on just three of the most common use cases.

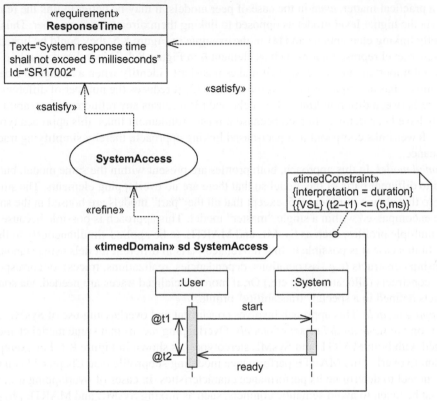

FIGURE 8.6

Example of combined use of SysML and MARTE to define requirements.

8.5.1 Use case: Supplementing SysML requirements with MARTE NFP specifications

This use case occurs when we are modeling in SysML, but need to have a means of specifying the concrete values of non-functional requirements in a precise and flexible way. We noted earlier that, while SysML provides the ability to describe requirements and also to capture relationships between them and corresponding model elements, it does not define a concrete language for specifying such values. We can fill this need by taking advantage of the non-functional modeling features of MARTE along with its VSL language. Note that, in that case, we need not apply the full MARTE profile, but only those parts of the non-functional modeling package that are needed plus the VSL subprofile.

This approach is illustrated in Figure 8.6, which depicts a fragment of a SysML model that utilizes a subset of the standard MARTE model library.[8] In this model, ResponseTime is a requirement specified using SysML. It stipulates that the response time of the system in question will not exceed

---

[8]The diagram in Figure 8.3 is a composite of several diagrams provided for illustrative purposes. In reality, it is generally not practical to show these types of relationships graphically, since there are typically too many of them. They are rendered much more conveniently in tabular form.

5 milliseconds. However, this is specified as informal natural language text, which cannot be easily recognized and processed by a computer-based tool. In the process of designing this system, a use case, SystemAccess, was defined, which represents user access to the system. To indicate that this use case must satisfy the response time requirement (among others), a SysML **Satisfies** dependency is added to the model, linking the use case to the requirement. Next, as the design is further elaborated, an interaction called SystemAccess (represented here by a sequence diagram) is added to the model. It refines the use case into a more concrete and detailed realization *scenario*. To capture the relationship between the scenario and the use case, a UML **Refine** relationship from the interaction to the use case is added.[9] Finally, using MARTE's time modeling features, two timed instant observations, @t1 and @t2, and a MARTE timed constraint to the interaction are added. The constraint is formulated as a VSL expression that precisely captures the original requirement. This specification is computer readable, opening up the possibility of subsequent computer-aided analysis of the timing characteristics of this design.

Because only the timing features of MARTE and VSL are used in this example, it is sufficient to apply just the **MARTE::Time** subprofile and the **VSL** profile to the SysML model.

This example covers the case of an overlapping or partitioned usage. Of course, there is a disjoint variant of it, which looks quite similar, except that the **Satisfies** dependencies would have to be replaced by external traceability links.

8.5.2 Use case: Transitioning between models at different levels of abstraction

The previous use case can be seen as a special case of the more general use case of moving between models that are at different levels of abstraction. In that case, SysML is used for high-level technology-agnostic modeling and UML-MARTE for the more detailed software-specific parts.

Typically, we first start with one or more high-level SysML models that capture the high-level system architecture, i.e., its decomposition into major subsystems and parts. One of the primary uses of such a model is to help select which implementation technologies to use for the various parts of the system (note that the technology assignment may not necessarily match the primary system decomposition; some conceptual system units may be realized by a combination of different technologies). Once these technological choices have been made, a set of more refined technology-specific models may be added to supplement the main system models as illustrated in Figure 8.4. These new models are more detailed and can, therefore, more accurately render the consequences of particular technology choices on the overall system design. It could easily happen that such a detailed model may reveal that a technology selection made at a higher level is impractical or too risky (e.g., due to technological limitations) for the intended purpose. In such situations, we may need to go back to the more abstract model and, possibly, modify the high-level design. This means that the transition from one model to the other can go in either direction, not just top down. For example, an analysis of the schedulability of a software subsystem, using the MARTE schedulability framework (see Chapter 10), could indicate that some critical timing requirements will not be satisfied by the chosen platform,[10] forcing a potential refactoring of the higher-level design [1,8,11].

---

[9]This relationship should not be confused with the SysML **refine** dependency, which must point to a SysML requirement. Instead, this **refine** stereotype is defined within the UML Standard Profile.

[10]By platform, we mean here a set of technologies chosen to run the application. It can be either software-based or hardware-based technologies or a mix of both (Chapter 6).

The following is a short review of possible strategies for dealing with specific transition issues that may occur when moving between models. Note that some of these transition steps could be partly supported through automated, or at least computer-aided, model transforms. Where that is possible, it is good practice to provide traceability information between the related elements (as illustrated in Figure 8.4), *supplemented with information documenting the nature of the transformation required.* Such traceability information may be useful and even essential, if the targeted system has to be certified against international standards and government regulations.

8.5.2.1 *When should we move to a more detailed model? [Advanced]*

In the case of transitions between high-level SysML models and more detailed models specified in UML-MARTE, one of the main design challenges is in deciding where to make the cutoff between the high-level and detailed models. A high-level model that has too much detail loses much of its appeal as a communication and reasoning vehicle. Large models are also often difficult to analyze by formal means since they pose scalability problems. A simple methodological guideline to follow is to make the choice based on where the SysML language runs out of expressive power or when it is obvious that no more value is obtained by further refinement of the high-level model. But how will we know when that point is reached?

The answer can be found by recognizing that one of the primary drivers of design is (or should be) engineering risk. *Engineering risk* is defined as the product of the cost of design failure (however that is defined) and the likelihood of it happening. Thus, even though we may be very uncertain about the success of particular design approaches, if the cost involved is small, we may decide to proceed anyway, since the risk may be low. The difficulty in making such a call lies in the fact that we may not know the risk associated with a given design choice. Barring some magical mathematical formula that can tell us, the only possibility is to delve deeper into the problem and understand it more fully. Understanding usually comes from direct experience, which means that we must follow through and elaborate our unknown design approach until we know enough about it to make a reasonably informed call. Consequently, if analyzing our SysML model does not provide us with the necessary degree of confidence that we understand the level of risk involved, we need to construct a more detailed model that will. If the technology involved is software, then a UML-MARTE model might be the appropriate choice for that detailed model.

The technical issue is, of course, to ensure that the refinement is an accurate representation of the corresponding high-level elements and, vice versa, that the high-level rendering properly abstracts the detailed model or set of models.

8.5.2.2 *Transitioning from SysML to UML-MARTE*

Elements of a SysML model that are expressed using diagram types shared with UML, such as state machines, can often be imported directly into the corresponding UML-MARTE model, using either the standard element or package import facilities of UML. In fact, when importing such elements into the UML-MARTE model it may be useful to retain the SysML profile application to preserve any SysML-specific data attached to the model. For example, a SysML block definition, when imported into a UML model, would not be differentiated from a UML class in a UML tool, but the additional block-specific information (e.g., whether or not a block is "encapsulated" in the SysML sense) would be retained, although it would not have any special meaning to a pure UML tool. This information could still be useful to modelers, and, of course, it would facilitate any transition in the opposite direction.

The following are the main issues that may be encountered when transitioning from SysML to UML-MARTE models:

1. *Requirements*. If requirements are specified via SysML requirement blocks, use case, or sequence diagrams (as described in Section 8.5), these can be imported directly into a UML-MARTE model. To a UML tool, they will appear merely as UML classes. However, if the SysML profile application is retained, the additional SysML-specific data (text and identifier) will not be lost in the process.[11]
2. *Blocks and internal decomposition*. SysML blocks and their decomposition map readily to structured classes provided by UML. SysML block diagrams map to UML class diagrams and internal block diagrams to UML structured class specifications or, in some cases, collaborations.
3. *Physical data types*. As noted earlier, a good strategy for dealing with physical types is to use MARTE library types with VSL, instead of the SysML equivalents. VSL enables more precise specification of values, dependencies, and constraints. However, if SysML data types are used, then most of them can be mapped to corresponding MARTE NFP types (described in Chapter 3 and Appendix B). It is even be possible and fairly straightforward to automate parts of this transformation using a model transform.
4. *Time model*. Since SysML reuses the basic time model of UML, it can be mapped "as is" to the more detailed and more precise models supported by MARTE (see Chapters 4 and 5). More likely, however, is that it would be mapped to a more refined model, allowing more sophisticated treatment of time.
5. *Parametrics*. In most cases, SysML parametric diagrams can be mapped into equivalent VSL constraints.
6. *Continuous phenomena*. These are unlikely to be of major significance in the MARTE model, but their presence may be recognized via mapping them to appropriate physical types (e.g., **NFP_Energy**).
7. *Discrete flows*. If the SysML model uses flow ports for discrete flows, these can map directly to MARTE flow ports. Otherwise, if SysML flow specifications are used, they can be readily mapped to their MARTE equivalent using model transformations.

It is conceivable that some of these transitions can be fully automated using suitable model transforms, or, more likely, partially automated with additional input from a modeler.

8.5.2.3 Transitioning from MARTE to SysML
As noted above, keeping the original SysML stereotypes in the UML-MARTE model can simplify some of the mappings required when transitioning from the detailed UML-MARTE model back to the high-level SysML model. Note that this transition is usually incremental, required only in cases where some change in the refined model needs to be reflected back in the more abstract model. Abstraction is a uniquely human activity that typically depends on viewpoint taken, which determines what is to be abstracted away and what is to be retained and, if so, what form it should take. So, even

---

[11]Note that UML *profile applications* are not named elements, which means that they cannot be imported with either a package or an element import. This, in turn, means that all stereotypes will be removed upon import, unless the receiving package already has the profile applied.

though some of this transition can be automated (e.g., by inverting the transformations performed for the downstream transition), most of it will require user intervention. Naturally, any information associated with the traceability links between the models in use will likely be of interest in this process.

8.5.3 Use case: Engineering analysis of a SysML model using MARTE analysis facilities

MARTE provides a generic framework for certain types of analyses that are not necessarily software specific (see Chapter 9). This framework can be reused in SysML by importing the appropriate portions of the MARTE profile and extended as necessary. One profile that can be reused directly is the performance modeling profile (see Chapter 11), since its core conceptual model is not specific to software. Schedulability analysis can also be performed on top of SysML model through specific transition schema as explained in Chapter 10.

8.6 SUMMARY

The combined use of SysML and MARTE provides a rich set of complementary capabilities that can be extremely useful in the design and validation of cyber-physical systems. Jointly, they provide a powerful and highly expressive facility to model, with a high degree of accuracy, most of what is required in such systems. However, because the definitions of the two languages are not yet fully synchronized with each other, special care needs to be taken to avoid possible syntactic and semantic conflicts. Specifically, what is required is a systematic approach, not only to prevent conflicts, but also to eliminate the possibility of confusing models with an indiscriminate mix of concepts from the two languages.

In this chapter, we outlined several techniques and scenarios for systematic joint usage of SysML and MARTE in some of the most common situations encountered in practice.

References

[1] Anssi S, Tucci-Pergiovanni S, Kuntz S, Gerard S, Terrier F. Enabling scheduling analysis for AUTOSAR systems. In: Proceedings of the 2011 14th IEEE International Symposium on Object/Component/Service-Oriented Real-Time Distributed Computing; 2011. p. 152–9.

[2] Espinoza H, Cancila D, Selic B, Gérard S. Challenges in combining SysML and MARTE for model-based design of embedded systems LNVSPaige R., Hartman A, Rensink A, editors. Proceedings of the fifth European conference on model-driven architecture foundations and applications (ECMDA-FA '09), vol. 5562. : Springer-Verlag; 2009.

[3] Friedenthal S, Moore A, Steiner R. A practical guide to SysML: The systems modeling language, 2nd ed. : Morgan Kaufmann; 2011.

[4] ISO/IEC/IEEE, systems and software engineering—Architecture description (Final Draft), ISO/IEC/IEEE; 2011.

[5] Mallet F. Logical time @ work for the modeling and analysis of embedded systems. LAP Lambert Academic Publishing; 2011.

[6] Modelica association, the, modelica®—A Unified Object-Oriented Language for systems modeling: language specification, version 3.3, https://www.modelica.org/documents/ModelicaSpec33.pdf; 2012.

[7] Morin E. Introduction à la pensée complexe, [Nouv. éd.]. Seuil; 2005.

[8] Mraidha C, Tucci-Piergiovanni S, Gerard S. Optimum: a MARTE-based methodology for schedulability analysis at early design stages. ACM SIGSOFT Software Eng Notes 2011;36

[9] Object Management Group, The, OMG Systems Modeling Language (OMG SysML™), version 1.2, OMG document formal/2010-06-01; 2010.

[10] Object Management Group, The, UML Testing Profile (UTP), version 1.1, OMG document formal/2012-04-01; 2012.

[11] Tucci-Piergiovanni S, Chokri M, Wozniak E, Lanusse A, Gérard S. A UML model-based approach for replication assessment of AUTOSAR safety-critical applications. In: Proceedings of the 10th International Conference on Trust, Security and Privacy in Computing and Communications (TrustCom); 2011. p. 1176–87.

System Analysis with MARTE

PART IV

Foundations for Model-Based Analysis

CHAPTER CONTENTS

9.1 INTRODUCTION

One of the primary purposes of models in traditional engineering is to help stakeholders understand and predict the key properties of a proposed design, e.g., Will the bridge bear the predicted load? Will the airfoil design provide the required lift forces? What braking distance characteristics can we expect from the new brake design? Will the provided safety barriers be sufficient for the system to achieve the desired safety integrity level?

Clearly, it is of great value to be able to accurately predict the salient characteristics of a design prior to committing substantial financial and human resources to its implementation. Using engineering models to predict the properties of a design is a classical risk mitigation strategy. It is what enables most classical engineering disciplines to avoid costly and possibly dangerous design failures. It is what allows implementation teams to proceed with a high degree of confidence that what they are asked to build is not only feasible but also that it will actually work as specified.

Obviously, *the veracity of model-based predictions is a direct function of the accuracy of the models*. Although the models used in traditional engineering disciplines are invariably approximations of the real systems, they are generally sufficiently accurate to support reliable predictions. The key to their success lies in abstraction: the ignoring of myriad details that have negligible influence on the predictions sought. It is what enables the construction of practical models that are both manageable and accurate. This is possible because the majority of traditional engineering systems are subject to the well-understood and relatively well-behaved laws of physics, which can be represented with sufficient precision using relatively straightforward mathematical formulae or by simulation.[1]

Unfortunately, when it comes to software-based systems, the picture is not nearly as simple. Software systems are typically highly nonlinear and complex, making them very difficult to model by analytical means. A single flaw in logic, an uninitialized pointer, or a misplaced decimal point could potentially cause a catastrophic failure [3]. If any fine-grained detail of this kind, lurking among thousands or even millions of lines of code, can potentially have such massive consequences, it seems to rule out abstraction (and modeling) as a useful prediction tool. Consequently, most of the focus has been on detailed analysis of code to ensure its *logical* consistency and correctness via formal model checking and theorem proving. However, these methods are applied to the implementation rather than to the design; that is, after all the significant design decisions, valid or not, have been made. What is needed is something that allows us to validate designs as early as possible in the development cycle and thus avoid costly fixes later in the cycle.

Fortunately, when it comes to real-time software, the laws of physics and statistics do have relevance and can be exploited to support practical predictive modeling. Many of the key system qualities are a direct consequence of the physical environment in which the software operates, such as the characteristics of the underlying hardware platform, the communications media, and the nature and frequency of physical inputs to the system. Hence, we are in a more predictable environment here, one that is more amenable to modeling and precise analysis.

A major portion of MARTE is dedicated to supporting model-based analyses—it is what the "A" in the MARTE acronym stands for. Central to this is a generic framework, *called the Generic Quantitative Analysis Modeling (GQAM)*, which was designed to be shared by a number of seemingly unrelated analysis methods [4].

9.2 The demand–supply analysis pattern

The fundamental problem of most quantitative analysis methods in engineering can be reduced to answering the seemingly simple question: Does supply meet demand?

We refer to it as the *demand–supply* analysis pattern. The pattern is composed of two fundamental elements:

- The *supply* side of this analysis pattern is represented by the system under analysis, consisting of both the application(s) and its supporting platform. As explained in Chapter 6, a platform comprises a set of *resources*, which can be either hardware or software, but all of which are ultimately rooted in some physical machinery (e.g., processor, memory, and communication devices).
- The *demand* side is represented by the load, or *workload*, imposed on the system by the environment in which it operates; i.e., the use cases side of things. These use cases are demands for the system to perform its functions. In the real-time domain, demand is often associated with stringent quality of service (QoS) requirements, such as maximal acceptable response time, reliability, safety, cost, or energy consumption. It is the responsibility of the supply side (i.e., the system), and, hence, its designers, to ensure that these requirements are met.

---

[1]Even the most basic foray into quantum physics reveals that the traditional "laws of physics" used in most engineering work are, in fact, merely high-level approximations of reality.

Simple as the basic supply versus demand question sounds—after all, it typically reduces to comparing two quantities—when it comes to software, it is generally not an easy one to answer. One of the primary sources of complexity is *resource sharing*, which characterizes many software-based systems, particularly those in the real-time and embedded domain. For example, a processor is shared by all by multiple concurrent tasks, which may have been designed independently of each other. Note that such resource sharing is used not only for reasons of economy (e.g., it would not be practical to dedicate a separate processor to each concurrent task). Applications sharing the same processor may need to interact with each other (e.g., the brake control system and the engine control system of a vehicle). By locating these applications on the same processor, it is generally much easier and more efficient to coordinate their activities, but activities. But, this means that such applications may conflict with each other trying to access the same resource at the same time. They may be driven by different and independent external inputs so that it may not be possible to control or know in advance the order in which resource demands will occur. This means that the problem is inherently complex with a very large number of different possible combinations. Of course, it grows exponentially in complexity as the number of concurrent applications sharing resources increases.

In addition, note that the difficulties stem not only from software; hardware is also a very rich source of complexity and unpredictability (e.g., component failures). For example, common mechanisms such as memory caches and instruction pipelines make it difficult or impractical to determine certain key quantitative characteristics such as actual execution times (or even their upper and lower bounds) with full precision. This greatly complicates analyses of such systems.

9.3 Model-based design analysis

There are many different types of analyses that can be performed on a UML design model, depending on which characteristics are of interest. Different analysis methods typically represent the systems to be analyzed using idiosyncratic constructs, which quite naturally tend to emphasize those aspects relevant to the specific analysis while ignoring or downplaying others. In fact, each analysis method usually involves an *analysis-specific modeling language* and corresponding *analysis-specific tools*. For example, in the domain of performance analysis based on queuing theory, a system is viewed as a network of interconnected server entities with explicit service queues. A significant body of theory has evolved to support this idiosyncratic model, but neither of these is explicitly supported in UML.

Moreover, designers and analysts often use different languages and, hence, work with different models, even though they all represent, at least partially, the same system. For obvious reasons, it is crucial to ensure that these models are mutually consistent. Since the design model is the original source for all analysis models, the issue comes down to ensuring that the analysis models are accurate renderings of the design model.

9.3.1 Design models versus analysis models

An obvious way to ensure consistency of these two kinds of models is to *formally* derive the analysis models from the design model. This requires formal transformations from UML to the different analysis languages. Once such a transformation has been defined and verified, it can be automated, thereby eliminating many potential sources of errors and providing faster turnaround.

However, it is usually the case that a pure design model does not provide all the information required for analysis. For example, in performance analysis, it is necessary to have specific data about the individual server queues such as their number, queuing discipline (e.g., FIFO, LIFO, priority based), and capacity. In addition, it requires the specification of explicit scenario models, which specify when and how system resources are used (see Chapter 11). Since they are analysis specific, such model fragments may not be included in the original design model and may contain information not present in that model.

This supplementary analysis-specific information can either be added to the original source model before the transformation takes place, or it can be added to the analysis model generated by the transformation. The latter approach is problematic, since it means that the reference information about the system is partitioned across multiple models. This makes it more difficult to ensure consistency. It also requires that the supplementary information is specified in terms of the transformed model and its elements rather than in terms of the original model to which the information directly applies. MARTE can help avoid these problems because it provides a set of analysis-specific annotation[2] subprofiles, which can be used to attach the necessary viewpoint-specific information directly to the design model.

This does not preclude the existence of separate design and analysis models, which may be required for organizational or pragmatic reasons (e.g., to avoid cluttering the design model with analysis-specific fragments and data, or to avoid large and cumbersome models). Figure 9.1 illustrates the two approaches. (Note that the case of disjoint models still allows a model transformation to be used to derive the analysis model from the design model).

9.3.2 Design space exploration with MARTE-based model analysis

Model analysis allows us to predict the key characteristics of proposed designs. However, unless we have extensive experience and expertise with a given type of problem, in practice we rarely get the design right the first time around. More often than not, we need to explore multiple design alternatives and configurations before making any hard commitments. The result is an iterative and incremental process, in which it is crucial to be able to predict the consequences of design choices rapidly and accurately.

The MARTE approach to model analysis was designed to support such a process (see Figure 9.2). It consists of an extensible generic framework (GQAM) for annotating models with analysis-specific data, and two specialized analysis profiles based on that framework: the *Schedulability Analysis Modeling (SAM)* subprofile (described in Chapter 10) and the *Performance Analysis Modeling (PAM)* subprofile (described in Chapter 11). Because it is based on computer languages (UML and MARTE) and models, some of the key steps can be automated, thereby enabling faster turnaround and more reliable results.

The process shown in Figure 9.2 starts with the design model, which is then annotated using the appropriate MARTE stereotypes. Note that these annotations can be dynamically removed by "unapplying" the profile (as explained in Chapter 2), leaving the original design model unaffected. Next, the annotated model is transformed into the appropriate analysis-specific model. This step can be automated if suitable model transforms are defined. The analysis model can then be "solved"

---

[2]See Section 2.2 for a discussion of *annotation* profiles.

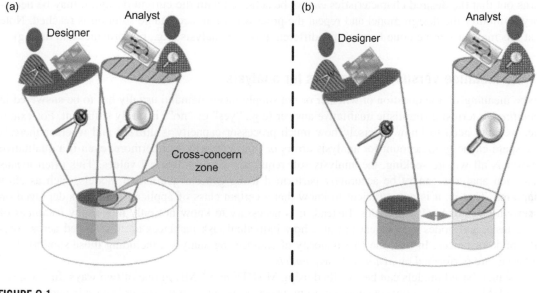

FIGURE 9.1

Overlapping (a) versus separate (b) analysis and design models.

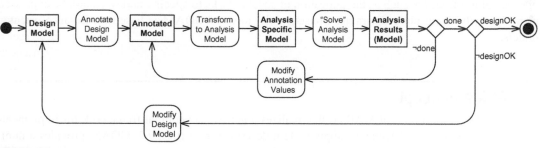

FIGURE 9.2

The general model analysis process based on MARTE.

(i.e., analyzed) either manually or with corresponding tools. These could either be simulators or formal analytical tools. An important advantage of analytical tools is that they can reduce or even eliminate the need for expertise with complex and highly specialized analysis methods. To assist in this, it may be useful to insert the analysis results directly in the appropriate location in the MARTE model and in a form that is better understood by the designers. This, of course, requires an "inverse" transform, which extracts the analysis results and injects them back into the source UML or SysML model.

The results of an analysis run are evaluated and, if desired, the cycle can be repeated using a different configuration of values for the annotations until a satisfactory combination is uncovered. If it turns out that the desired characteristics cannot be achieved with the current design, it may be necessary to modify the design model and repeat the process until an acceptable solution is reached. Note that this may have to be done for multiple different types of analysis (e.g., performance and timing).

9.3.3 Instance versus class models for analysis

To be meaningful, the question of whether or not supply meets demand usually has to be answered in *quantitative* terms; a simplistic qualitative answer (e.g., "yes" or "no") is rarely sufficient. For example, we may need to know precisely how much processor capacity is utilized and whether there is any spare capacity to account for analysis errors or future growth. Furthermore, even if a qualitative answer is all we are seeking, the analysis still requires precise numerical values. This often means that such analyses cannot be accurately performed using generic qualitative models, such as class diagrams. That is, it is not sufficient to know that a certain class of application tasks is deployed on a certain class of hardware nodes. Instead, it is necessary to know not only how many *instances* of those tasks and nodes are present but also how individual task instances are distributed across specific node instances. In fact, the vast majority of engineering analyses, including those supported by MARTE, are performed on *instance-based models*.

Instance-based models can be specified using MARTE and UML in one of two ways. In one case, we use UML modeling concepts that represent instances as opposed to classes. These include objects, links, parts, roles, and lifelines. These are found in object diagrams, structure diagrams, collaborations, and the various interaction diagrams, respectively (e.g., sequence diagrams). Alternatively, we can simply use class-based models, but in this case we must annotate the classes with information on how many instances are involved. Note, however, that even this may not be sufficient, since certain topological information, such as the allocation of specific tasks to specific nodes, cannot be expressed unambiguously using class diagrams. Consequently, most of GQAM is based on instance-oriented models.

9.4 GQAM concepts

The GQAM is a subprofile of MARTE that realizes a generic conceptual framework for implementing analyses based on the demand–supply pattern described in Section 9.2. GQAM provides a number of stereotypes that are intended to be specialized (via subclassing) to produce analysis-specific variants. These specific stereotypes are packaged in separate subprofiles. MARTE provides two such specialized sub-profiles:

- *SAM* is a profile for analyzing the schedulability characteristics of certain categories of mostly cyclical real-time systems, using established methods such as rate-monotonic analysis [2].
- *PAM* is a profile for analyzing the performance characteristics of systems based on queuing theory (see Chapter 11).

Of course, additional subprofiles for new or more specialized kinds of analyses can be added, as illustrated in Figure 9.3 For example, GQAM includes a generic **GaAnalysisContext** stereotype, which is specialized by the stereotype **SaAnalysisContext** in the standard SAM subprofile. This stereotype adds some features that are specific to schedulability analysis. As shown in Figure 9.3, modelers can

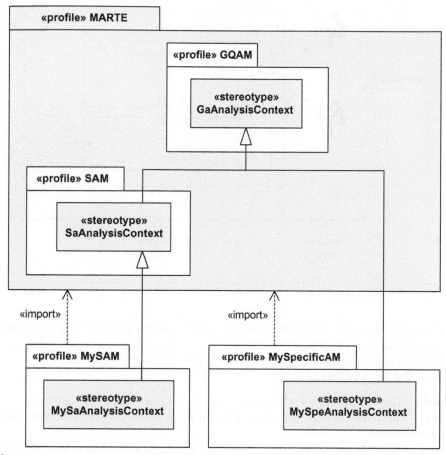

FIGURE 9.3

Specializing GQAM profiles.

use this subprofile directly, or, if it is insufficiently precise for the problem on hand, it can be further specialized (e.g., **MySaAnalysisContext**) in a custom subprofile (**MySAM**). If a new type of analysis such as safety or timing analysis is desired, then a new custom profile (e.g., **MySpecificAM**) can be derived from GQAM in a similar way.

9.4.1 The analysis context

The central concept of the GQAM is the above-mentioned *analysis context*. This concept represents a situation that needs to be analyzed and serves as the starting point for analysis. A typical example of an analysis context is a sequence diagram describing a scenario or set of scenarios whose timing or performance characteristics need to be analyzed. A logical representation of this concept is depicted in Figure 9.4.

In GQAM, the analysis context is represented via the generic **GaAnalysisContext** stereotype, whose definition is shown in Figure 9.5 It is a stereotype of the UML Package and

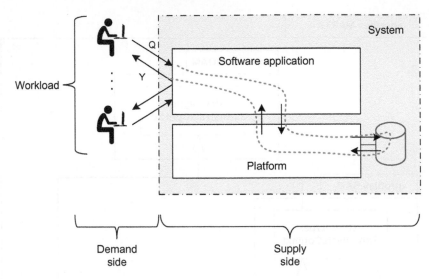

FIGURE 9.4

Analysis context (conceptual view).

StructuredClassifier concepts. The latter represents a fairly general category of UML modeling concepts, but it is primarily used to tag interactions (e.g., sequence diagrams representing scenarios) or collaborations and object diagrams (e.g., representing deployment specifications).

It has the following attributes:

- **workload** — This specifies the workload imposed on the system (i.e., the "demand").
- **platform** — This points to a resource that represents the platform on which the real-time application executes.
- **contextParams** — This specifies an optional set of parameters to be used in analysis (see below).
- **mode** — This points to a state in a UML state machine that represents a mode of operation of a system in which the analysis context applies (e.g., a "Running" state of an engine); this allows modeling of systems whose behavior can vary significantly with the operating mode.

An example of a high-level analysis context using this general stereotype is provided in Figure 9.6[3] In this example, the context is captured in a package, AnalysisPkg1, which contains an interaction, Scenario1, which captures the workload, and a class, Processor, which represents the platform. The context declares the rep parameter, which specifies the repetition factor of the loop in Scenario1.

The **contextParams** string specifies a VSL expression specified by the following BNF:

```
<variable-declaration> ::= [<variable-direction>] '$' <variable-name>
[':' <type-name>] ['=' <init-expression>]
```

The definition of two auxiliary stereotypes used in the definition of the analysis context, **GaWorkloadBehavior** and **GaResourcesPlatform**, is provided in Figure 9.7.

---

[3]This is a rather contrived example intended to illustrate the basic concepts used; in practice, a more analysis-specific specialization of the generic stereotypes is more likely.

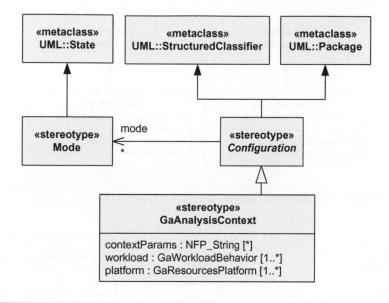

FIGURE 9.5

The **GaAnalysisContext** and related stereotypes.

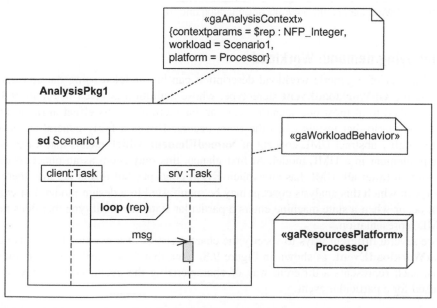

FIGURE 9.6

A simple analysis context in the form of a stereotyped package.

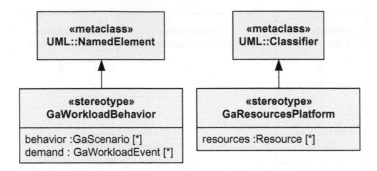

FIGURE 9.7

The **GaWorkloadBehavior** and **GaResourcePlatform** stereotype definitions.

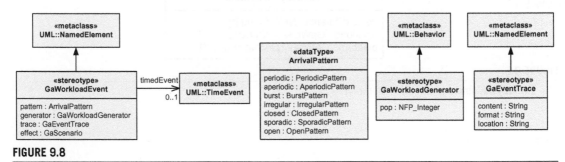

FIGURE 9.8

The definitions of GaWorkloadEvent, GaWorkloadGenerator, and GaEventTrace.

9.4.2 Specifying demand: Workload

The demand aspect of a generic workload description can be modeled using the concept of workload event via the **GaWorkloadEvent** stereotype, whose definition is given in Figure 9.8. A workload event is linked to at most one scenario (e.g., an interaction) via its **effect** attribute and is used to specify the scenario that results when the event occurs. This is a fairly general stereotype, since it extends the highly abstract UML concept of **NamedElement**, which means that it can be attached to almost any element in a UML model. At first glance, this may seem as an unnecessarily unconstrained definition (after all, UML has an explicit **Event** concept), but this is because there are many different ways in which this analysis concept may be manifested in a design model. For example, the event might occur when a state machine enters a particular state, an event type that does not have an explicit UML representation.

There are several different ways to specify the characteristics of a workload event using the attributes of **GaWorkloadEvent**, as shown in Figure 9.8. Note that these attributes are mutually exclusive; that is, each represents a different way of characterizing the event. Hence, only one of them should be used for a particular event:

- **pattern** is used to specify events whose occurrence is characterized by the MARTE library type **ArrivalPattern** (see Chapter 3).

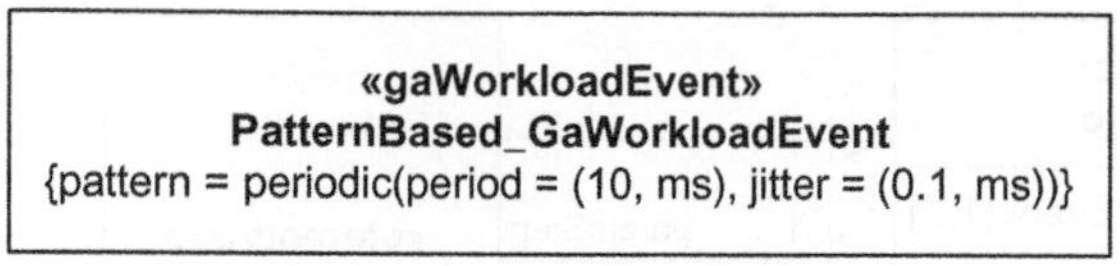

«gaWorkloadEvent»
PatternBased_GaWorkloadEvent
{pattern = periodic(period = (10, ms), jitter = (0.1, ms))}

FIGURE 9.9

Workload event specified as a periodic pattern.

«gaWorkloadEvent»
GeneratorBased_GaWorkloadEvent
{generator = OneGaWorkloadGenerator}

«gaWorkloadGenerator»
OneGaWorkloadGenerator

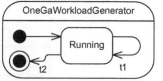

FIGURE 9.10

Workload event specified using a workload generator.

TraceBased_GaWorkloadEvent

«gaEventTrace»
EventTraceSpecification
{content = <This field includes the trace itself>,
format = ctx,
location = C:\MyModel\MyTrace.ctx}}

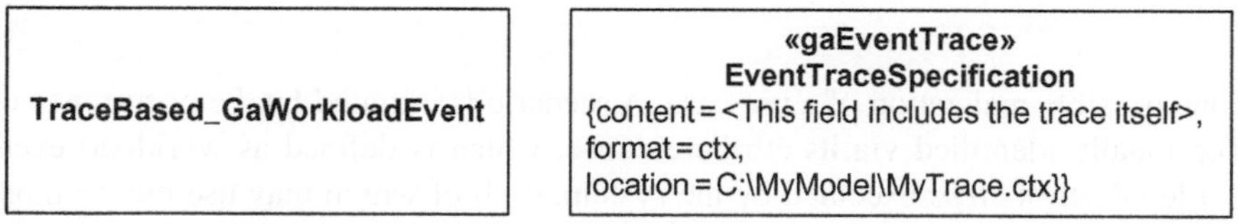

FIGURE 9.11

Workload event specified by an existing externally defined trace.

- **generator** is used when the event is specified in the form of a UML behavior (e.g., state machine, activity) that is stereotyped as a **GaWorkloadGenerator**.
- **trace** is used for cases where the occurrence of the event is described by a UML behavior stereotyped as **GaEventTrace**.
- **timedEvent** is used in situations where the event occurs at a specified time, as defined by the UML **TimeEvent** concept.

The following are all examples of workload event specifications:

- Case 1: The workload event is specified using predefined pattern: the effect scenario is stimulated periodically every 10 ms with a jitter equal to 0.1 ms (see Figure 9.9).
- Case 2: The workload event is specified using a workload generator specified by a state machine. Each transition of the state-machine (t1 and t2) specifies a stimulus that triggers the workload scenario (see Figure 9.10).
- Case 3: The workload event is specified using a trace specified outside the model (see Figure 9.11).

9.4.3 Specifying the supply side: Scenarios and steps

The supply side of a system in GQAM is represented by a *scenario* (or a set of scenarios) that captures how the analyzed system utilizes resources to perform its functions (services). Most often, it

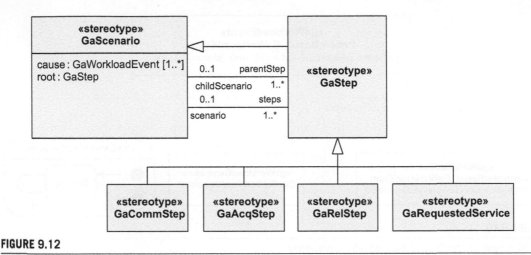

FIGURE 9.12

The definitions of **GaScenario**, **GaStep**, and its specializations.

represents one possible realization of a use case. A scenario is initiated by the occurrence of an *external event* (optionally identified via its attribute **cause**, which is defined as workload event). It consists of an ordered set of *steps* executed by the system, each of which may use one or more platform resources.

A high-level scenario model can consist of just a single step, which may be sufficient for some basic analyses. Since a step is defined as a kind of scenario (see Figure 9.12), it can be decomposed into finer-grained steps. A complex scenario may even include conditional branches or concurrency forks and joins.

In addition to its **cause** and **root**[4] attributes shown in Figure 9.12, the **GaScenario** stereotype includes the following attributes, which specify its real-time characteristics (see Figure 9.13):

- **hostDemand** and **hostDemandOps** are two attributes whose values denote the CPU demand, respectively, in time units (type **NFP_Duration**) or in the number of basic CPU operations (**NFP_Integer**). Notice that these values only make sense if all the steps of the scenario are executed on the same CPU. Moreover, both the **NFP_Duration** and the **NFP_Real** data types are specializations of **NFP_CommonType**, which means that it is possible to specify if their values represent estimated, calculated, required, or measured quantities (see Chapter 3 and Appendix B). Finally, the value of **hostDemand** can be identified as a nominal, worst, or best value.
- **utilization** and **utilizationOnHost** are two attributes whose values are instances of **NFP_Values** and denote, respectively, the occupancy of the **GaScenario** and the occupancy of the resource hosting the scenario (assuming that all the steps of the scenario are allocated to the same host).

Note that the **GaScenario** stereotype has four additional attributes (**interOccT**, **throughput**, **respT**, and **timing**). However, since the same information is provided by **GaWorkloadEvent** (e.g., via its pattern attributes), *we advise that they not be used*.

---

[4]**root** identifies the initial step of a scenario.

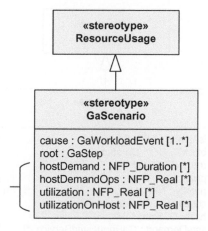

FIGURE 9.13

Some details of the **GaScenario** stereotype.

Finally, the **GaScenario** stereotype inherits from the **ResourceUsage** stereotype (see Section 4.3.4). Since the latter is a stereotype of UML **NamedElement**, it can, in principle, be applied to almost any element in a UML model. Once again, this is because a scenario can be manifested in different ways within a design model, some of which may be implicit. A scenario may involve the use of one or more resources. This can be specified via the **usedResource** property, which it inherits from **ResourceUsage**, by pointing to the set of used resources. Finally, a **GaScenario** can also specify additional properties related to memory and energy usage.

As noted previously, a simple scenario may either be a simple step or a set of multiple steps for denoting more complex behaviors. If the step models software in execution, it will require a *host* processor. (Note, however, that a step at a high level of abstraction may be hosted on multiple processors.) As shown in Figure 9.14, a step has additional attributes related to its usage of resources and its real-time specific properties. The explanations of those attributes are not given here, but are described in the chapters on the two specific analysis subprofiles, SAM and PAM (see Chapters 10 and 11 respectively).

To differentiate certain kinds of steps of particular interest to analysis, the **GaStep** stereotype (see Figure 9.14) is specialized into four categories of steps: **GaCommStep**, **GaRequestedService**, **GaAcqStep**, and **GaRelStep** (see Figure 9.15) These represent steps that model a communications action, a service request, a resource acquisition step, and a resource release step, respectively. The latter two have additional attributes for specifying the type and number of resources involved.

A workload scenario specifies a demand for the services provided by the resources involved in the scenario (including computing resources). The original service demand is thus transmitted via the scenario to the ultimate supplier: the physical resources that do the actual work. Consequently, the original event, with its demands, and the resulting scenario jointly constitute the full *workload* that is imposed on the resources (see Figure 9.16).

9.4.4 Platforms

To completely specify an analysis context, at least one platform needs to be defined. Note that, by using VSL variables it is possible to specify different platform and variants using a single

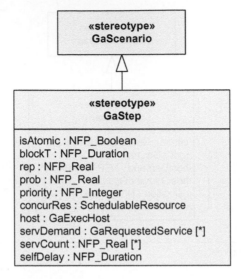

FIGURE 9.14

About attributes of the **GaStep** stereotype.

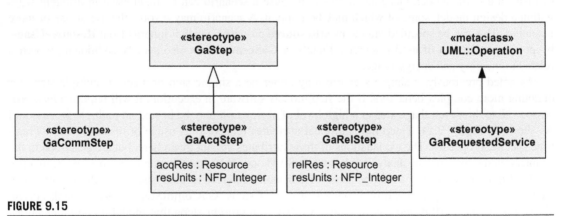

FIGURE 9.15

The **GaStep** stereotype and its specializations.

analysis context. A platform description consists of a set of resources as described in Chapter 4 and Chapter 6. For analysis purpose, three general concepts have been specialized (see Figure 9.17): **GRM::ComputingResource**, **GRM::CommunicationMedia**, and **GRM::SchedulableResource**.

Both **GaCommHost** and **GaCommChannel** were added in order to represent communications related elements of the platform. **GaCommHost** is used to specify the throughput of the data exchanged and the utilization of physical communication channels. **GaCommChannel** is used to specify the size of the data packets and the utilization rates of logical communications channels between tasks executing on the platform.

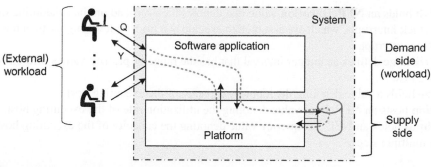

FIGURE 9.16

The total workload imposed on the platform.

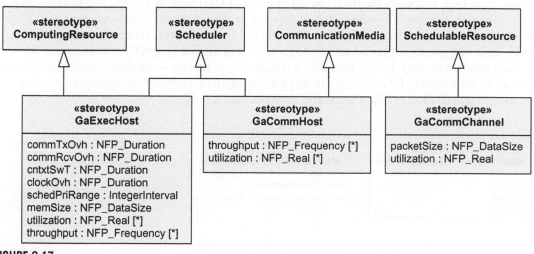

FIGURE 9.17

UML extensions for GQAM: **GaExecHost**, **GaCommHost**, and **GaCommChannel**.

The **GaExecHost** stereotype is used to specify the characteristics of the processing resource that executes scenario steps. It can represent a physical processor or, at a more abstract level, the operating system supporting an application. It includes the following attributes:

- **commTxOvh** holds an **NFP_Duration** value that denotes the overhead involved in sending a message.
- **commRcvOvh** holds an **NFP_Duration** value that denotes the overhead involved in receiving a message.
- **contxtSwT** holds an **NFP_Duration** value that denotes the context switching overhead involved in multitasking.

- **clockOvh** holds an **NFP_Duration** value that denotes the overhead on the scheduling due to system clock interrupts, which are assumed to execute at a priority level higher than the highest application interrupt.
- **schedPriRange** defines an integer interval that has the range of priority values offered by the executing host.
- **memSize** holds a value denoting the memory capacity of the executing host.
- **utilization** hosts an **NFP_Real** value denoting the utilization rate of the executing host.
- **throughput** holds an **NFP_Frequency** value denoting the capacity of the executing host to support multiple steps.

9.4.5 Defining timing constraints using time observers

MARTE stereotypes and their attributes are based on standard design and analysis patterns encountered in the design of real-time systems. For example, the **hostDemand** attribute of the **GaScenario** stereotype is used to specify the host demand in terms of CPU time of a scenario executing on processor, since that is the information that is required in most standard situations. However, despite the comprehensive coverage provided by MARTE and its stereotypes, there will always be exceptional cases that are not supported directly (e.g., when it is desired to specify constraints on intervals between arbitrary events). To deal with this, it is necessary to provide some more general mechanisms that can be used flexibly by modelers. For this purpose MARTE provides the concept of time observers, using a special form of **Nfp_Constraint** shown in Figure 9.18.

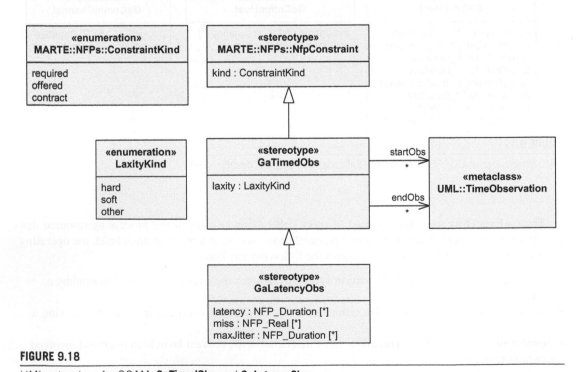

FIGURE 9.18

UML extensions for GQAM: **GaTimedObs** and **GaLatencyObs**.

The **GaTimedObs** stereotype, which specializes **Nfp_Constraint**, has two attributes, **startObs** and **endObs**. These may be used to specify latencies between an ordered set of *start events* and a correspondingly ordered set of *end events*. A start event and its corresponding end event represent an interval pair, whose laxity property (**hard**, **soft**, or **other**) can be specified via the **laxity** attribute of the constraint.

A refinement of **GaTimedObs** and **GaLatencyObs** provides additional attributes:

- **latency** is a duration value that specifies the latency between **GaTimedObs::startObs** and **GaTimedObs::endObs** time observation pairs.
- **miss** is a real value denoting the tolerated percentage of required (or measured or calculated, respectively) deadlines that can exceed (or have exceeded) the laxity constraints. Of course, this concept of miss ratio makes sense only if the laxity constraint has been specified to be a soft one; otherwise it is not allowed to miss any deadline.
- **maxJitter** represents a maximum deviation in the range of possible values for the observed latency. The output jitter is calculated as the difference between a worst-case latency time and the best-case latency time for the observed event (**GaTimedObs::endObs**) measured from a reference event (**GaTimedObs::startObs**).

The sequence diagram shown in Figure 9.19 is an example of usage of the **GaLatencyObs** stereotype. It represents an interaction between two subsystems. Subsystem subS1 receives a start message at time t1. After a delay, this results in execution of an action that sends a synchronous initialize message to subsystem subS2. This subsystem, in turn, executes its initialize method that sends a displayStatus message and terminates execution at t2. Both t1 and t2 represent timed instant observations as described in Section 4.2.6. A **GaLatencyObs** constraint is applied to the interaction, which specifies a hard timing constraint that requires the latency between the receipt of the start message by subS1 and the completion time of the initialize behavior executed by subS2 is ≤100 ms.

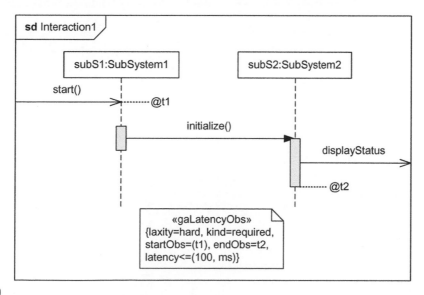

FIGURE 9.19

An example of use of the **GaLatencyObs** stereotype.

9.5 SUMMARY

This chapter describes the common foundations supporting the MARTE analysis framework (GQAM) [4]. It is based on the demand–supply pattern that can support a variety of different kinds of analyses. GQAM is not intended to be used as is; it is designed to be refined for each specific analysis type. The MARTE standard provides two concrete profiles, PAM and SAM, dedicated to performance analysis (see Chapter 11) and schedulability analysis (see Chapter 10), respectively. However, it is expected that GQAM will be specialized for other kinds of analyses such as dependability analysis or safety analysis. An example of this type of extension for dependability can be found in the work of Bernardi et al. [1]

References

[1] Bernardi S, Merseguer J, Petriu DC. A Dependability Profile within MARTE. J Softe SystModel 2011;10(3):313–36.

[2] Klein M, et al. A practitioner's handbook for real-time analysis: guide to rate monotonic analysis for real-time systems. Kluwer Academic Publishers; 1993.

[3] Lee L. The day the phones stopped. : Donald I. Fine Inc; 1991.

[4] Object Management Group, The, The, Clause 15 in A UML Profile for MARTE: Modeling and Analysis of Real-Time and Embedded Systems, Version 1.1, OMG document no. formal/2011-06-02, 2011.

Model-Based Schedulability Analysis

10

CHAPTER CONTENTS

10.1 INTRODUCTION

In real-time systems that take advantage of multitasking, it is often required that the tasks conform to explicit timing constraints. These may be *hard* constraints, for which the consequences of missing even a single deadline are considered unacceptable. Alternatively, they may be *soft* constraints, where exceeding the occasional constraint is tolerated as long as the percentage of such misses is below a preset threshold. The goal of the *scheduling* is to ensure that such timing constraints will be met. In safety-critical systems it may even be required to provide formal proof that hard timing constraints will not be exceeded. This is a prototypical example of where schedulability analysis is useful, since it provides a systematic formal framework for predicting the schedulability properties of multitasking software systems.

MARTE supports schedulability analysis through its Schedulability Analysis Model (SAM), a custom subprofile. It is a specialization of the general analysis framework (Generic Quantitative Analysis Modeling, GQAM) described in Chapter 9. In this chapter we describe the primary concepts and corresponding stereotypes of the SAM subprofile and explain how it is used in conjunction with the MARTE Non-Functional Property (NFP) capability (see Chapter 3). Since this book is an introductory text, not all of the concepts are described in full detail and the examples provided cover only some prototypical cases. Readers interested in a more comprehensive view of SAM should refer to the official MARTE specification [5].

10.2 Basic SAM concepts

In this section, we describe the most frequently used SAM concepts. An example showing how they can be used for schedulability analysis is provided in Section 10.3.

10.2.1 Analysis context

As already noted, SAM is built on the foundations defined within the GQAM framework. Consequently, the starting concept of any schedulability analysis will be its context description i.e., a model element stereotyped by **SaAnalysisContext**. This stereotype is a specialization of the GQAM **GaAnalysisContext** stereotype (see Figure 10.1). Therefore, it inherits all the features of that general stereotype (see Section 9.4.1) and adds the following ones that are specific to schedulability analysis:

- **isSched** — This is a Boolean value that is used to store the result of the analysis. If true, the specified configuration of schedulable resources defined in the analysis context is said to be *schedulable*,[1] otherwise it is not.
- **optCriterion** — This attribute, typed by the **OptimalityCriterionKind** enumeration shown in Figure 10.1, is used to specify which criterion is to be used for the analysis.

The **SaAnalysisContext** stereotype can be applied to any kind of UML NamedElement. This gives the user a lot of flexibility in choosing which element will represent the context for analysis. Note that, as a kind of expression context, the schedulability analysis context serves as the namespace for any VSL variables required in the analysis (see Appendix A). Variables can be used to parameterize the model, enabling exploration of multiple alternatives using a single model, by specifying different values for the variables.

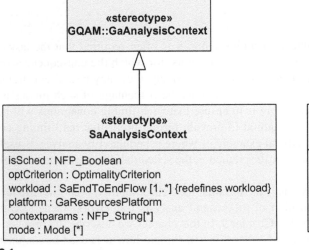

FIGURE 10.1

Definition of the **SaAnalysisContext** stereotype.

[1] A system of tasks is said to be "schedulable" if all of its deadlines are guaranteed to be met.

Like any analysis context based on MARTE's general analysis framework, a schedulability analysis context needs to specify at least a computing platform and a workload behavior. These are defined via the attributes, **platform** and **workload**, inherited from **GaAnalysisContext**. The former refers to a set of possible platforms to be considered for the analysis and the latter refers to a set of behaviors defined as inputs to the analysis. An example of its use is shown in Figure 10.2, in which it is applied to a UML package.

The next two sections describe how workloads and platforms are modeled for schedulability analysis using SAM.

10.2.2 Specifying workloads for schedulability analysis

To perform schedulability analysis on an application model, it is necessary to explicitly model the set of behaviors of that application that typify how it is used. These are collectively referred to as the *workload*. In SAM, the **SaEndToEndFlow** stereotype is used to identify such behaviors. This is a specialization of the GQAM **GaWorkloadBehavior** stereotype as shown in Figure 10.3. It adds several properties specific to schedulability analysis and also redefines some of the inherited ones to

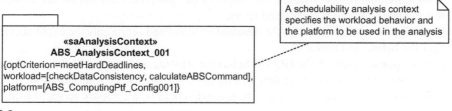

FIGURE 10.2

Example of a Schedulability Analysis Context Specification.

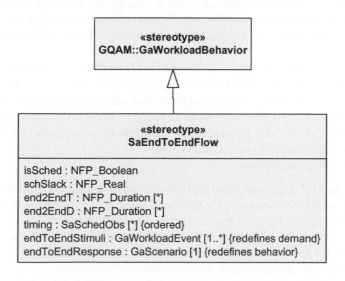

FIGURE 10.3

Definition of the SaEndToEndFLow stereotype.

conform to standard schedulability analysis terminology. The stereotype is typically applied to behavioral models representing sequences of steps (behavior fragments), such as interactions (sequence diagrams) or activities.

As shown in Figure 10.3, the **SaEndToEndFlow** stereotype provides the following additional attributes:

- **isSched** is a Boolean property used to store the result of the analysis that identifies whether or not that flow meets the imposed real-time schedulability requirements.
- **schSlack** is a computed percentage, expressed as a real value, denoting the variation (i.e., slack) in actual execution time of a step in the flow that can be tolerated without jeopardizing schedulability.
- **end2EndT** is an **NFP_Duration** value denoting the total response time of the flow measured from the instant it is triggered.
- **end2EndD** is an **NFP_Duration** value denoting the required deadline for the flow measured from the instant it is triggered.
- **timing** denotes a set of real-time constraints, either estimated or required durations, which are imposed on individual behavior fragments (steps) of the flow; these constraints are expressed in terms of scheduling observers (explained later).
- **endToEndStimuli** redefines the GQAM **demand** attribute and represents the event occurrences that trigger the behavioral flow.
- **endToEndResponse** redefines the GQAM **behavior** attribute and represents the actual scenario that characterizes the workload (note that, to simplify the analysis, the multiplicity of this attribute is reduced to exactly 1; however, the scenario could be a complex scenario with nested sub-scenarios).

Note that using both **end2EndT** and **end2EndD** *makes sense only if the flow has both a start and a finish event*. In that case, **endToEndStimuli** refers to exactly one workload event that represents the start event occurrence. If the end-to-end flow specification consists of multiple workload events, then the **timing** attributes should be used to specify more complex real-time characteristics of the end-to-end flow.

The **endToEndResponse** property of the **SaEndToEndFlow** stereotype must refer to a **GaScenario** stereotype element. In GQAM, a scenario may be specified either as a single unrefined step or as a series of more detailed computational and communication steps. To satisfy the needs of schedulability analysis the two general stereotypes intended for this purpose, **GaStep** and **GaCommStep**, are specialized into **SaStep** and **SaCommStep**, respectively (see Figure 10.4). These are used to annotate individual steps in a scenario flow.

SaStep adds the following attributes:

- **deadline** holds an **NFP_Duration** value that denotes the maximum computation time of the step.
- **spareCap** holds an **NFP_Duration** value that denotes a possible additional computation time (spare capacity) relative to the time specified in the **deadline** attribute.[2]
- **schSlack** holds a computed **NFP_Real** value that denotes a percentage (slack) by which the execution time of the step can vary (either increased in case of a positive value, or reduced in case of a negative one) without jeopardizing schedulability.

---

[2] **spareCap** is particularly useful for sensitivity analysis.

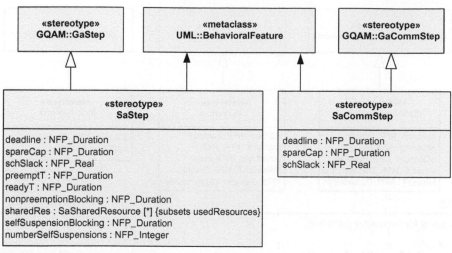

FIGURE 10.4

Definition of the **SaStep** and **SACommStep** stereotypes.

- **preemptT** holds an **NFP_Duration** value denoting how long the step might be preempted by the execution of a higher priority step.
- **readyT** is used only for cases where periodic tasks are involved; it holds an **NFP_Duration** value that specifies how much delay can be tolerated between the commencement of the time interval allocated to the step and its actual start of execution.
- **nonpreemptionBlocking** is an **NFP_Duration** value that specifies the maximum amount of time that a step can tolerate waiting for the execution of a lower priority step to complete (i.e., during priority inversion).
- **selfSuspensionBlocking** is an **NFP_Duration** value specifying the maximum time that a step can remain suspended after it has suspended itself (i.e., relinquished the processing resource).
- **numberSelfSuspensions** is an **NFP_Integer** value specifying the maximum number of times a step may suspend itself. If the value of the **selfSuspensionBlocking** attribute is greater than zero, then the **numberSelfSuspensions** value has to be provided.
- **sharedRes** refers to all resources that the step shares with at least one other step.

GaCommStep has also been specialized into a **SaCommStep** in order to allow specifying its **deadline**, **spareCap** and **schSlack**, which have the same meaning as their counterparts in **SaStep** described above.

10.2.3 Specifying platforms for schedulability analysis

As explained throughout this book, the design of most kinds of real-time systems is often very much dependent on the characteristics of the underlying platform. Naturally, schedulability analysis must properly account for the influence of platforms on timing characteristics. For that, SAM defines several schedulability-specific specializations of certain platform modeling stereotypes as shown in Figure 10.5.

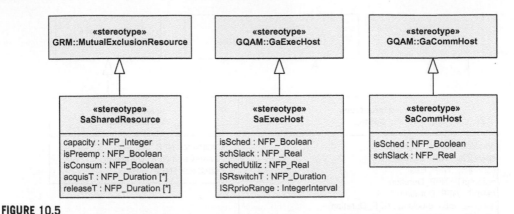

FIGURE 10.5

SAM extensions for modeling platforms.

The general **MutualExclusionResource** stereotype is specialized via the **SaSharedResource** stereotype. This stereotype offers the following new attributes:

- **capacity** holds an **NFP_Integer** value denoting the maximum number of steps that simultaneously share the exclusion resource.
- **isPreemp** is an **NFP_Boolean** value, which, if true, indicates that a step using the resource can be preempted.
- **isConsum** is an **NFP_Boolean** value, which, if true, indicates that the resource is consumed when it has been accessed.
- **acquisT** holds an **NFP_Duration** value denoting the maximum delay that a step may encounter while attempting to acquire the resource.
- **releaseT** holds an **NFP_Duration** value denoting the maximum time required to release the resource.

The **GaExecHost** stereotype has been similarly extended via the **SaExecHost** stereotype to support following properties:

- **isSched** is an **NFP_Boolean** value for storing the result of an analysis. If true, it means that the executions of all steps allocated to this host will meet their real-time constraints.
- **schSlack** holds a computed **NFP_Real** value that denotes a percentage (slack) by which the execution time of all steps allocated to the execution host can be varied (either increased in case of a positive value or reduced in case of a negative one) without jeopardizing schedulability.
- **schedUtiliz** holds an **NFP_Real** value that represents the utilization when all steps allocated to the host are executed.
- **ISRswitchT** holds an **NFP_Duration** value denoting the context switching time of interrupt service routines (ISRs).
- **ISRprioRange** defines the minimum and maximum priority levels for the ISR; this is an **NFP_IntegerInterval** value (note that different operating systems may provide different priority ranges).

Finally, **GaCommStep** from GQAM is specialized via the **SaCommStep** stereotype. This stereotype serves to identify if all steps allocated to the communication resource satisfy the schedulability constraints (attribute **isSched**). As with the **SaExecHost** stereotype described above, a communication step can also indicate the scheduling slack resulting from all its allocated steps via the attribute **schSlack**.

10.3 **An example of schedulability analysis**

This section illustrates how the schedulability analysis features of MARTE can be used to determine the schedulability properties of a real-time system. The example used in is a simplified antilock braking system (ABS).

10.3.1 **A simple ABS system**

We introduce a simple ABS example to illustrate how the SAM concepts described previously can be used for schedulability analysis. The methodological approach used for analysis in this particular case is a simplified version of a more comprehensive method called *Qompass* [4].[3] It advocates creating three distinct views of the system model, representing a series of refinements, as shown in Figure 10.6.

10.3.1.1 The black-box view

The initial view is the most abstract and it captures the use cases and the environment (i.e., the actors) in which the application operates. For the simple ABS system in our example there are two independent use cases (Figure 10.7):

1. calculateABSCommand, which periodically calculates the ABS command to be sent to the brake system, based on the input received from a data sensor.
2. checkDataConsistency, which periodically checks the sensor by checking the consistency (i.e., validity) of the data that it generates.

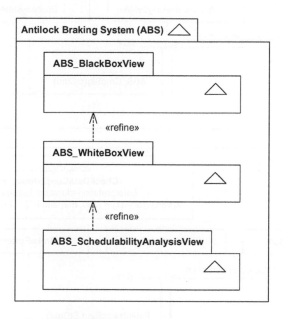

FIGURE 10.6

Organization Outline of the ABS modeling project.

---

[3]This method was developed by the Laboratory of Model-Driven Engineering for Embedded Systems at CEA, LIST (Gif sur Yvette, France).

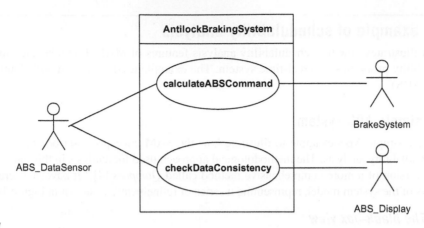

FIGURE 10.7

ABS Use Case specifications.

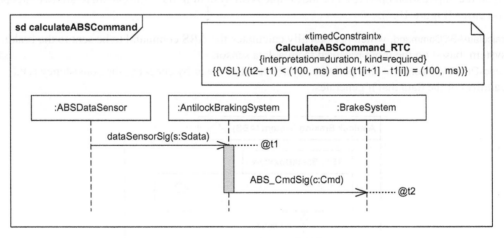

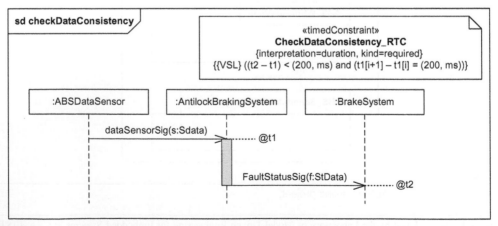

FIGURE 10.8

The interactions corresponding to the two ABS use cases.

The environment includes three actors: ABS_DataSensor, BrakeSystem, and ABS_Display.

Also included in this black box view are interactions that specify the sequences of events associated with the use cases, as shown in Figure 10.8.

In these sequence diagrams, there are two constraints stereotyped by the **TimedConstraint** stereotype, which is described in Section 4.2.7. The first constraint, CalculteABSCommand_RTC, specifies that the duration between time observations t1 and t2 is required to be less than 100 milliseconds and that the interval between two successive sensor signals is equal to exactly 100 milliseconds. Similarly, the second constraint, checkDataConsistency_RTC, requires that the distance between observations t1 and t2 must be less than 200 milliseconds and that the interval between two successive sensor value samples is equal to exactly 200 milliseconds.

10.3.1.2 The white-box view

Once the black-box view model is defined and validated, it is then refined into a set of additional views called *white-box* views, which deal with the internals of the system. These views are grouped into a number of distinct packages, as shown in Figure 10.9.

Package ABS_WBV_RefinementView captures the refinement relationships between elements of the black-box model and corresponding elements of the white-box model. This provides explicit traceability between the two views. For example, Figure 10.10 specifies that the interaction calculateABS-Command in the white-box model is a refinement of the eponymous interaction in the black-box model (and analogously for the checkDataConsistency interaction).

Packages ABS_InternalStructureView, ABS_Interfaces, and ABS_SignalTypes contain various model fragments that capture the application.[4] This part of the model may either be imported directly from the design model or defined separately. The ABS_InternalStructureView package includes a specification of the internal architecture of the system, represented by a structured class with internal parts and connectors, as shown in Figure 10.11. (This diagram captures the static architecture of the system. It

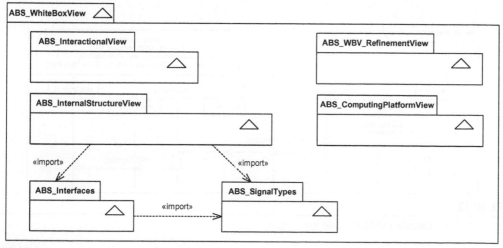

FIGURE 10.9

Example organization of the white-box view.

---

[4]This example is only one possible packaging structure for the application. Other organizational groupings are possible and typically depend on the design model.

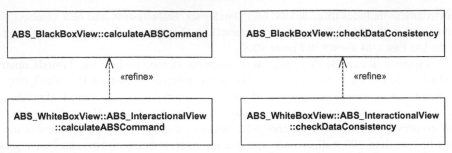

FIGURE 10.10

Fragment of the refinements view package.

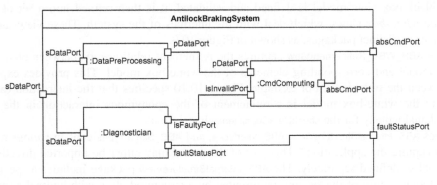

FIGURE 10.11

The internal structure of the ABS application.

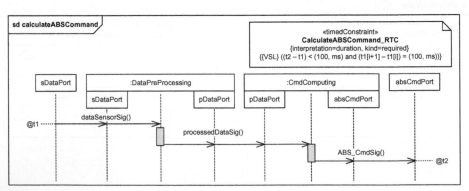

FIGURE 10.12

Refinement of the **calculateABSCommand** interaction.

identifies the constituent parts of the system their interconnections. This structural model is complemented by additional diagrams that specify the behaviors of this system, e.g., Figure 10.14.)

Package ABS_InteractionalView contains the refined representations of the use case interactions depicted in Figure 10.8. These more detailed versions are shown in Figure 10.12 and Figure 10.13.

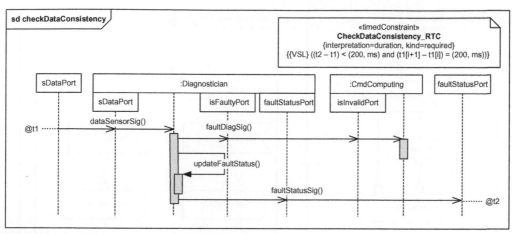

FIGURE 10.13

Refinement of the **checkDataConsistency** interaction.

Note that both of these interactions play an important role in schedulability analysis. As explained later, they are used as workload behavior descriptions.

For each of the parts shown in Figure 10.11, an activity diagram in the ABS_InteractionalView package is used to model their classifier behaviors. Figure 10.14 depicts the activity diagram representations for the behaviors of the PreProcessing and the CmdComputing components. These models capture their dynamic architecture, which specifies what they do and how they react to the receipt of signals arriving on their input ports. As explained later, these activity diagrams will be annotated with supplementary information required needed for schedulability analysis.

In this particular realization of the system, the computeCmd and the setErrorMode actions of CmdComputing share an internal attribute of the class, isDataError, which is used to flag the occurrence of errors in the system. The interaction of these two concurrent activities is represented by the sequence diagram in Figure 10.15.

Finally, package ABS_ComputingPlatformView contains a model of the computing platform on which the application runs. The contents of this package are shown in Figure 10.16.

The platform has a software layer, ABS_SwPlatform, representing the operating system supporting the application. This contains two concurrent tasks, theABSTasks[0] and theABSTasks[1], whose type is **BasicTask**, which share a common resource, computeCmdCS of type **Resource**. The shared resource is used to protect the data shared by the computeCmd and setErrorMode actions of the CmdComputing behavior shown in the right-hand activity diagram in Figure 10.14. Finally, underlying the operating system platform is the hardware platform ABS_HwPlatform, consisting of a single processor (ecu[5]).

We can be more specific if desired and provide additional details about the elements of the platform, for example, using the MARTE annotations described in Chapter 6. Alternatively, we can use predefined library types. One such library that might be particularly appropriate for the ABS example is the **OSEK/VDX_Library**, which is included in the standard MARTE model library and which contains a MARTE-based model of the standard OSEK embedded operating system. OSEK/VDX

---

[5]ECU stands for Electronic Control Unit, a standard term used in the automotive domain.

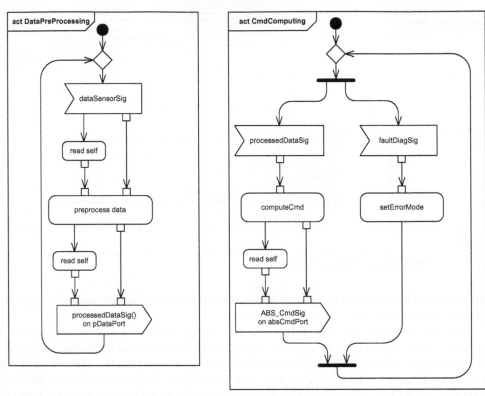

FIGURE 10.14

Activity diagrams denoting the Classifier Behavior of part of the ABS.

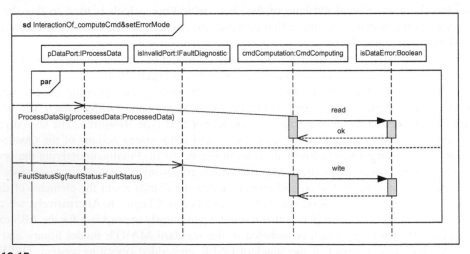

FIGURE 10.15

Sequence diagram showing the shared use of the **isDataError** attribute of **CmdComputing**.

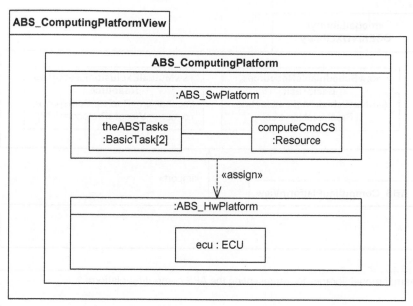

FIGURE 10.16

Details of the ABS computing platform.

(Offene Systeme und deren Schnittstellen für die Elektronik in Kraftfahrzeugen/Vehicle Distributed eXecutive) is a European consortium of automotive manufacturers and suppliers.[6] Included in this library are definitions for the **BasicTask** and **Resource** classes used in our platform model. These definitions utilize MARTE stereotypes to provide more information about their characteristics. They can be made available to our platform model by importing the library, as depicted in Figure 10.17.

10.3.2 Schedulability analysis example

The schedulability analysis view shown in Figure 10.18 denotes how the information needed to carry out schedulability analysis on the ABS model might be organized. In this example, we have chosen to group it into three packages: ABS_AnalysisContexts, ABS_AnalysisPlatform, and ABS_WorkloadBehavior. These packages contain the different analysis contexts, analysis platforms, and workload behaviors that are of interest. Each analysis context specifies one or more combinations of platform models and workloads.

The analysis proceeds as follows:

1. We first define the set of platforms and workloads to be used in the analysis (i.e., the contents of packages ABS_AnalysisPlatforms and ABS_AnalysisWorkloads). These are models derived from and

---

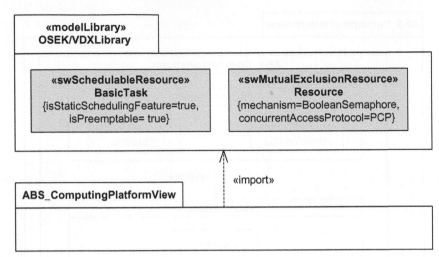

FIGURE 10.17

The use of external model libraries for representing the ABS computing platform.[8]

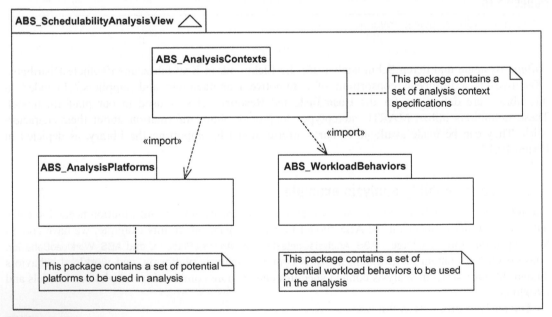

FIGURE 10.18

Outline of the structure of the ABS schedulability analysis view.

---

[8]Actually, the name of the library class **Resource** is misspelled as "**Ressource**"; however, we have chosen to use the correct English spelling here to avoid distracting readers.

consistent with the design model and are annotated with supplementary information required for the analysis. Practical methods for creating these model fragments are illustrated in Sections 10.3.3 and 10.3.4.

2. One or more analysis contexts are created for the platform/workload combinations of interest (i.e., the contents of the ABS_AnalysisContexts package). These can be combined in various ways: a number of different workloads can be applied to a given platform model or, alternatively, multiple platform configurations may be combined with a given workload. Construction of analysis contexts is illustrated in Section 10.3.5.

3. Analyses are performed for each of the analysis contexts defined. This can be done manually, but, of course, it is best if a suitable analysis tool can be used. In that case, it is necessary to define a formal model-to-model translation procedure that transforms the contents of the schedulability analysis view into a corresponding model that the analysis tool understands. An example of such an analysis based on the widely-used Rate Monotonic Analysis (RMA) approach is provided in Section 10.3.6.

4. The results of the analyses runs are reviewed. If none of the configured platform/workload combinations can satisfy the schedulability requirement, additional combinations (analysis contexts) can be tried. In that case, the use of VSL variables for key analysis parameters can be extremely helpful, since it can greatly reduce the effort required to produce new combinations. However, if no suitable combination can be uncovered by the analyses, it may be necessary to change the design model and repeat the analysis process.

This amounts to an iterative exploration of the design space. Ideally, the analysis should take place as early as possible using relatively high level models to ensure earliest possible detection of inappropriate design choices.

10.3.3 **Creating a platform model for analysis**

To perform schedulability analysis, it is necessary to define models that are suitable for analysis. These models are derived from and consistent with the design model. Unfortunately, it is not always possible to simply annotate a copy of the design model, since it may not be in a suitable form. For example, the software platform model in Figure 10.16 depicts an array of **BasicTasks** (theTABSTasks), represented by a single model element. However, in our example, the scheduling parameters for each instance of the array are different. Consequently, we need a model that allows us to differentiate the individual instances.

As discussed in Section 6.5.3, there are a number of instance-oriented models that can be used. In this case, we have chosen to represent the platform configuration as a UML collaboration stereotyped by **GaResourcePlatform**. One such configuration, ABS_ComputingPtf_Config001, is depicted in Figure 10.19. The set of platform resources are listed via **resources** attribute of the stereotype. These comprise the two tasks, theABSTasks[0] and theABSTasks[1], the critical section, computeCmdCS, and an ECU, ecu. Note the similarity of the names used in the collaboration model to those used in the design model to emphasize that this analysis-specific model is derived from the corresponding design model.

As shown in Figure 10.19, in this particular platform configuration we have selected a fixed priority scheduling policy. Accordingly, the two tasks have fixed priority levels (1 and 2, respectively). Finally, a priority ceiling policy is defined for the mutual exclusion device.

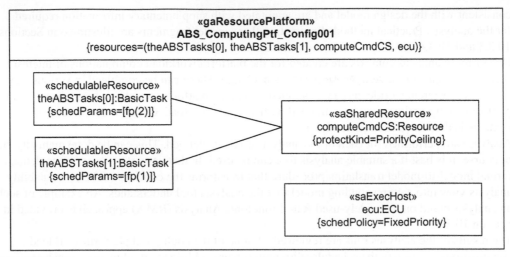

FIGURE 10.19

Example of one possible analysis platform configuration for the ABS application.

10.3.4 Creating workload descriptions

A workload consists of one or more end-to-end flows. An end-to-end flow represents the behavior of the system (response) activated by an external stimulus. In the ABS model, end-to-end flows are obtained by refining the two use-case inspired interactions calculateABSCommand (see Figure 10.12) and checkDataConsistency (see Figure 10.13), which are owned behaviors of the AntilockBrakeSystem class.

Refinement here consists in annotating the interactions with workload information using SAM stereotypes (see Figures 10.12 and 10.13).

As shown in Figure 10.12, the real-time constraint of the calculateABSCommand interaction states that it is a periodic interaction (every 100 ms) and that its deadline is also 100 ms. The refinement of this real-time constraint for the schedulability analysis view is done in two steps:

- First, the **GaWorkloadEvent** stereotype is applied to the dataSensorSig() message. This stereotype allows specifying the arrival pattern of the message that triggers the system response. In this case, a **periodic** arrival pattern is specified, with a period equal to 100 ms.
- Second, the **SaEndtoEndFlow** stereotype is applied to the whole interaction in order to specify the deadline for the flow. This is done through its **end2endD** attribute. In this case, the deadline is equal to the period of the external stimulus i.e., 100 ms.

To characterize the worst-case execution times of the behaviors involved in the interactions, the **SaStep** stereotype is applied to the individual behavior steps and the **execTime** attribute of this stereotype is used to specify their worst-case execution times.

Each step of the flow is further characterized by specifying the task used to execute its behavior. The **concurRes** attribute of **SaStep** is used to set which task is executing the step. Note that, for the calculateABSCommand end-to-end flow, the execution of each step is assigned to task theABSTasks[0] (see Figure 10.20).

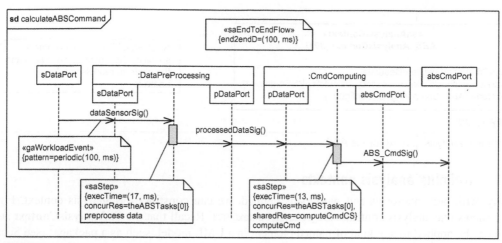

FIGURE 10.20

Refinements Examples of the ABS **calculateABSCommand** interaction for schedulability analysis.

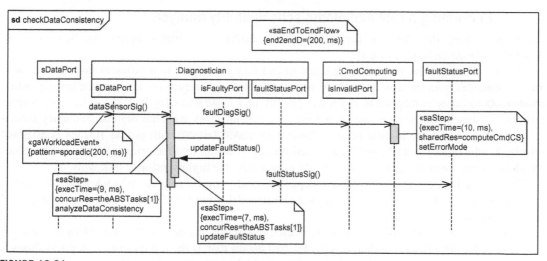

FIGURE 10.21

Refinements Examples of the ABS **checkDataConsistency** interaction for schedulability analysis.

We do a similar refinement for the second ABS interaction as shown in Figure 10.21, checkData-Consistency, with appropriate values for periods, deadlines, and execution times.

If a step traverses one or more critical sections in mutual exclusion, the **sharedRes** attribute of the **SaStep** stereotype can be used to specify that. In these end-to-end flows, both steps computeCmd and setErrorMode, belonging, respectively, to the flows calculateABSCommand and checkDataConsitency, share the same resource, computeCmdCS. Therefore, the **sharedRes** attribute of the **SaStep** stereotype for each of them refers to the same critical section.

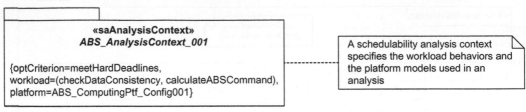

FIGURE 10.22

An example analysis context for the ABS.

10.3.5 Defining analysis contexts

Finally, with both platforms and workloads defined, we can construct the analysis context. Figure 10.22 shows one analysis context, ABS_AnalysisContext_001. Recall that the **SaAnalysisContext** stereotype can be applied to any kind of named element in a UML model, such as a package[7] (see Section 10.2.1). This particular analysis context consists of two workloads, checkDataConsistency and calculate-ABSCommand, and just one platform, ABS_ComputingPtf_Config001.

10.3.6 Performing a rate monotonic schedulability analysis

Before presenting the formulas for schedulability analysis, we first examine the Schedulability Analysis View described previously.

First of all it must be noted that each end-to-end flow is mapped to a different task. Specifically, the calculateABSCommand flow is entirely mapped to the higher priority task theABSTasks[0], while checkDataConsistency is mapped to the lower priority task theABSTasks[1]. In RMA ([1,2,3]) priorities tasks are assigned following a rate-monotonic assignment: tasks with the highest frequency (shortest period) are given the highest priority. Thus, task theABSTasks[0] with period 100 ms is assigned priority 2, while task theABSTasks[1] is assigned priority 1. Recall that the priority of a task determines which tasks run when multiple tasks are ready to execute—the highest priority task wins.

The two tasks are assumed to have independent and periodic activations: task theABSTasks[0] is activated with a period of 100 ms, and task theABSTasks[1] is activated with a minimum inter-arrival time of 200 ms.

Note that a mutual-exclusion semaphore is used to serialize the access of setErrorMode (writer) and computeCmd (reader) steps to a shared variable. This means that, if the low-priority task theABSTasks[1] locks the semaphore to access the critical section, the higher priority task, theABSTasks[0], may have to wait until the lower priority task, theABSTasks[1], releases the lock.

An examination of the model reveals that the following assumptions hold:

- Tasks activations are independent and periodic, i.e., activation of one task does not depend on the activation of the other task because it is triggered by an external independent stimulus.
- The task deadlines are equal to their periods.
- A single resource is shared between the two tasks.

---

[7]Using packages as the base for analysis contexts has the advantage that packages, like analysis contexts, have no run-time manifestation. Of course, these packages are normally empty and merely serve as carriers of stereotypes.

We also assume that the *infinite preemptability assumption* holds; that is, a lower priority task can be preempted immediately when a higher priority task becomes ready to run. This assumption holds for the access to the CPU (execution host), whereas the above-mentioned blocking time occurs when a lower priority task is in a critical section and cannot be preempted because it is accessing a shared resource [2].

Under these assumptions, the following standard RMA formula with blocking time can be applied [2]:

$$\sum_j \frac{C_j}{T_j} + \max\left(\frac{B_1}{T_1}, \ldots, \frac{B_{n-1}}{T_{n-1}}\right) \leq n\left(2^{\frac{1}{n}} - 1\right)$$

Note that C_j is the worst-case execution time of task t_j, T_j is its period, and n is the number of tasks. B_j is the blocking time for task t_j; that is, the worst-case (longest) time that the task can be prevented from executing by a lower priority task that is holding to a shared mutual-exclusion resource. If the inequality is true, then the system is schedulable; the system always meets its deadlines.

In order to compute the blocking term B_j, we have to consider that the critical section is accessed using a *priority-ceiling protocol*. The priority-ceiling protocol is a synchronization protocol for shared resources to avoid unbounded priority inversion and mutual deadlock due to incorrect nesting of critical sections. In this protocol each resource is assigned a priority ceiling, which is the priority equal to the highest priority of any task that can potentially lock the resource. In our case, only one variable is shared. Consequently, only one critical section is needed, and its priority ceiling (PS) is equal to 2. If D_j denotes the critical section duration of task t_j, and P_j is the priority of task tj then:

$$B_i = \max\{D_j : P_j < P_i \text{ and } PS \geq P_i\}$$

The following table summarizes the analysis parameters for the analysis context ABS_AnalysisContext_001:

t_i	P_i	C_i	T_i	D_i
t_1	2	17 (preprocessDataMethod) + 13 (computeCmd) = 30	100	13
t_2	1	9 (analyzeDataConsistency) + 7 (updateFaultStatus) + 10 (setErrorMode) = 26	200	10

Where t_1 corresponds to theABSTasks[0] and t_2 corresponds to theABSTasks[1].

From these parameters values, it follows that:

- $B_1 = 10$
- $B_2 = 0$
- $\max\left(\frac{B_1}{T_1}, \ldots, \frac{B_{n-1}}{T_{n-1}}\right) = 0.1$
- $\sum_j \frac{C_j}{T_j} + \frac{30}{100} + \frac{26}{200} = 0.3 + 0.13$
- $n\left(2^{\frac{1}{n}} - 1\right) = 2(1.4 - 1) = 0.8$

- The system *is schedulable* since: $\sum_j \frac{C_j}{T_j} = \frac{30}{100} + \frac{26}{200} + \max\left(\frac{B_1}{T_1}, \ldots, \frac{B_{n-1}}{T_{1n-1}}\right) = 0.413 < 0.8$

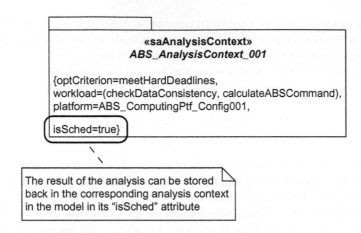

«saAnalysisContext»
ABS_AnalysisContext_001

{optCriterion=meetHardDeadlines,
workload=(checkDataConsistency, calculateABSCommand),
platform=ABS_ComputingPtf_Config001,

isSched=true}

The result of the analysis can be stored
back in the corresponding analysis context
in the model in its "isSched" attribute

FIGURE 10.23

Results of the Schedulability Analysis of the ABS system.

If the analysis is performed by a tool that would be connected to the UML tool as shown in the Figure 9.2, it is possible in principle to insert the computed results provided by the analysis tool back into the original model. In our example, the analysis tool checks to determine whether the system is schedulable or not. The place for inserting this information is the **isSched** attribute of the **SaAnalysisContext** stereotype. Figure 10.23 shows how this might look in our ABS example for the analysis just described.

10.4 SUMMARY

This chapter describes the extensions defined in the SAM sub-profile of MARTE, which are used for schedulability analysis. These are based on domain-specific specializations of the stereotypes defined in the general analysis framework (the GQAM subprofile) described in Chapter 9. The application of these concepts for schedulability analysis is illustrated using am ABS as a concrete example.

References

[1] Klein M, Ralya T, Pollak B, Obenza R, Harbour MG. A practitioner's handbook for real-time analysis: guide to rate monotonic analysis for real-time systems, 1st ed. : Springer; 1993.

[2] Liu J. Real-time systems, 1st ed. : Prentice Hall PTR; 2000.

[3] Liu C, Layland J. Scheduling algorithms for multiprogramming in a hard real-time environment. J. ACM January, 1973;20(1):46–61.

[4] Mraidha C, Tucci-Piergiovanni, S, Gerard S. Schedulability analysis at early design stages with MARTE. In: Sangiovanni-Vincentelli H, Di Natale M, Marwedel P, editors. Embedded systems development: from functional models to implementations. (in preparation). Springer; 2014. p. 91–109.

[5] Object Management Group, The, Clause 16 in A UML Profile for MARTE: Modeling and Analysis of Real-Time and Embedded Systems, Version 1.1, OMG document no. formal/2011-06-02, 2011.

Model-Based Performance Analysis

(with Dorina Petriu and Murray Woodside)

11

11.1 INTRODUCTION

In this chapter, we examine the Performance Analysis Modeling (PAM) subprofile of MARTE and describe how it is used. The primary objective of this subprofile is to support the early analysis of the performance characteristics of systems and software application designs, using established performance analysis methods. Some of these methods are quite sophisticated and usually require highly specialized and relatively rare domain expertise. For that reason PAM was designed to allow automation of much of the analysis process, so that it can benefit even those who may not have ready access to such experts. Of course, it can also be used even if the automation is not available.

11.2 Concepts of performance analysis

Performance is a concern for many software-based systems and, in particular, for real-time systems, in which there are stringent requirements for timely responses to inputs from the environment.

The performance of software applications is determined by a number of factors, including the characteristics of the underlying platform and the design of the application, as well as external factors such as the imposed workload (see Figure 11.1). One aspect that makes performance prediction particularly challenging is the fact that a platform may simultaneously support multiple concurrent tasks or even multiple applications, all of which share its resources, often vying for the same resources at the same time. It can be further complicated if the workload imposed on the system is dynamic, varying over time.

Many real-time systems have a part with non-deterministic workloads and response requirements based on average or percentage-based delays; some systems (notably in communications systems and distributed systems, and all Web service systems) are entirely in this class. Menascé et al. [4] described methods of analyzing this type of system. Performance analysis provides estimates of *statistical measures* of delay, throughput, and resource utilization, based on *statistical descriptions* of workloads, behavior, and resource demands. The most important performance measures to be estimated are the following:

- The *response time average value R*, or its 95th or 99th percentile (*R95* or *R99*), as used in quality of service (QoS) contracts (i.e., the probability of exceeding *R95* is 5%, for *R99* it is only 1%)
- the *average throughput*
- the *maximum throughput capacity for a given R, R95 or R99*
- the *average utilization* of some resource

The workload, that is, the stream of requests or trigger events for execution of system functions, is modeled in one of three ways:

1. An *open* workload, representing a stream of events with a given mean rate f and a statistical description of the variation. The prime example is a Poisson process, in which the probability of an arrival event in any small interval of length dt is $f$dt (and the distribution of times between events is exponential with mean $1/f$).
2. A *closed* workload, that is, a stream of request events coming from a fixed number N (the "population") of users or sources. In this case, there is a random delay (the "think time") between receiving a response and initiating the next request, with mean Z.
3. A specific source model (not discussed further here); for example, a user population that alternates between requesting service A (with a short think time) and service B (with a long one).

Performance analysis is based on a *performance model*, which is abbreviated henceforth as *Pmodel*, which specifies how the system behavior uses resources. *Resource* in performance analysis

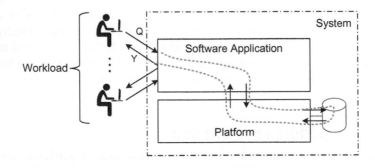

FIGURE 11.1

The performance analysis context.

means either a physical resource, such as a CPU, disk device, or a network link, or a logical resource such as a mutual exclusion mechanism or buffer. This conforms to the MARTE model of resources described in Section 4.3.

11.3 MARTE performance analysis example

The basic concepts will be demonstrated on a representative three-tier Web-based service system, consisting of a Web-server tier, an application tier, and a database tier. Figure 11.2 shows the software structure at the level of concurrent processes, which is a suitable level of detail for performance analysis, and the deployment of application elements to corresponding platform elements. Greater structural detail (objects within a task) may also be included. Some assumption of an execution environment is essential.

Physical resources are shown in a collaboration or object diagram, in which any device that can execute operations is modeled as a *host*, indicated by the stereotype **ExecHost**. Elements of the model are annotated with resource characteristics (host multiplicity **resMult** for multi-core, host **speedFactor**, host messaging overhead **commTxOvh**, **commRcvOvh**, and network latency (the attribute **blockT** for the link)). If these are not annotated they have default values that are 1, 1, 0.0, 0.0, and 0.0, respectively. The hosts can also have annotations for the scheduler. Note a peculiarity of MARTE terminology: latency is called **blockT** for "blocking time"; anywhere this attribute appears in performance modeling it represents a latency. Since the units of LAN capacity are "per second" they are given as GHz (billions of bits per second).

The key information about resource usage is annotated on a behavior diagram showing a *scenario*. Figure 11.3 shows a sequence diagram for one usage scenario. Each lifeline represents the behavior executed by a task instance corresponding to a deployed instance in Figure 11.2, so it is stereotyped as **PaRunTInstance**. The execution occurrence specifications are stereotyped as **PaStep**s and annotated with the CPU usage (**hostDemand**) of each. (Alternatively, the **PaStep** stereotype can be attached to the invoking message instead, if the execution occurrence specifications are omitted from the model.)

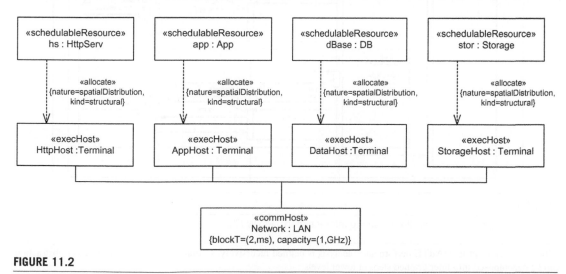

FIGURE 11.2

Example of a structural model used for performance analysis.

An **alt** block can also be stereotyped as a "high-level" **PaStep** with a nested scenario[1] (its contents) and a probability annotation **prob**, specifying the probability of occurrence. (The sum of the probabilities of all the **alt** alternatives must equal 1.) Similarly, the **loop** block also is stereotyped as a **PaStep** with a nested scenario, and a repetition count **rep**. The workload driving the scenario is a population of N users, each of whom spends Z milliseconds between the end of one response, and the next request. The variables N and Z that occur in the annotations are declared as *analysis variables* in the **contextParams** attribute of the stereotype **GaAnalysisContext** for the model as a whole. In the declarations, the "$" signifies declaration of a variable, as explained in Section A.3.2.3 in Appendix A.

The MARTE annotations must be sufficient to fully specify a performance analysis, which might be by a simulation model. From Figures 11.2 and 11.3 we can imagine a simulation in which

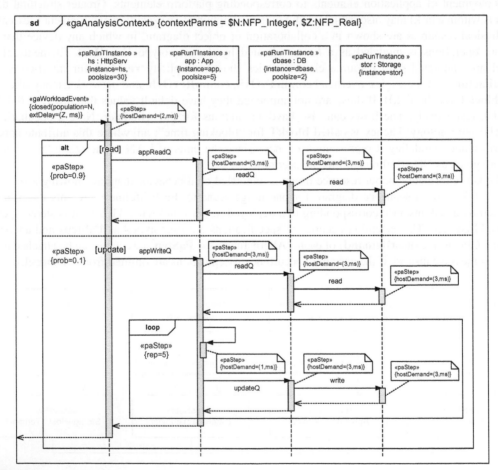

FIGURE 11.3

Sequence Diagram based on the browsing interaction in TPC-W [7].

---

[1] The "step" concept in MARTE performance analysis is defined recursively, so that a step at a higher level of abstraction can be decomposed into finer grained steps at lower levels.

primitive steps (those with no nested scenario) are scheduled to "run" on their hosts for a time (computed as: host demand/host speed factor), in a sequence determined by the sequence of steps in Figure 11.3 with random choices for **alt** and **opt** blocks, and by the host schedulers. After a response ends, a new arrival from the same user occurs after a simulated delay of mean z. When a message is sent, the sending communications overhead execution is scheduled first on the sending host, then the latency gives a pure delay, and finally the receive overhead execution occurs.

With these annotations, simulation models as well as a variety of analytic models can be constructed, following a methodology such as those described in [4,3] for queuing network (QN) models or in [1,2] for layered queuing network (LQN) models.

11.4 Key stereotypes for performance analysis

A few stereotypes and attributes are sufficient for most performance analyses of non-deterministic systems. The PAM subprofile refines some of the general MARTE stereotypes and UML concepts. These include the following (see Figure 11.4)[2]:

- **PaStep** is a specialization of the more general **GaStep** stereotype (see Section 9.4.3) and it typically applies to a UML action or a message that invokes a behavior. It defines a unit of behavior (a step in a scenario) that usually requires some resources. A primitive step has the following attributes:
  - **hostDemand** — This is a CPU demand attribute, and possibly a probability
  - **prob** — This is an optional probability attribute used for optional steps
  - **rep** — This is a repetition count for a repeated operation, and other demands

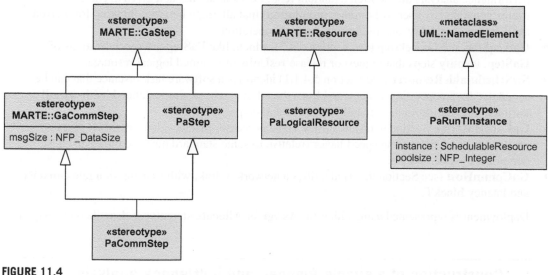

FIGURE 11.4

Definitions of some key PAM stereotypes.

---

[2]For the full set of PAM-specific stereotypes, readers should refer to the MARTE specification [5].

A higher level step has nested behavior defined by a nested **GaScenario**, defined by the operand of a UML **CombinedFragment** or of a UML StructuredActivity.

- **PaCommStep** is a specialization of the more general **GaCommStep** (see Section 9.4.3) and **PaStep** and represents a communications activity.
- **PaLogicalResource** is a specialization of the general **Resource** stereotype (see Section 4.3), and it identifies a resource that is needed, with a mechanism or discipline for granting it, and the possibility of blocking the behavior until it is obtained. This could be a semaphore, a lock, or a buffer. It has an attribute **resMult** for multiplicity (e.g., the size of a buffer pool or the maximum value of a counting semaphore).
- **PaRunTInstance** is a part of a behavior (typically a UML Lifeline in an interaction diagram, or a UML ActivityPartition in an activity diagram) representing the behavior of a task. It includes the following attributes:
    - **instance** — This is a **SwSchedulableResource** that executes the behavior
    - **poolsize** — This is an optional attribute that defines a thread pool size

In addition, the following stereotypes defined in other parts of MARTE are also frequently used for performance analysis:

- **GaAnalysisContext** (see Section 9.4) applies to any UML diagram with MARTE annotations with **contextParams** to define variables that govern the analysis.
- **GaScenario** (see Section 9.4.3) applies to a UML behavior model and identifies it as a behavior scenario to be analyzed.
- **GaWorkloadEvent** (see Section 9.4.2) defines the event stream that drives a scenario. For performance analysis this is often a random (e.g., Poisson) stream at a given average rate, or events generated by users (of number **population**) that alternate between thinking for a given average time **extDelay**, and requesting a system operation.
- **GaAcqStep** and **GaRelStep** (see Section 9.4.3), which, like **PaStep** are specializations of **GaStep**, identify steps that request or release **resUnits** of a named logical resource.
- **SwSchedulableResource** (see Section 5.4.1.1) identifies a software task instance that can be scheduled by an operating system, and has a thread pool whose size is defined by the **result** attribute inherited from the general **Resource** stereotype.
- **GaExecHost** (see Section 9.4.4) identifies a host processor instance, with **resMult** cores or processors and a processing speed factor (relative to some standard host used to define host demands) of **speedFactor**.
- **GaCommHost** (see Section 9.4.4) identifies a network or link, with transmission rate **capacity** and latency **blockT**.

Deployment is represented using either the **Assign** or **Allocate** stereotypes described in Chapter 7.

11.5 Construction of a simple Pmodel, and bottleneck analysis

To illustrate the end-to-end analysis process and show how some insight can be gained early in the development cycle, in the following section a simple QN model is constructed and solved, including a quick investigation of potential bottlenecks.

11.5.1 **Creating a QN model**

The general procedure for constructing a QN model consists of the following:

1. Identify all the hosts, and number them by $h=1, 2, 3$.
2. For every step i determine its host demand $d(i)$ and its execution frequency $y(i)$ per user request. To find $y(i)$, trace the scenario from the beginning, keeping track of multiples due to loops, and fractions due to **alt** or **opt** blocks.
3. For each host h, call the set of steps that are executed on it $S(h)$ (each step has exactly one host, or none). Add up the total demand for host h: $D(h) = \Sigma_{i \text{ in } S(h)} y(i)d(i)$.

The QN has a *queue server* for each host h. A quick analysis (bottleneck analysis) gives the maximum user throughput that can be achieved as $1/\max(D(h))$. An analysis with contention delays needs a QN solution, and (assuming it is separable, see [3]) the parameters $D(h)$ and Z are sufficient for a solution. It can be found, for instance, using the Web service Weasel[3] (you will need to specify your QN in a language called PMIF [6]).

Figure 11.5 shows the QN results for the mean response time R against the user request arrival rate f, found by varying the number of users N (the figure also includes some other results described below). Since no logical resources are modeled in the QN, it assumes that task thread pools are unbounded.

Because the QN ignores contention for logical resources it may overestimate performance; an Extended QN model such as LQN is needed. Thus, the LQN curve in Figure 11.5 shows the increased response time due to limited thread pool sizes and resulting contention delays. LQN models and their solving tools are described in [2]. The dashed line for messaging latency is another result, for a case described below.

This type of model can be constructed either manually, by examining the corresponding UML model, or it can be generated by first annotating the UML model with the MARTE stereotypes described above and then transforming that model into an equivalent PMIF model that can be analyzed by appropriate tools. Examples of such annotations can be seen in Figures 11.7 and 11.8

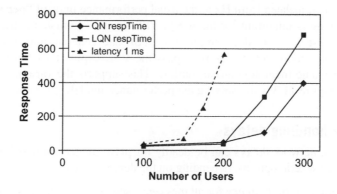

FIGURE 11.5

Results for the example, for varying sizes of the user population N.

---

[3] http://weaselinux.univaq.it/.

11.6 **More complex annotations**

More complex annotations can be useful. Here, we describe five useful features of MARTE: parameterized values, NFP types, messaging delays, logical resources (such as thread pools, locks, and mutexes), the importation of defined services, and multiple versions of a value coming from different sources.

11.6.1 **Parameterized values**

The quantitative annotations (NFPs) in MARTE can be specified using VSL (see Appendix A). The NFPs in Figures 11.2 and 11.3 are written in the form (**value, units**), but they could also take the more complex form: (**VSL expression, units**). For instance, the value (3, ms) in Figure 11.3 for host demand could be replaced by the following:

hostDemand = ((1.2 + XactSize*2.4), ms) for a linear relationship to the analysis variable XactSize, or

hostDemand = ((Startup + 13*(ListSize.^0.5)), ms) for a sorting operation with square-root complexity (in VSL, "a.^0.5" denotes the square root of a)

In the above two examples, the variables XactSize, Startup and ListSize must also be declared as **contextParams** of the given **GaAnalysisContext**.

11.6.2 **NFP types**

Apart from **NFP_Integer** and **NFP_Real**, the most important NFP types used for performance analysis are the following[4]:

- **NFP_Duration**, for a time interval or an execution time demand (**hr, s, ms, us**)
- **NFP_DataSize**, for the size of a block of data (**byte, KB, MB, GB**)
- **NFP_Frequency**, for a throughput (or a data rate or capacity) (**Hz, KHz, MHz**)

Throughputs can be translated from **Hz** to the usual performance units of "**per second.**"

Interpretation tooling is important for the use of VSL. In the automated extraction of the performance model there must be a tool that can parse the VSL and generate numerical values. It is also possible (but sometimes more complicated) to pass the VSL expressions through into the performance model, and evaluate them at solution runtime. This supports the variation of problem parameters like N and Z in Figure 11.3 while solving the performance model.

11.6.3 **Message handling delays**

In distributed systems, network delays can be deadly for performance, so it is important to estimate them. The modeler has several options, depending on the depth of the concern.

1. The simplest option is a *fixed latency* for all messages, specified by a latency parameter applied to the link in the deployment diagram. The link would carry a stereotype **GaCommHost** with a **blockT** attribute, for example {blockT = (latency,ms)} would define it by a variable latency.

---

[4]These data types are described in Chapter 3 and in Appendix B.

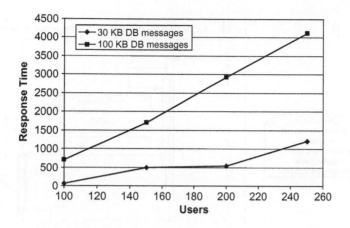

FIGURE 11.6

The impact of the size of database write messages on response time.

Figure 11.5 includes a curve with a dashed line that illustrates the impact of a 1 millisecond latency on all messages, in the LQN model for the example in Figures 11.2 and 11.3.

2. *Separate latencies* may apply to individual messages, and can be specified by a **blockT** attribute for a **PaCommStep** stereotype applied to the message.

Using VSL expressions, these message-specific latencies can also be made dependent on parameters such as the message size. Figure 11.6 shows a graph for the response time with the database write message latency defined as (2 + msgSize*0.2), ms) and msgSize equal to 30 and 100 KB (other latencies on links between hosts are fixed at 2 milliseconds).

3. If network saturation is a concern, it is necessary to model network congestion effects, which requires creating a queuing center for the network in the Pmodel (corresponding to the **GaCommHost**, with its latency and capacity) and extracting the message occurrences and their sizes to model its traffic in the Pmodel.

4. More detailed models of messaging delays could include specifying an external operation (see below) invoked by **PaCommStep** to convey the message, which could model middleware operations and multiple steps in conveying the message. However, this is beyond the scope of this introductory text.

11.6.4 Logical resources

Semaphores, locks, buffers, task thread pools, and any other entities that can make the program wait when they are busy or occupied are represented for performance analysis by an element stereotyped as a **PaLogicalResource**. Apart from task thread pools, they have explicit acquire/release actions indicated by stereotypes **GaAcqStep** or **GaRelStep** on steps, with attribute **acqRes** or **relRes** to identify the resource. The holding time of the logical resource is the time to execute the steps between the two (including the acquire and release steps). Note that a behavior element can be stereotyped by both **PaStep** and **GaAcqStep** or **GaRelStep**.

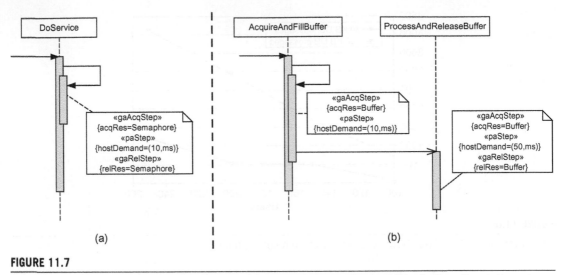

FIGURE 11.7

Examples of Annotations on Logical Resources: (a) a protected operation and (b) a buffer with overlapped operations to fill and process it.

Figure 11.7 shows annotations on two sequence diagram behavior fragments involving logical resources. In Figure 11.7a the multiple threads of the task DoService must queue up for a critical section protected by a semaphore (Semaphore). Semaphore can be a performance-critical resource if its holding time is long enough. In Figure 11.7b, Buffer is a pool of buffers (a resource with a multiplicity) used by two multithreaded processes. A request is made for one buffer, followed by a step to fill it from an arriving message. It is passed to a different host to task the data concurrently with buffering the next arrival (double buffering). If all buffers are full the next acquisition must wait.

11.6.5 Importation of external operations

External operations are offered by subsystems that are not specified in the UML model, but are used by the specified behavior (i.e., some step calls an external operation). The external subsystems could be system infrastructure, middleware, storage systems, or Web services. A modeling infrastructure with libraries of performance submodels of such external systems can be built up to make modeling faster and to reuse previously constructed Pmodels.

In MARTE a **PaStep** that uses external operations has an attribute **extOpDemand**, which is a list of the names of such services, and a matching attribute **extOpCount**, which is a corresponding list of how many times (on average) the service is invoked by the step. For example, if a step uses extOpA 19 times on average, and extOpB 1.5 times, its stereotype could be specified as follows:

```
PaStep {extOpDemand = (extOpA, extOpB),
  extOpCount = (19, 1.5),...}
```

This assumes that (1) the performance tool chain has a submodel for the operations extOpA and extOpB, which it can add to the overall Pmodel, and (2) the operation names used in the MARTE annotation are known to the tool chain.

An external operation can be as simple as a local disk operation. For instance, in Figures 11.2 and 11.3, the database storage is modeled as a single StorageHost, which might just be a local disk. An external operation submodel might be used in its place to describe a more complex storage back-end, including the hardware and software of the file server, the effect of multithreaded operation, read and write caching, the storage subsystem (possibly modeling a RAID array), and network messaging. Going further, the database subsystem (dbase:DB and sto:Storage) could be made external, allowing the specification in Figures 11.2 and 11.3 to focus only on the application.

If the external operation performance (for example, the database performance) depends on parameters of the transaction they must be defined in the Pmodel by the MARTE modeler.

11.6.6 Required values and other sources of values

To specify that a performance measure is a required value (rather than a value estimated for the specification as it is defined) one can use the long-form syntax for the NFP value with a **source** qualifier (see Section 3.2). To specify a response time variable R with required value 500 milliseconds, for example, this attribute is added to the **Workload** stereotype:

```
{R = (value = 500, units = ms, source = req)}
```

If we also wanted to show a value of response time or 275 milliseconds that had been measured on the system, we could define R with both values and different sources:

```
{R = (value = 500, units = ms, source = req),
(value = 275, units = ms, source = meas)}
```

Other sources for a value can also be used as explained in Section 3.2.

11.7 Modeling with multiple scenarios

Actual computer systems support many scenarios, and performance analysis usually selects just a few of these in the usage profile for the analysis. Each scenario is specified separately, but the resources are shared. The usage profile for multiple scenarios defines the groups of users (called *classes* in performance analysis) with a top-level usage scenario for each class showing how it uses the individual system scenarios. There is an overall workload for each class (showing its *population* and *thinkTime*) rather than for each system scenario. For example, Figure 11.8 shows a class of users of a Web shopping service that involves a Browsing interaction (an average of 15 times) followed by a Buy interaction in 30% of cases, or termination. Each interaction use is stereotyped as a **PaStep** with a nested **ref** combined fragment for each scenario. Browse_sd and Buy_sd are two alternative interaction models for those system scenarios. (The MARTE diagrams for those scenarios are not shown, but they too Would be annotated in a similar manner.)

11.8 The typical performance analysis process

Like any realistic engineering process, performance analysis is an iterative process, as depicted by the activity graph in Figure 11.9. This process is a specialization of the general analysis process introduced in Section 9.3.2.

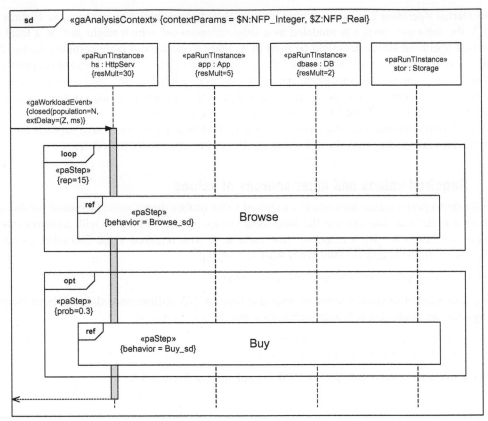

FIGURE 11.8

Top-level scenario for a usage profile combining two scenarios **Browse** and **Buy**.

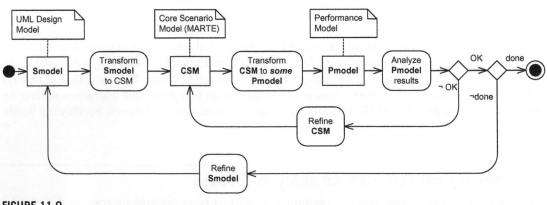

FIGURE 11.9

Iterative performance analysis of software [8].

Ideally, the reference source for performance analysis is the original UML design model (Smodel). This reduces the likelihood of discrepancies between the design and the models used in the analysis. For performance analysis, we need to annotate the input model with the appropriate performance-related MARTE annotations. This typically involves focusing on a subset of the model that is relevant to performance, such as the structural deployment submodel in Figure 11.2 and the scenario (sub)model in Figure 11.3. (If such models are not available in the design model the best approach is to add them to that model, to ensure that they remain consistent with any design changes.) Once the annotations are in place, we have a *Core Scenario Model* (*CSM*), which can be used in performance analysis. The elements that constitute the CSM can be extracted from the full model by starting with elements tagged by the **GaAnalysisContext** stereotype and transitively following all dependencies in those. This operation can be automated. The CSM is then transformed into an appropriate Pmodel, such as a queuing network model. This too can be automated using standard model transformation tools. The performance model is then given to a specialized performance analysis tool, which generates the performance values of interest (response time, throughput, etc.). This tool might use simulation or some analytical approach (or both) to generate the desired results. At this point it may be desired to explore the solution space by varying the input values (MARTE annotations) in the CSM and repeating the process as long as necessary. In addition, the performance characteristics of different design alternatives can also be explored by varying the Smodel.

11.9 SUMMARY

Understanding the performance implications of design choices is fundamental in the development of cyber-physical systems. Naturally, the earlier this can be done in the development cycle, the better. To support a structured and more dependable method for this purpose, MARTE provides the Performance Analysis Modeling (PAM) subprofile, which is designed to support a semi-automated formal performance analysis process. It is based on established analysis methods for the case of non-deterministic workloads.

References

[1] Franks G, Petriu D, Woodside M, Xu J, Tregunno P. Layered bottlenecks and their mitigation. In: Proceedings of third international conference on quantitative evaluation of systems QEST'2006, Riverside, CA, September 2006, p. 103–114.

[2] Franks G, Al-Omari T, Woodside M, Das O, Derisavi S. Enhanced modeling and solution of layered queueing networks. IEEE Trans Soft Eng 2009;35(2):148–61.

[3] Jain R. The art of computer systems performance analysis. : John Wiley & Sons Inc.; 1991.

[4] Menascé DA, Almeida VAF, Dowdy LW. Performance by design: computer capacity planning by example. Prentice Hall; 2004.

[5] Object Management Group, The, Clause 17 in UML Profile for MARTE: Modeling and Analysis of Real-Time and Embedded Systems, Version 1.0, OMG doc. formal/2009-11-02, Dec. 2009.PMIF.

[6] Smith CU, Llado CM. Performance model interchange format (PMIF 2.0): XML definition and implementation. In first international conference on quantitative evaluation of systems (QEST '04), Enschede, 2004, p. 38–47.

[7] Transaction Processing Council, TPC Benchmark W (Web Commerce) Specification, Version 1.8, 2002.

[8] Woodside M, Petriu DC, Petriu DB, Shen H, Israr T, Merseguer J. Performance by unified model analysis (PUMA). In: Proceedings of the fifth international workshop on software and performance (WOSP'2005), Palma de Mallorca, Spain, July 2005, p. 1–12.

Extending MARTE

Extending MARTE

Extending MARTE [Advanced]

12

CHAPTER CONTENTS

12.1 INTRODUCTION

Users of MARTE working within a particular application domain may find that MARTE is not always precise or complete enough to meet their needs for expressing the concepts in their project or application domain. For example, while MARTE provides facilities for modeling operating system threads, these are relatively general, covering the common features of threads across a broad range of different operating systems. However, when it comes to implementation-level detail, most operating system implementations of threads differ from each other. If there is a need for models to include platform-specific details (e.g., for automated code generation), then a general MARTE concept will have to be extended to incorporate the missing information. It may even happen that some unique application domain concept may not even have a MARTE equivalent, in which case it is the UML itself that needs to be extended. In this chapter we examine the various ways in which we can deal with these situations.

As explained in Chapter 2, the Unified Modeling Language was designed to be extensible. This is achieved via the *profile* mechanism [3]. Informally, a profile is a domain-specific interpretation of UML (MARTE itself is a notable example of a profile). The core idea behind profiles is to allow standard UML concepts to be extended with additional domain-specific semantics. One critical characteristic of such extensions is that they must be both *syntactically and semantically compatible* with the extended base UML concept. This ensures that a profile will be compatible with the UML standard and with the tooling that supports it—a key benefit of the profile mechanism. This means not only that standard UML tooling can be reused but also that modelers who are familiar with standard UML can reuse that knowledge and only need to learn about the increment provided by the profile, reducing both training and tooling costs.

12.2 How to add missing modeling capabilities to MARTE

In general, when a domain-specific concept is missing from MARTE, there are three methods for adding that construct:

1. *Application-level construct.* This consists of adding application-specific constructs that represent the missing concepts (e.g., a class representing a semaphore as discussed in Section 2.3.3). If the concept is to be reused in multiple applications, then it can be stored in a custom model library.
2. *New language construct.* In this approach, a new first-class language construct is added using stereotypes (refer to Section 2.3.3 for the explanation of "first-class").
3. *Hybrid approach.* This is some combination of the approaches 1 and 2.

The first method involves straightforward modeling and is the simplest to realize since it does not require any knowledge of the UML metamodel. As noted earlier, it has the drawback that any special semantics of such entities will not be recognized and, therefore, may not be processed appropriately by programs such as code generators or model analyzers. The second approach avoids this problem, but, unless care is taken, it can lead to an excess of highly specialized language concepts resulting in a complex domain-specific language that is difficult to learn and cumbersome to use. Consequently, in practice it is often the third approach that works best. In that case, the main unique characteristics of the concept are included in the stereotype definition, but other lesser characteristics are left to be defined by the application modeler. This approach reduces the number of domain-specific concepts, resulting in a simpler language.

Nevertheless, it is not possible to formulate hard and fast guidelines that clearly delineate which of the three approaches to use in a given situation. In general, the first approach may suffice when the special semantics behind the concepts are of no special interest. For example, if there is no intent to automatically generate code or to analyze the model in some way using computer-based tools. In all other cases either the second or third approach should be used. In the rest of this section we concentrate on the latter two approaches, which involve explicit language extension. We illustrate these through a case study.

12.3 Extending the MARTE domain-specific language—a case study

Annex A of the MARTE specification includes a worked out example of how the profile can be used to define another profile: the AADL profile. The "Architecture Analysis & Design Language (AADL)" is a domain-specific modeling language developed to support the analysis, design, and implementation of a common category of performance-critical real-time systems characterized by statically defined cyclical tasks [4]. AADL was designed to support various kinds of engineering analyses, such as predicting the schedulability, performance, or safety characteristics of systems. In this sense, it shares some of the same core objectives of MARTE. Like MARTE, AADL incorporates higher level concepts for specifying software applications and hardware platforms as well as concepts for describing deployment. It also supports precise specification of key quantitative and other characteristics needed for analysis.

Given the above, it may perhaps seem rather pointless to define one domain-specific language (AADL) using another (i.e., MARTE). However, recall that MARTE has the potential to reuse various UML tools, whereas the number of AADL tools is quite limited.[1] Hence, such a language-to-language mapping may make sense in some situations.

Note that mappings of this type are typically more complex than simple one-to-one concept translations. With its more specialized focus (relative to MARTE), AADL concepts tend to be more specific and more precise than their nearest MARTE or UML equivalents. Therefore, the mapping task involves selecting one or more appropriate base MARTE and UML concepts and then refining them to reach the same level of precision as their AADL counterparts.

12.3.1 A quick overview of AADL

AADL is a component-oriented language with facilities to specify a software application, its underlying hardware platform, and the deployment of software to elements of the platform. Various types of domain-specific components are defined for modeling software (processes, threads, data, subprograms, etc.) and hardware (processors, memories, busses, etc.). It is a concurrent language in the sense that it directly supports concurrency-related concepts encountered in most real-time operating systems such as processes and threads. Each of these can be annotated with corresponding properties, which provide concrete information that can be used for analyses, such as code size, execution time, period, scheduling policy, etc. Interaction between AADL components takes place through a network of ports and connections of various types. A powerful feature of AADL is the ability to specify end-to-end flows of data and control through the system along with their performance characteristics, such as latency and throughput. This helps us to reason about full end-to-end properties of a system.

An AADL *system model* is a composite of (1) a software application model and (2) a platform (hardware) model. The latter includes a specification of the deployment (binding) of software elements to underlying hardware components (e.g., threads to processors).[2]

12.3.2 Mapping of AADL concepts to MARTE

The conceptual similarity between AADL and MARTE simplifies the mapping between them. To illustrate how such a mapping is achieved and how MARTE can be extended, we examine in detail the mapping of the core AADL "thread" concept into a MARTE-based equivalent.

In AADL a *thread* is defined as representing "a sequential flow of control that executes instructions within a binary image produced from source text [4]." It also states that a "thread models a schedulable unit." Moreover, a thread is a subcomponent of a *process*, which, according to the AADL specification, "represents a virtual address space." Clearly, this concept is inspired by the conventional notion of concurrent thread, such as the one defined in the POSIX operating system standard [1]. This is useful to know, since it helps identify the closest UML or MARTE conceptual equivalent that can serve as the base for the extension. It is important to repeat here that "closeness" between concepts is measured primarily in terms of semantic similarity as opposed to syntactic similarity [2].

---

[1] https://wiki.sei.cmu.edu/aadl/index.php/AADL_tools.
[2] Although the MARTE specification includes in its Annex A a definition of a full AADL subprofile, the AADL stereotypes and other constructs described in this chapter are different from those found in the standard. They were chosen for their pedagogical value instead of for accuracy.

Further examination of the thread concept in AADL reveals that it is defined as a specialization of the general abstract *component* concept, which serves as a base for many different software and hardware concepts (e.g., processes, processors, memories, busses). In AADL, a component can define a set of *features*, a set of *flows*, and a set of *properties*. Features are model elements that define the interfaces of a component (e.g., ports, data), flows specify how information and control pass through a component, and properties characterize the component in various ways (e.g., resource requirements, timing properties). Through a mechanism known as "extension"[3] any of these characteristics can be inherited by another component similar to how UML generalization works (albeit AADL limits extension to at most one parent component). As with UML, it is possible to refine (or, redefine) characteristics inherited from an ancestor component.

This suggests that either the UML's Class concept or some MARTE extension of it might be the right starting point for defining the MARTE equivalent of AADL threads. However, before committing to that choice, we must account for one important difference between the AADL components and UML classes. Namely, AADL makes a clear distinction between a *component type* and a *component implementation*. In essence, a component type is a "black-box" view of a component, shorn of any internal detail. A component implementation, on the other hand, which must conform to a component type, captures the internals of a particular implementation of the component type (there can be many different implementations for a given type). Neither UML nor MARTE support this distinction as a first-class notion, although it can be easily realized with either language.

Fortunately, it is possible to get around this by defining two different specializations of the same base concept, one corresponding to component type and the other to a component implementation. A component type equivalent can be realized in MARTE simply by defining a stereotype of the UML Class concept called **AADLThreadType**, which includes an OCL constraint that prevents any internal elements in its decomposition:

```
self.base_Class.part- > isEmpty()) and
(self.base_Class.feature- > forAll(f|not f.oclIsTypeOf(Connector)))
```

This is saying that a UML class tagged with the **AADLThreadType** stereotype cannot have

- any internal parts (specified by the collection **part**, which is a feature of the UML Class concept and which, according to the above constraint, must be an empty collection) or, similarly,
- any features that are connectors.

In addition, since threads represent concurrent entities, it is helpful to add the following constraint to ensure that the extension will have the desired concurrency semantics:

```
(self.base_Class.part- > isActive)
```

Further details on how such constraints are specified are given later in this chapter.

Without loss of generality, we will confine ourselves in the remainder of this section to describing only the mapping of a simplified version of the AADL thread type concept (**AADLThreadType**). Our objective here is to illustrate the methods used to extend MARTE and not to encumber readers with the details of a complete AADL-to-MARTE mapping. To that end, we use the following

---

[3]Not to be confused with the UML concept of "extension" used for defining stereotypes.

simplified AADL language specifications expressed using the Backus-Naur form (BNF; AADL keywords are in **bold** script):

```
<thread_type> :: = thread < thread_type_id >
  [ports ({ < port > } + | none;)]
  [properties ({ < property_association > } + | none;)]
     end < thread_type_id > ;
```

where < thread_type_id> is a user-defined identifier, { < port > } + denotes a list of one or more port specifications, and { < property_association > } + is a list of one or more properties and their value specifications. The keyword **none** represents the absence of any ports or properties respectively.

AADL ports are similar to the UML concept of ports, but are slightly more refined. They are categorized according to the direction of information flow relative to the component to which they belong: input (**in**) ports, output (**out**) ports, or input–output (**in out**) ports. Also, based on the form of information that flows through them, they are characterized as **data** ports, **event** ports, or **event data** ports. For data and event data ports it is also necessary to specify the type of data that flows through them.

In addition, AADL defines many different properties for threads, but, for our needs, the following two exemplars are sufficient:

- The **Dispatch_Protocol** property of a thread, which specifies scheduling information, can be either **Periodic, Aperiodic, Sporadic,** or **Background.**
- The **Period** property of a thread identifies the time interval between successive dispatches and is expressed in terms of a predefined type **Time**. (Time in AADL can be expressed in standard units such as nanoseconds, microseconds, milliseconds, seconds, minutes, or hours).

Our task then, is to define MARTE equivalents of these AADL concepts, starting with the basic notion of *thread*. The obvious starting point seems to be the UML concept of an *active class*, since it has the right core semantics. However, since we are extending MARTE and not UML, we first need to check whether MARTE has a more suitable starting point. In fact, this turns out to be the case: MARTE includes a concept that already extends UML in the desired direction, the stereotype **SwSchedulableResource**.

This concept has a rather complex derivation, based on a hierarchy of extensions and generalizations rooted in the UML concept of Classifier, as shown in the model fragment in Figure 12.1. It is instructive to follow the rationale behind this complex definition stack.

The fundamental MARTE concept of Resource is described in detail in Chapter 4. To make it more generally useful, it is defined as an abstract stereotype in the General Resource Modeling Package (GRM) package of MARTE where it is derived from the more general UML Classifier concept rather than the narrower Class concept. (Actually, as we explain later, there is more than just one base UML concept involved. For the time being, we shall only consider the Classifier root of this stereotype.) As explained in Chapter 4, this very general concept has three attributes:

- **resMult** is used for modeling resources that have some form of multiplicity associated with them, such as, a circular buffer pool, which can only store a certain number of entries before it either overwrites a previous value or blocks further access.
- **isProtected** is used to identify whether the resource is protected in some way from the effects of uncoordinated concurrent access. For example, when full, a circular buffer might block further

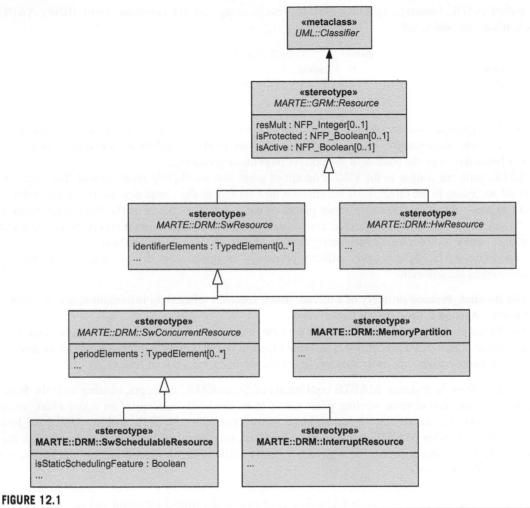

FIGURE 12.1

The derivation of the **SwSchedulableResour**ce stereotype.

writes until the oldest stored item is safely extracted. At this level of abstraction nothing is said about the form of protection.

- **isActive** indicates that the resource has properties that are reminiscent of a hardware processing device; i.e., it is capable of autonomously (and, hence, asynchronously) initiating behavior. In essence, this duplicates the role of the **isActive** attribute of a UML Class, but allows it to be applied at the more abstract level of a UML Classifier (as well as for the other base metaclasses of this stereotype.)

Note that the lower multiplicity bound of each of these stereotype attributes is zero, implying that they are all optional. This is particularly useful for situations where an attribute of some higher level (i.e., abstract) stereotype is not required or not meaningful for a given concept. For example, if we would prefer to eliminate the **resMult** attribute for some specialization of the **Resource** stereotype, we can do so by attaching the following OCL constraint to this new stereotype:

```
self.resMult- > size( ) = 0
```

This strategy is a common way of avoiding unwanted inherited properties.[4]

The **Resource** stereotype is quite abstract and is used to model both hardware and software resources. Hence, at the next level of refinement, this abstract concept is partitioned into hardware resources, characterized by a physical nature, and software resources that are at least one level removed from hardware. Refining software resources further, we note the introduction of concurrency through the abstract stereotype **SwConcurrentResource**. Most of its attributes are inspired by the POSIX standard. Those that are not needed can be eliminated by constraining their size to zero, as explained above. Some of these attributes, however, map directly to equivalent AADL properties (e.g., **stackSizeElements**, **heapSizeElements**). This last refinement finally gets us to MARTE's **SwSchedulableResource** stereotype, which was, in fact, designed to serve as a general base for representing different variants of operating system threads and processes.

At this point, we are much closer to the AADL **thread** concept than had we started with just the UML Class or Classifier concepts as a base. This is because **SwSchedulableResource** incorporates the necessary characteristics of resources in general as well as notions such as concurrency and concurrency protection. We get all of this for free by reusing the MARTE concept. However, even this far down in the MARTE hierarchy, we are still not fully matched to the AADL thread concept. For instance, there is no attribute to help us deal with the dispatch protocol property of AADL threads. And, although **SwSchedulableResource** includes a generic collection attribute called **periodElements** (see Figure 12.1), intended for capturing various characteristics related to periodic execution of tasks, these are not quite precise enough to capture the very specific AADL concept of **period**. Consequently, we will define our new **AADLThreadType** stereotype as a subclass of **SWSchedulableResource**, by adding the missing AADL attribute equivalents, as shown in Figure 12.2.

In this case, we have chosen to redefine the abstract **periodElements** attribute inherited from the **SwResource** stereotype. That ensures that they are not accidentally misused, since, in their standard form, they are not meaningful in the AADL context. Other attributes, such as the **isStaticScheduling-Feature** inherited from **SwSchedulableResource**, which identifies whether the scheduling parameters of the resource are defined statically, might be given fixed default values (in this case, **true**, since AADL supports only static scheduling). Finally, any remaining unwanted attributes will be removed by constraining their sizes to zero.

As shown in Figure 12.3, the new stereotype is defined in a different profile package outside of MARTE (the **AADL** profile package). This is the preferred way of introducing extensions to MARTE as it leaves the original standard profile unchanged. Of course, to obtain access to the necessary base stereotypes, the new profile must import the MARTE profile.

---

[4]The presence of an attribute in an ancestor class that is not shared by all its descendants indicates an improper generalization, typically because it is located too far up in the generalization hierarchy. The preferred method for dealing with those situations is to move the problem attribute downward to a subclass. However, in practice this is not always possible, particularly when it comes to extending industry standards such as UML and MARTE. The definition of these languages and their class hierarchies are not easily modified, so pragmatic workarounds such as the one described above are often the only practical solution.

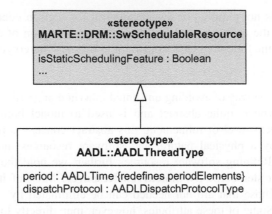

FIGURE 12.2

Definition of the **AADLThreadType** stereotype as a specialization of an existing MARTE concept.

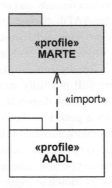

FIGURE 12.3

Defining the AADL profile package.

The new **AADLThreadType** stereotype has two attributes, **period** and **dispatchProtocol**, corresponding to the **Dispatch_Protocol** and **Period** properties of AADL threads, which are typed by AADL specific types, **AADLTime** and **AADLDispatchProtocolType**. The first of these is a defined as a new NFP type (see Chapter 3), while the second is a simple UML enumeration containing a list of dispatch protocols unique to AADL. In general, such domain-specific types are used both in the definition of the stereotypes as well as in user models based on those stereotypes. As explained in Section 2.5, the UML profile mechanism provides the concept of a model library package.

For our example, we can define a model library called **AADL_Library**, where these and other related types will be defined. The library will be included along with the AADL profile itself making it available to anyone who chooses to apply the profile.

The definition of the **AADLDispatchProtocolType** enumeration is shown in Figure 12.4.

Although MARTE has a ready-built model library for expressing time, this does not quite match what exists in AADL (e.g., AADL supports specifications with a resolution of picoseconds, whereas MARTE only goes down to nanoseconds). For this reason, and also to demonstrate how new NFP

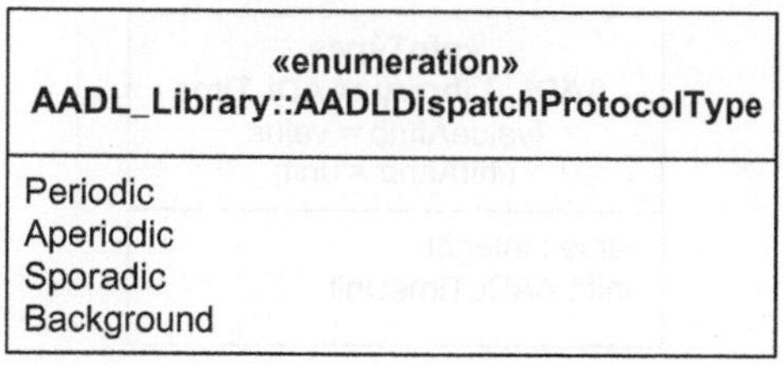

```
                    «enumeration»
      AADL_Library::AADLDispatchProtocolType

  Periodic
  Aperiodic
  Sporadic
  Background
```

FIGURE 12.4

The **AADLDisptachProtocolType** definition.

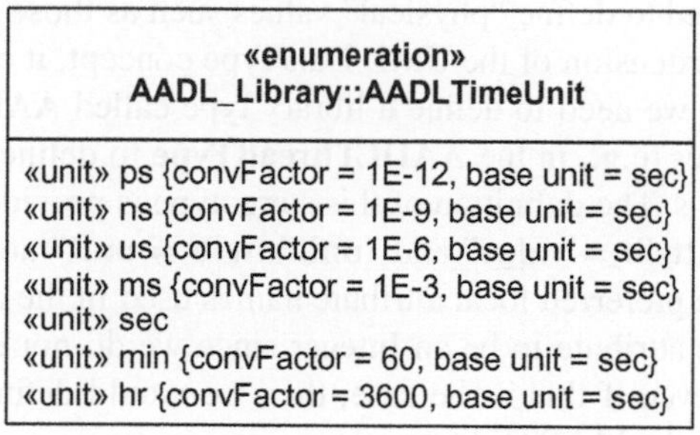

```
                    «enumeration»
          AADL_Library::AADLTimeUnit

  «unit» ps {convFactor = 1E-12, base unit = sec}
  «unit» ns {convFactor = 1E-9, base unit = sec}
  «unit» us {convFactor = 1E-6, base unit = sec}
  «unit» ms {convFactor = 1E-3, base unit = sec}
  «unit» sec
  «unit» min {convFactor = 60, base unit = sec}
  «unit» hr {convFactor = 3600, base unit = sec}
```

FIGURE 12.5

Defining the AADL time units.

types are defined in MARTE, we will define new types to be used with AADL-MARTE models. These definitions would also be included in the **AADL_Library**.

First, we define the time units recognized in AADL as shown in Figure 12.5. This definition takes advantage of the MARTE stereotype, **Unit**,[5] which is an extension of the UML **EnumerationLiteral** concept. It specializes the latter by adding optional conversion attributes: a conversion factor (**convFactor**) relative to a chosen "base" unit (**baseUnit**), as well as an optional offset to be used in the conversion (not required in our example). For example, the picosecond unit is signified by the literal "**ps**" which is 10^{-12} times the size of the base unit (seconds).

Now that we have the time units defined, we need to have a time value that is expressed as a pair consisting of a value and a time unit. As explained in Chapter 3, MARTE provides a generic stereotype to be used for this purpose called **NFPType**. This is a refinement of the standard UML **DataType** concept with three added attributes:

- **valueAttrib** is a property that defines the actual value of the data item; this may be a number, string, Boolean value, or some other type of data item such as an enumeration literal.
- **unitAttrib** defines the dimensional unit of the data item (i.e., second); in our example this is going to be one of the AADLTimeUnit literals.
- **exprAttrib** is used to specify values in the form of VSL expressions as an alternative to specifying **valueAttrib**.

---

[5] The modeling of NFP types is described in Section 3.2.

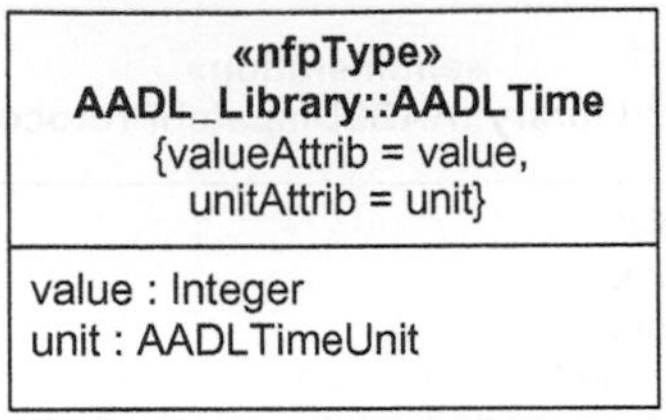

FIGURE 12.6

Definition of the **AADLTime** data type.

This stereotype can be used to define "physical" values such as those required to express time values in AADL. Since it is an extension of the UML DataType concept, it can be applied to instances of data types. For our example, we need to define a library type called **AADLTime**, which can be used in the definition of stereotypes (e.g., in the **AADLThreadType** to define the type of the **period** attribute) as well as in user models. The definition of this stereotype is provided in Figure 12.6.

The expressions "**valueAttrib = value**" and "**unitAttrib = unit**" are used to bind the stereotype default attribute names to the preferred local attribute names used in the data type definition. We have chosen the type of the **value** attribute to be an Integer since we do not expect there to be a need for fractional time values. However, if this is the case, then we would define the type as Real, which is another data type provided in the MARTE library.[6]

12.3.3 Extending multiple base classes

As noted earlier, a stereotype instance is a kind of attachment linked to the underlying base UML element that it specializes, but a stereotype instance can only be attached to an instance of a base class that its definition extends. Thus, since our **AADLThreadType** is a subclass of a stereotype that extends the UML Classifier concept, it can only be attached to elements that are kinds of Classifier (i.e., instances of Class, Actor, Behavior, etc.). However, especially when working with profiles that are used for analysis, it often happens that a single domain-specific concept is manifested in many different forms in a given model. For instance, a workload generator for some performance analysis method may be represented by a message in an interaction model, by a role in a collaboration, or by a transition in a state machine. Each of these is represented by a different UML base class.

As explained in Section 2.3.8, if a stereotype were permitted to only extend a single base class, it would be necessary to define a different stereotype for each possible manifestation of the domain-specific concept in a UML model. Each of these stereotypes would have a different name but would define the exact same set of stereotype features. This would not only complicate the definition of a profile, requiring cloning of the same features across different stereotypes, but would also create a maintenance problem.

To get around this, the UML profile mechanism allows a stereotype to extend more than one base class. For example, the **Resource** stereotype in MARTE extends five different UML concepts, since the concept may manifest itself differently in different models and situations (see Figure 12.7).

---

[6]More recent releases of the UML standard have added a Real primitive data type.

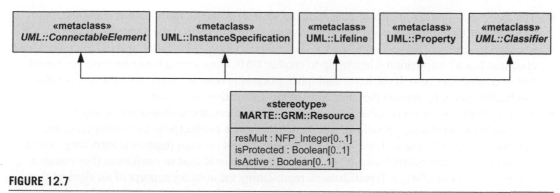

FIGURE 12.7

The different base classes of the MARTE Resource stereotype.

There is one crucial difference here between UML extension and UML generalization. In the case of generalization, the different generalizations are conjunctive, meaning that an instance of the subclass with multiple ancestors simultaneously possesses the features of all of its ancestors. However, for extensions the opposite, disjunctive, interpretation applies, meaning that a particular stereotype instance extends only one of its base class instances. In a sense, each base class of a stereotype represents a different use case of the domain concept.

The advantage of this mechanism is that the domain-concept needs to be defined only once, even though it may be used to tag different types of UML model elements. We have already seen why it makes sense for the resource concept to extend Classifier. Allowing it to extend the UML Lifeline concept enables a resource to appear in an interaction diagram. Extending ConnectableElement permits resources to be represented by roles in a collaboration or parts in a composite structure. InstanceSpecification enables its use in instance diagrams, which is particularly useful in analysis.[7] Finally, extending Property is useful to represent resources as attributes of some complex system represented by a Classifier.

12.3.4 Selecting base classes for stereotypes

Selecting the most appropriate base classes for a stereotype definition is one of the most important and most challenging tasks facing a profile designer. As already noted, it is most important that the selected base class is *semantically aligned* with the domain concept. This can be broken down into the following individual criteria:

- The domain concept and the base class should represent the "same kind" of entity. It does not make sense, for instance, to use UML Package as a base class for a concept that has a run-time manifestation, simply because UML packages, by definition, do not represent any run-time entities. (Packages in UML are either used to group static model elements or, alternatively, to model design-time groupings of model elements.)

---

[7]This is because many types of analyses require instance-based models (see Section 9.3.3). For example, for schedulability analysis, it is not sufficient to know which classes are involved, but also precisely how many instances of a particular class exist, since each instance adds incrementally to the overall load on the underlying platform.

- The base class should not include constraints or abstract syntax definitions that contradict the semantics of the domain concept that is represented. For example, if the domain concept is intended to represent some kind of atomic (i.e., non-decomposable) entity, it should not use a base class that has a composition relationship to another UML class with a lower multiplicity bound that is greater than zero. If the lower multiplicity bound is zero, however, then the composition can be eliminated by forcing the cardinality of the association end to zero.
- Since stereotypes cannot redefine the features of a base class, there should not be any base class features (attributes, operations, receptions) that are in conflict with the semantics of the domain concept. Of course, if the lower multiplicity bound on such features is zero, they can be eliminated by a constraint. However, be warned that this could lead to confusion. (For instance, in the definition of UML, a TypedElement, representing the abstract concept of an element that conforms to a type can be typed by *zero* or more types. By forcing the upper bound on the number of types to zero (using a constraint), we end up with the seemingly paradoxical concept of a typed element that cannot have a type).

The intent behind these three basic guidelines[8] is to increase the likelihood that the desired language extension is truly compatible with the UML. This ensures that neither UML tools nor people with UML expertise will be misled when working with the domain-specific language. It is of course, quite difficult to guarantee true semantic compatibility even if these guidelines are adhered to.

There will undoubtedly be situations where these guidelines cannot be fully followed. In such cases, it may be a better choice to define a new domain-specific language, as opposed to extending a UML-based language. Although the concepts of UML are quite general and cover a lot of very different possibilities, the profile mechanism should not be stretched outside its semantic envelope.

12.4 Who should define language extensions?

As can be seen from the descriptions in this chapter, extending MARTE and UML is no simple task and should not be undertaken lightly with little preparation. Designing computer languages in general is a complex task requiring deep expertise and experience. Moreover, in contrast to the well-researched field of programming language design, the theory of modeling language design is much less advanced. Without a proper theoretical underpinning, it is difficult to ensure a clean design that satisfies all formal requirements.

When it comes to defining profiles, there is even less theory and less experience. It requires a thorough understanding of the UML metamodel and its design rationale (which, unfortunately, is not documented very well) as well as an understanding and facility with the profile mechanism. It also requires, in equal measure, a deep understanding of the problem domain, its purpose, ontology, and common design and usage patterns.

Consequently, the most practical approach to extending UML or MARTE is to involve a multidisciplinary team that includes language design experts and domain experts. Experience has shown that an imbalance on either side typically leads to an inadequate result. There are at present very many bad UML profiles (even those produced by standards bodies) and very few good ones.

---

[8]Since semantics are often described informally, it is typically not possible to define these as hard and fast rules that can be checked by formal means. Hence, they are referred to as "guidelines."

12.5 SUMMARY

MARTE is designed to cover a broad spectrum of real-time phenomena. Unfortunately, one of the costs behind this level of generality is that it may not always be able to provide the degree of precision that may be required in a given problem or domain. One possible solution in such situations is to specialize MARTE further, using refinements of its stereotypes.

In this chapter, we used an example to illustrate some of the key techniques that are used in refining profiles such as MARTE. However, as explained in Section 12.4, language design and profile specialization in particular are complex topics that, in addition to detailed domain knowledge, also require deep understanding of the UML metamodel and the profile that is extended. Therefore, the decision to extend MARTE should only be undertaken if such expertise is readily available.

References

[1] Institute of Electrical and Electronics Engineers, The (IEEE), IEEE Standard 1003.1-2008 – IEEE Standard for Information Technology—Portable Operating System Interface (POSIX®), 2008.

[2] Noyrit F, Gérard S, Terrier F, Selic B. Consistent modeling using multiple UML profiles Petriu DC, Rouquette N, Haugen Ø, editors. Model driven engineering languages and systems. : Springer; 2010. p. 392–406.

[3] Object Management Group, The, Clause 18 in OMG Unified Modeling Language™ (OMG UML), Superstructure, Version 2.4.1, OMG document no. formal/2011-08-06, 2011.

[4] SAE International Group, "Architecture Analysis & Design Language (AADL)," Aerospace standard AS5506 (Issued 2004-11).

Appendices

Appendices

The Value Specification Language (VSL)

A.1 Why VSL?

Basic standard UML provides very limited facilities for specifying complex expressions that are sometimes needed to specify the kinds of values encountered in cyber-physical systems.[1] In particular, it does not provide any concrete syntax for specifying values that

- represent complex physical data types (described in Chapter 3 and Appendix B)
- are computed by mathematical functions
- are dependent on other values through some functional relationship

The Value Specification Language (VSL) was defined to fill this void. It is an integral part of the MARTE and is essential to the definition of physical (NFP) data types. Like MARTE, it is an extension of UML and recognizes the UML abstract syntax. Consequently, VSL expressions can directly refer to elements of a UML model in which they appear, such as class attributes and operations.

The ultimate purpose of any VSL expression is to specify a value associated with some model element. This could be, for example, the initial or default value of an attribute or parameter, an upper or lower multiplicity bound, a term in an arithmetic or Boolean expression, an argument in an operation call, and so forth. Note that values are not always strictly numeric, and include things such as enumeration literals, string values, clock readings, and calendar dates. The ability to specify concrete values is necessary for analysis, when it is desired to predict the key qualitative and quantitative characteristics of proposed designs (response times, safety integrity levels, availability metrics, timing characteristics, etc.).

---

[1] The recent adoption of the Alf action language [1] has eliminated this shortcoming. However, the practicality of its use with MARTE is unproven as yet. We discuss Alf briefly in Section A.4.1.

VSL is a formal computer language in the sense that it is defined by a precise grammar and well-defined semantics. It is not a self-contained language, however, because of its limited role (i.e., to specify values). Hence, it exists in and depends on the greater context defined by UML and MARTE. Although VSL language statements can be used purely for their documentation value, the full power of the language emerges when it is used with appropriate *VSL language evaluators*. These are used to validate the well formedness of VSL expressions and to evaluate them when required.

A.2 Where to apply VSL

VSL is used most often in the following situations:

- Assigning a value to a class or stereotype attribute
- Writing constraints, typically ones that involve values of object and class attributes
- Defining complex data types

Note that VSL is defined as a separate profile in its own right that is independent of MARTE.[2] This means that it can be used for other Object Management Group (OMG) modeling languages, such as SysML (see Chapter 8) [2], in addition to MARTE.

A.3 Quick (abbreviated) VSL user guide

The following sections highlight the most commonly used elements of VSL. For the full specification of the language, readers should refer to Annex B of the official MARTE specification [3].

A.3.1 Modeling structured data types with VSL [Advanced]

For modeling complex data, VSL goes beyond the core capabilities of UML. This includes:

- The ability to represent new *patterns* of structured data types that are not supported directly by standard UML: *choice types*, *interval types*, *tuple types*, and *collection types*.
- A concrete syntax for specifying the *values* of these data types using VSL expressions.

Since standard UML does not prescribe concrete syntactical forms for specifying data values except for primitive type literals, the ability to do so for these complex data structures is particularly important for various types of MARTE-based formal model analyses (see Chapter 9).

This capability is realized in VSL via stereotypes that extend the basic UML DataType concept. This is reminiscent of the way that the standard UML Enumeration is defined, except that extension is used instead of specialization. Figure A.1 illustrates this method, using the example of one of the VSL types, the **IntervalType**. The UML Enumeration metaclass is not itself an enumeration; instead, it specifies a pattern for constructing enumeration types in user models. Similarly, **IntervalType** defines *a pattern for constructing new user-level interval data types*.

---

[2]Except that it relies on the MARTE Primitive Types library package, which can be imported independently of other packages in that standard MARTE library.

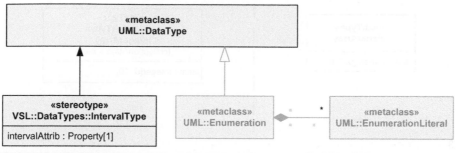

FIGURE A.1

Definition of the VSL **IntervalType** stereotype.

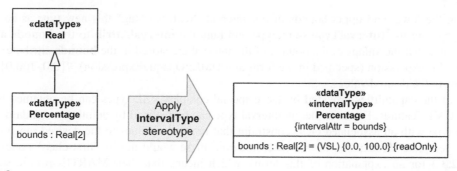

FIGURE A.2

Defining an interval type composite data type using the **IntervalType** stereotype.

As an example of how such a definition is used, consider the case where we want to define a new **Percentage** data type to be used in our models. Percentages, of course, can be represented by real numbers and a simplistic solution would be to use the type **Real** for this purpose. However, this is not sufficient since we would like to restrict the values of this type to the range between 0 and 100.

As can be seen from Figure A.1, the **IntervalType** metaclass has a solitary denotational attribute (see Section 2.3.7 for an explanation of denotational attributes), **intervalAttrib**, which points to a single instance of the UML metaclass Property. This metaclass is used to specify the attributes of classifiers such as data types. This means that **intervalAttrib** is pointing to an attribute (a kind of property) in some user-defined classifier. In this case, we want it to point to the attribute that actually defines the interval of valid values. This indirect approach frees us from committing to a particular type of that attribute, which allows us to define intervals of different types (e.g., real numbers, integers).

In case of the **Percentage** data type, we first need to create an appropriate user-level data type to which we will apply the **IntervalType** stereotype. Since percentages are expressed using real numbers, we create a subclass of the MARTE **Real** primitive type,[3] as shown in Figure A.2. We name this new user-level type **Percentage**. In its definition, we include a read-only collection attribute, **bounds**,

---

[3]Note that this is the MARTE library type Real and not the standard UML Real primitive type. This is because the UML version of Real was added to UML only after MARTE was adopted.

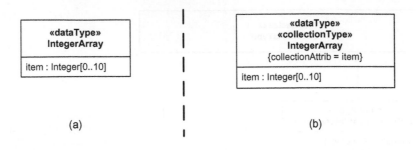

(a)   (b)

FIGURE A.3

Example of using the **CollectionType** stereotype.

for storing the lower and upper bounds of our interval. Next, we "tag" this new type as an interval type by applying the **IntervalType** stereotype and bind the **intervalAttrib** to the **bounds** attribute. This indicates that the values of the bounds of the interval are stored in the **bounds** attribute. Finally, we add a VSL expression (specified in the form of a UML::OpaqueExpression), "{0.0, 100.0}," to set the bounds to the desired values.

Most of the capabilities provided by these special complex VSL types can be obtained by using standard UML features. For example, an interval type can be realized by defining a standard application data type with an associated OCL constraint that limits the values to the desired range or using the UML template mechanism. In that case, however, these would not be "first-class" concepts (see Section 2.3.3 for an explanation of this term), which means that their MARTE-specific semantics would not be recognized readily by external tools and code generators.

Some of the more useful VSL types are described in the following sections.

A.3.1.1 IntervalType

As explained previously, this stereotype is used to define a valid range of data values of the base type. The base type can be any system or user-defined data type whose value ranges can be meaningfully described by two boundary values. In the **Percentage** example above, we used the primitive type **Real** as the base type. For an enumeration type that lists the seven days of the week, for example, it might make sense to define a **Weekend** interval type, spanning the range from **Saturday** to **Sunday**.

IntervalType is used to define several additional utility types in the standard MARTE model library, including **IntegerInterval** and **RealInterval**, which can be used as supertypes for other custom interval types. (In fact, our example **Percentage** data type could have been defined as a subtype of **RealInterval**.)

A.3.1.2 CollectionType

Although UML supports the notion of *attributes* that are collections (e.g., attribute x:Integer[10]) it does not provide the ability to define *types* that are collections (e.g., **IntegerCollection**). Consider, for example, that we need to have a data type that represents an array of up to 10 Integer values. We can do this, of course, by defining a new data type that includes an Integer attribute with a multiplicity of 0..10 as shown in Figure A.3a. Alternatively, we can do it using the VSL **CollectionType** stereotype as depicted in Figure A.3b.

The difference between these two forms is relatively minor from a modeler's viewpoint: it is primarily in how the individual items are accessed. Thus, if we have an attribute, x, typed by **IntegerArray**, in the first case, the ith item would be accessed using the expression x.item[i] versus x.at(i) in the second. Note that in the latter expression there is no explicit reference to the attribute **item**; its purpose is simply to help define the type, size, ordering, and uniqueness of the collection. It is bound to the stereotype attribute, **collectionAttrib**, which serves the same purpose as **intervalAttrib** did for **IntervalType**; that is, as a "pointer" to the attribute where the actual parameters of the composite type are defined.

CollectionType is used to define a number of utility types in the standard MARTE model library. These include data types such as **IntegerMatrix**, **RealMatrix**, **IntegerVector**, **RealVector**, and the template data type **Array**. The latter has two parameters: the type of element in the array (e.g., **Real**) and the size of the array, expressed as an Integer. It is possible to define different types of arrays by binding different values to these two parameters.

A.3.1.3 ChoiceType

The **ChoiceType** stereotype is analogous to the union type in the C language, and is used to combine multiple structurally unrelated data types into a single type. It is typically applied in situations where some feature needs to be typed by any single one[4] of the combined types. It is particularly handy in cases where no common supertype exists for the alternatives, or in situations where some of the subtypes of the shared supertype need to be excluded.

A typical example of this is the standard MARTE model library type **ArrivalPattern**, which can be used to characterize probabilistically-distributed workloads in some types of analyses. The library provides a number of commonly used arrival patterns, defined as individual data types (periodic, aperiodic, sporadic, irregular, etc.). In this case, there are no common features that span the full range of these patterns, so that it would be rather contrived to declare them as subtypes of a common (empty) supertype.[5] Instead, the **ArrivalPattern** type is defined as a choice type as shown in Figure A.4.

The **ChoiceType** stereotype has two attributes:

- **choiceAttrib** is a collection of pointers to UML Properties (i.e., it is a denotational attribute), each one representing one alternative data type.
- **defaultAttrib** is an optional denotational attribute (multiplicity 0..1), which can be used to point to one of the alternative data types that will serve as a default choice. Of course, if no default is desired, this attribute is omitted.

Choice types are used to define various utility types in the standard MARTE model library.

A.3.1.4 TupleType

VSL tuple types (**TupleType**) are conceptually analogous to standard data types: they are simply ordered collections of typed attributes. At first, this may seem like a duplication of an existing UML capability. However, the VSL tuple type provides two important capabilities that are not available in standard UML. First, it allows special MARTE-specific semantics to be assigned to key attributes of certain tuple types, such as the **NfpType** concept, which is central to how MARTE represents

---

[4]The types are mutually exclusive, in the sense that only one of the choices applies in any given case.
[5]Although this is a possible alternative to using MARTE choice types.

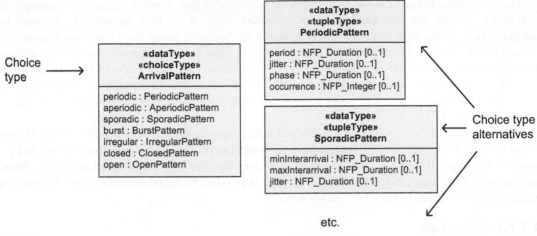

Choice type

Choice type alternatives

etc.

FIGURE A.4

Example of using the **ChoiceType** stereotype (not all alternative types shown).

physical types and other non-functional properties (see Chapter 3). Second, it also provides a direct and convenient means for specifying values of complex data types using VSL expressions.

The **TupleType** stereotype has a single open-ended collection denotational attribute, **tupleAttrib[*]**, of type UML Property. Each item in this collection points to a feature of the tagged model element that defines the type, size, and other characteristics of the composite type. For example, the right side of Figure A.4 shows two concrete examples of **TupleType: PeriodicPattern** and **SporadicPattern**.

As noted previously, the **NfpType** stereotype, which is a subtype of **TupleType**, takes advantage of the tuple type concept to associate special semantics with some of its attributes (see Figure A.5):

- **valueAttrib** is a denotational attribute that defines the quantity of the physical data type instance.
- **unitAttrib** is a denotational attribute that defines its specific physical measurement unit.
- **exprAttrib** is an optional denotational attribute, which can be used to capture a VSL expression that defines a value of the type (this expression can be a simple number or a complex expression of the appropriate type).

A typical example of how this stereotype is used can be seen in the fragment from the standard MARTE model library shown in Figure A.6.[6] In this case, the common features of all NFP types are captured in the **NFP_CommonType** (abstract) data type, including the attribute, **expr:VSL_ Expression**. This attribute is bound to the **exprAttrib** attribute of the **NfpType** stereotype, to denote that it is the attribute that contains the value expression. It is by these means that the **expr** attribute is given its special semantic significance and which distinguishes it from other attributes of its type. The common stereotype is then further refined into a number of different abstract data types according to the type of the value (**Boolean, Real**, etc.), with their **value** attribute bound to the **valueAttrib** of **NfpType**. Finally, a concrete non-functional data type (e.g., **NFP_Frequency**) is derived from these value-specific types, with the **unit** attribute of the concrete type bound to the **valueAttrib** of **NfpType**.

---

[6]For clarity, some of the less frequently used attributes of these library types have been omitted from the diagram.

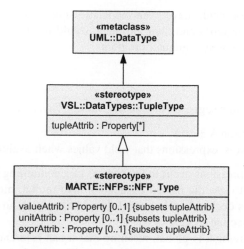

FIGURE A.5

MARTE definition of the **NfpType** stereotype as a tuple type.

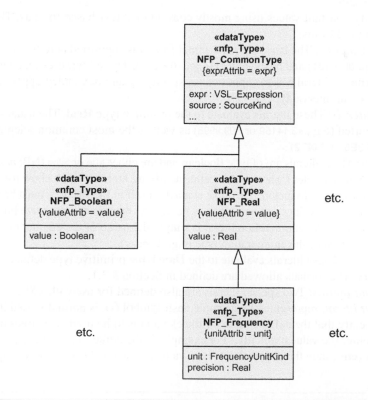

FIGURE A.6

A fragment of the standard MARTE model library showing the use of the tuple type **NfpType**.

As noted previously, these could have been modeled using standard UML data types, but then the special semantics of these types and their attributes would not have been easily recognizable to human observers and even less so to computer programs.

A.3.2 VSL expressions

The purpose of VSL, as its name suggest, is to specify values. This can be done in one of two ways:

- As literal values (see Section A.3.2.1)
- As value expressions, that is, expressions that yield values when evaluated (see Section A.3.2.2).

As noted earlier, VSL expressions occur in the context of a containing UML model. Consequently, a VSL expression can refer to specific named elements in that model, most often attributes or operations of classes or data types declared in the model. In addition, such an expression can also refer to special *VSL variables* (see Section A.3.2.2).

The *scope* of a VSL expression is global, meaning that it can reference any attribute or operation in the model, although it may need to use qualified names in case of naming conflicts. (Note that the scoping rule for VSL variables is slightly more elaborate, as explained below).

A.3.2.1 VSL literals

VSL literals specify constant values using mostly conventional text-based formats. The following are the most common used forms:

- *Integer number literals*: The basic signed decimal format is supported here (e.g., 1345 or –22) as are binary (e.g., 0b00101) and hexadecimal (e.g., –0 × 5F4). These literals evaluate to the primitive type Integer. The "*" literal is also supported for specifying an open-ended upper value where appropriate (e.g., in interval types).
- *Real number literals*: These literals evaluate to the primitive type **Real**. The usual signed decimal format is supported (e.g., +3.14159 or –99.9995) as well as the most common scientific exponential format (e.g., 5.3E5 or 2.0E-2).
- *Boolean literals*: These literals are of type **Boolean** and are either true or false (NB: *not* capitalized).
- *String literals*: Single quotes (') are used to delineate **String** literals, which allow use of any character in the character set used. To include the quote character itself in the string, it must be preceded by a backslash character (\). Strings can be as long as necessary; there is no upper size limit.
- *Enumeration literals*: An enumeration literal is simply the name of the enumeration literal as listed in the definition of the enumeration type (e.g., Sunday).
- *DateTime literals*: These literals evaluate to the **DateTime** primitive type defined in the standard MARTE library. The formats allowed are defined in Section 3.3.1.
- *Null and default literals*: Two special literals are also defined for use with VSL:
  - The *default literal,* represented by a simple dash symbol (-), is normally used in composite types to specify that the default value for the element is to be used. This frees users from having to enter the value explicitly.[7] For example, if the default unit for length is the centimeter (**cm**), then the physical data type value (5, cm) can be written as simply (5, -).

---

[7]One should always be careful when relying on defaults, since they may not always be what we expect. Errors caused by this are often difficult to detect.

• The *null literal*, represented by the string null, is used to denote an absent (i.e., undefined) value. This can be used to specify that a value for some optional attribute has not been provided; i.e., that it is not present.

A.3.2.2 *VSL expression types*

In this section we illustrate the most common VSL expression types using typical examples. For the complete formal specification of these types, readers are referred to Annex B of the official MARTE specification [3].

VSL expressions, like VSL literals, can be inserted in any location in the model where a value specification is expected. Since a VSL expression specifies a value, each expression has a corresponding type. Consequently, they are classified on the basis of the type they return when evaluated.

Tuple expressions: Tuple expressions are probably the most common VSL expressions used in practice. They serve to specify the values of VSL tuple types (**TupleType**, see Section A.3.1.4), including, notably, the various **NFP** types (see Chapter 3 and Appendix B). As one might expect, the type of a tuple expression must match the type of the tuple whose value it defines.

Tuple expressions are enclosed by parentheses and contain a comma-separated ordered list of *labeled* VSL expressions specifying the values of individual attributes in the tuple. Each value expression is preceded by a label consisting of a name and an equals (=) sign.[8] The label matches the name of the tuple attribute whose value is being defined. For example, the following fragment from the definition of some application class, includes a tuple expression that defines the initial value of attribute, **arrPattern**, which is typed by the **PeriodicPattern** tuple type (refer to Figure A.4 for a definition of this type):

```
arrPattern :PeriodicPattern = (period = (value = 2, unit = s), jitter = (value =
0.1, unit = s))
```

In the above example, only the values for **period** and **jitter** attributes are defined explicitly (they are both of type **NFP_Duration**), while the remaining attributes (**phase** and **occurrence**) are automatically initialized to their defaults. If no default is provided, then the values are set to **null**. Note that this example includes nested tuple expressions.

Since labels are used to associate the expressions with their corresponding attributes, there is no set order in which the attribute expressions must be listed when this option is used.

A special *shorthand* form of tuple expressions is supported by some VSL parsers for physical data types (specifically, NFP types that are subtypes of **NFP_Real**). This form omits the attribute labels and only specifies the values for the **value** and **unit** attributes in that order; all other attributes are automatically set to their defaults. The following are examples of this kind of tuple expression:

```
(2.5, ms) // an NFP_Duration value of 2.5 milliseconds
(100, cm) // an NFP_Length value of 100 centimeters
(2000, W) // an NFP_Power value of 2000 Watts
(5, Mb/s) // an NFP_DataTxRate value of 5 megabits per second
```

---

[8] Standard VSL syntax actually allows omission of the labels in tuple expressions, relying on the order of attributes as a means of identifying which value expression applies to which attribute. However, with the exception of the special shorthand cases described in this section, we advise against using this label-less form since it is error prone and cumbersome to use in situations where tuple types have a large number of attributes (such as most of the NFP types in the standard MARTE library).

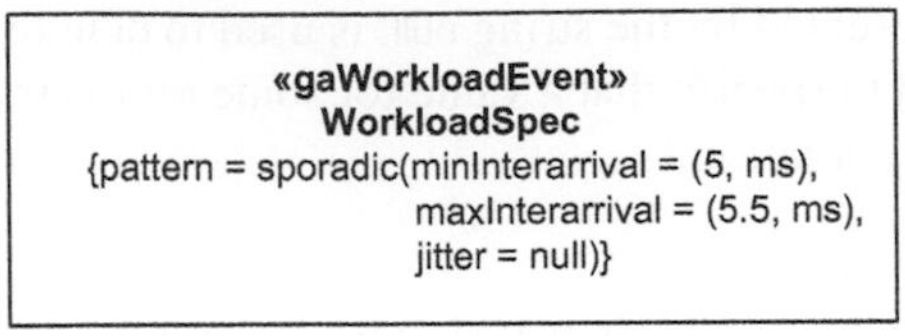

```
            «gaWorkloadEvent»
              WorkloadSpec
{pattern = sporadic(minInterarrival = (5, ms),
                    maxInterarrival = (5.5, ms),
                    jitter = null)}
```

FIGURE A.7

Example of a **Choice** expression involving a **Tuple** expression for the value.

This shorthand form is, by far, the one that is used most frequently in models. It not only saves time and effort[9] but also enhances readability and reliability.

Choice expressions: Choice expressions are used to specify a value for a choice type (**ChoiceType**, described in Section A.3.1.3). As explained choice types are types that unify a number of different types, such that any particular usage of the choice type has to be one of its "member" types.

Consider, for instance, the case where we want to define the initial value of the pattern attribute of some class (WorkloadSpec) tagged with the MARTE **GaWorkloadEvent** stereotype. This attribute happens to be typed by the choice type **ArrivalPattern** shown on the left side of Figure A.4. In this example, we would like the initial value to be a sporadic pattern, which means that we must choose the **sporadic** attribute of the choice type. Since **sporadic** is typed by the **SporadicPattern** tuple type (see the right side of Figure A.4), we need to define an instance of the latter type with a given set of values. The result is depicted in Figure A.7. In this case, the **minInterarrival** attribute of the sporadic pattern is an instance of the type **NFP_Duration**, which is also a tuple type, with a value of 5.0 milliseconds. Similarly, the **maxInterarrival** attribute of this sporadic pattern instance has a duration of 5.5 milliseconds. Finally, there is no jitter in this case, so we have assigned a null value to the **jitter** attribute.

Collection expressions: Collection expressions are used to specify values of VSL collection types (**CollectionType**, see Section A.3.1.2). They consist of an ordered list of comma-separated value expressions enclosed within braces ({}).[10] Each expression in the list specifies the value for the collection item in the corresponding position in the collection. For example, the following fragment of some data type specifies the initial value of an attribute, arr, typed by the **IntegerArray** collection type shown in Figure A.3b:

```
arr :IntegerArray = {1, 1, 1, 2, 2, 2, 3, 3, 3, 0}
```

Interval expressions: Interval expressions represent the full set of values between two boundary values. These expressions are enclosed within square brackets ([]) and consist of two expressions separated by two successive periods (..). The first expression specifies one bound and the second

---

[9]Most physical data types, such as **NFP_Duration**, have between 10 and 11 attributes, most of which are rarely used.
[10]This choice can be confusing sometimes, since standard UML encloses such collections between simple parentheses. On the other hand, OCL also uses braces to enclose collections of literals [4].

the other. Naturally, the type of the two expressions has to match the type of the interval. For example, the following example defines an integer interval type that represents the set of integers between 0 and the value of the variable max (an integer) less 1, *inclusive*:

```
[0..(max-1)]
```

VSL syntax provides the option to exclude one or both limit values from the interval. This is indicated by inverting the appropriate bracket; e.g., the **Real** interval expression]0..5.0] defines the full range of real numbers between 0 and 5 except for the excluded lower bound value 0.
Conditional expressions: A conditional expression works like a standard "if-else" type of statement. The syntax is borrowed from C: it involves a parenthesized Boolean VSL expression followed by a question mark separator (**?**) and two alternative value expressions: a "true" and a "false" expression, separated by a colon symbol (**:**). If, upon evaluation, the Boolean expression evaluates to true, then the "true" expression is evaluated, otherwise, the "false" expression is evaluated. The type of the alternative expressions must match the type of the value being specified. The following conditional expression returns the value of attribute (or variable) flow, of type **Real**, unless the value of flow exceeds the threshold value of 10, in which case it returns 10:

```
(flow > = 10) ? 10 : flow
```

Clearly, to be useful, the Boolean expression should involve some kind of variable element, either a reference to property in the model or a VSL variable (see Section A.3.2.3).
Feature access expressions: Feature access expressions are VSL expressions that access either an attribute of some model element (*property call expressions*) or one of its operations that return data type values (*operation call expressions*).[11] The type of these expressions is defined by the type of the feature being accessed. In either case, the basic form of these expressions is simply a reference to the name of the accessed feature. Operation call expressions also need to specify, between parentheses, any argument values corresponding to the parameters of the invoked operation. However, to disambiguate such references, it may be necessary to use a partially or fully qualified name of the feature. For example, for a class ClassA defined in package Pkg with an attribute arr of type **PeriodicPattern** (see Figure A.4), the following expression would be used to access the value of the **period** attribute of arr:

```
Pkg.ClassA.arr.period
```

Note that VSL uses the dot (.) operator for specifying qualified names instead of the double colon operator (::) used in the rest of UML.
The standard MARTE model library defines a set of common operations for the basic primitive types: **Boolean**, **Integer**, **UnlimitedInteger**, **String**, and **Real**. These include all the usual arithmetic operators (+ , − , *, etc.) and comparison operators (= = , > , < , > = , etc.). VSL allows such basic operators to be specified using an infix notation. Thus, the expression a + b is equivalent to an invocation of the + operation with b as an argument, i.e., a. + (b).

---

[11] VSL also allows invocation of "classifier behaviors," but this is needed only in more advanced cases, so we do not discuss it further here.

A.3.2.3 *VSL variables [Advanced]*

VSL allows the declaration of local VSL variables to represent values. These are typically used in the following situations:

- *When it is inappropriate to commit to a specific value in a (generic) model.* This might happen, for instance, in case of a *product line* model in which different versions of the product will have different default values for some attributes. Rather than have a separate version of the model for each possible value, it is clearly more efficient to have a single model with a single variable representing the different values possible. This is also useful in design analysis when we may want to experiment with different values for certain model parameters in order to determine the most appropriate ones.
- *When we desire to capture dependencies between different VSL expressions associated with different model elements.* For example, we may have a situation where the initial value of one attribute must always be 10 times greater than another. Since these would typically be specified by separate VSL expressions, to avoid having to enter the appropriate values in multiple places (an error-prone activity), it makes sense to declare a single variable to represent the value and then refer to it in all the places where it is required.
- *When a complex VSL expression is reused in multiple other expressions.* In this case, the repeated expression is used to specify the initial value of the variable. Note, however, that this is not the equivalent of either a macro or procedure, since the evaluation of the expression is done only once at the start of VSL evaluation and the computed value is then inserted in all the places where the variable is referenced.

All VSL variables need to be declared explicitly. This is done through a *variable declaration expression*. Although the VSL syntax leaves a lot of flexibility in how variables are declared, the most reliable and reader-friendly way is to specify both their type and their direction. The *type* of a variable is simply the type of value that it represents. The *direction* of a variable identifies whether the variable is intended as an input or as an output variable. It is defined by one of the following VSL keywords:

- **in** — The variable represents an independent (i.e., input) variable.
- **out** — The variable represents a dependent (i.e., output) variable.
- **inout** — The variable is used first for input and, eventually, for output (it is generally best to avoid using this type of direction, since it can be confusing and is prone to errors).

An optional *initial value expression* can follow the name of the variable in a variable declaration, to specify how the initial value of the variable is to be computed. Clearly, this option should be used only for output variables (although VSL does not prevent in variables from having initial values). However, as explained below, the values of output variables do not necessarily have to be computed by a VSL expression evaluator.

The syntax for variable declarations requires that the name of the variable be preceded by a dollar sign (**$**) as in the following two examples:

```
in $d1 : Real                    // input Real type variable d1
out $delay :Real = (1.3*d1 + 15.5)   // an output Real type
                                 // variable dependent on
                                 // d1
```

Note the use of a VSL initial value expression in the second example to compute the value of the output variable delay. The second example also illustrates how variables (e.g., d1) can be used in expressions by simple name reference.

VSL does allow for disambiguation of variable names in cases where they conflict with each other or where they conflict with the names of referenced model attributes or operations. The rules for this, including name scoping rules, are given in Annex B of the MARTE specification [3]. As a practical measure, however, it is best to give unique global names to VSL variables that are not in conflict with any other names in the model.

The presence of VSL variables makes a model generic. However, if we need to work with a specific (non-generic) model, for, say, analysis purposes, we must specify concrete values for its input variables. Neither MARTE nor UML specify how this is to be done, but it clearly requires some type of transformation of the generic model (this is sometimes referred to as *configuring* a model). This transformation typically involves providing values for the input variables followed by evaluation of all VSL expressions that can be evaluated,[12] including any associated with output variables. As noted earlier, the values of the output variables need not be computed using VSL expressions.

In fact, in many if not most practical cases, output values are computed by external means (e.g., by some specialized analysis program) and the results inserted back into the model.

A.4 Alternatives to VSL

As noted earlier, the VSL language was specifically designed to work with MARTE. It takes advantage of the MARTE Model Library and its primary focus is to specify values and constraints for models that use MARTE. However, it is possible to use other languages for the same purpose. Three of these are of particular interest since they have both been standardized by the OMG:

1. The Action Language for Foundational UML (Alf) [1]
2. The constraint blocks (also known as "parametrics") "language" of the systems modeling language, SysML [2]
3. The Object Constraint Language, OCL [4]

Although there is nothing preventing using these jointly with VSL, unless there is a specific need to do so, it is generally better to choose one and use it throughout a given model.

A.4.1 The Alf language [5]

Alf was adopted relatively recently by the OMG (in 2010) and is still in its "Beta" version. It is intended to provide a user-friendly front end to UML activities and actions, whose graphical representations tend to get unwieldy when specifying detailed or complex *flow-based* behaviors. To minimize learning hurdles, it has a familiar looking text-based concrete syntax that is quite similar to Java. Most important, it is fully aligned with OMG's "Semantics of Foundational Subset for Executable

---

[12]Note that it is not necessary for all input values to be specified at once, since we may still need to leave some variables unspecified for later substitution. The resulting model in those cases would still be a generic model even after the transformation.

UML Models" (also known as "fUML[13]") [6]. Because of that, valid Alf program fragments are fully consistent with fUML semantics. This stands in contrast to other programming languages that one might use in UML models, which, given that they are defined independently of UML, allow code to be written that can violate UML semantics. Such conflicts can be quite subtle and difficult to spot, and can be the source of much grief during debugging. For example, the use of pointers in C code embedded in OpaqueAction or OpaqueExpression fragments of UML models can easily circumvent any carefully designed constraints defined by class diagrams.

The introduction of Alf allowed UML, or, more precisely, fUML, to be used as a fully fledged programming language, if desired. It even includes a textual equivalent of class diagrams. For use with MARTE, it would mostly be used to specify values (including expressions and functions) and constraints. For these purposes, in a UML model it would be embedded in an OpaqueExpression with the **language** attribute set to **Alf** and the **body** attribute containing the Alf code. This will be parsed and converted to corresponding fUML model elements (or directly to generated code) by a UML tool that supports Alf. Such tools are starting to emerge from both commercial vendors and open source groups.

It is also possible for Alf to be used in conjunction with the MARTE Model Library, but note that this library requires the use of VSL, which it applies as a profile.

Lastly, it is worth noting that there is an ongoing initiative to unify VSL and Alf, after which VSL would emerge as a kind of dialect of Alf [1]. This is the most likely scenario for the evolution of VSL.

A.4.2 SysML parametrics and physical types

Clause 10 of the OMG Systems Modeling Language (SysML) standard includes a facility for specifying constraints using a graphical syntax [2]. This facility is briefly described in Section 8.3. However, as explained there, VSL has some important advantages, including a concrete syntax for specifying complex functional expressions, which might include variables. Remember that it is possible to use VSL with SysML without necessarily including the rest of MARTE.

SysML also provides a standard set of physical types using a simple pairing of standard "quantity kinds" (e.g., time, volume, mass, temperature, or even electric current) and corresponding standard units (e.g., second, cubic meter, kilogram, degrees Celsius, volt). These are similar to the physical types of MARTE, but MARTE provides an extended form whereby additional information can be attached to these types, such as their source (e.g., measured, estimated) and precision.

A.5 SUMMARY

VSL is a statically typed textual language defined in a separate profile so that it can be used with other OMG languages besides MARTE, such as SysML. It is designed to allow the specification of detailed functional relationships that may exist between various values in a model, such as the values of attributes of classes and objects. It also provides a library of standard meta-types that can be used in such expressions, including tuple types, collection types, choice types, and interval types. In particular, these meta-types are used to define the NFP types included in the standard MARTE library.

---

[13]fUML is a precisely defined subset of UML that supports the creation of executable models. However, this subset does not cover some important modeling features of UML such as state machines or structured classes, with their ports and connectors.

At present, tool support for VSL is limited to only a few UML tools. However, it is anticipated that VSL will be revised in the near future as an extension the Alf standard.

References

[1] Cuccuru A, Gerard S, and Terrier F, Defining MARTE's VSL as an Extension of Alf. In: Model driven engineering languages and systems, proceedings of the 14th MODELS conference, Wellington, New Zealand, 2011, Lecture Notes in Computer Science, vol. 6981; 2011. p. 699–13.

[2] Object Management Group, The, OMG Systems Modeling Language(OMG SysML™), Version 1.3, OMG document no. formal/2012-06-01, 2012.

[3] Object Management Group, The, A UML Profile for MARTE: Modeling and Analysis of Real-Time and Embedded Systems, Version 1.1, OMG document no. formal/2011-06-02, 2011.

[4] Object Management Group, The, Object Constraint Language (OCL), OMG document no. formal/2012-01-01, 2012.

[5] Object Management Group, The, Action Language for Foundational UML (Alf) Concrete Syntax for a UML Action Language, OMG document no. formal/2012-08-43, 2012.

[6] Object Management Group, The, Semantics of a Foundational Subset for Executable UML Models (fUML), Version 1.1, OMG document no. ptc/2012-10-18, 2012.

MARTE Library Types—Quick Reference

B

CHAPTER CONTENTS

B.1 Introduction

MARTE incorporates a set of convenient standardized utilities, including the VSL language profile (see Appendix A) and a set of concepts for modeling physical data types in the NFP profile (see Chapter 3), as well as a set of generally useful data types collected in the MARTE model library. The relationship between these elements is shown in Figure B.1. Both VSL and the NFP framework are defined as stand-alone UML profiles, which allows them to be used with other profiles than MARTE (although both rely on the MARTE primitive types package). The standard MARTE model library consists of specialized modules (packages) some of which are shown in Figure B.1.

In this appendix we provide a convenient overview of the most commonly used data types from the MARTE library. The full specification can be found in Annex D of the MARTE specification [3].

B.2 The MARTE library primitive types

Except for the MARTE-specific DateTime type, these are expanded forms of the basic UML primitive types incorporate the most arithmetic and other utility operations (see Figure B.2).

B.3 The MARTE library measurement units

These are enumeration data types representing physical units. They are all tagged with the **Dimension** stereotype defined in the NFPs profile. For an explanation of this stereotype, refer to Section 3.2 and Figure B.3.

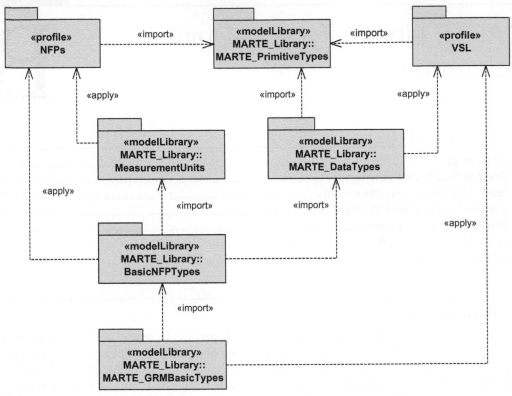

FIGURE B.1

Structure of the MARTE model libraries definition (including the NFPs and VSL profiles).

B.4 The MARTE library basic NFP types

These are probably the most commonly used MARTE physical data types (see Figure B.4). They serve to describe the physical characteristics of platforms and applications. Also included in this package are specifications of arrival patterns and probability distributions, which are used in analysis. Note that this package makes use of both the **NFPs** profile (the **NfpType** stereotype) and the **VSL** profile (**ChoiceType** and **TupleType**).

Probability distributions are defined as class (i.e., static) operations of the shared **NFP_CommonType** as shown in Figure B.5. As can be seen from Figure B.4, this data type is the common ancestor of most of the basic NFP types and, therefore, these operations can be used with any of these types.

B.5 The MARTE library time types

There are two basic library packages associated with time modeling in the standard MARTE library: **TimeTypesLibrary** and **TimeLibrary** (see Figure B.6). The first includes an enumeration that

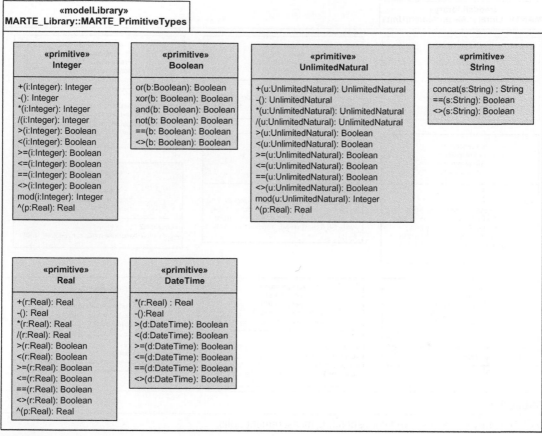

FIGURE B.2

Basic MARTE primitive data types and their operations.[1]

specifies a variety of time standards, which can be used when defining clocks using the **Clock** stereotype. The second includes a definition of the ideal clock and an instance of that type that can be used as a standard reference (see Section 4.2.5).

B.6 Other MARTE library types

In addition to the types described above, the standard MARTE library includes the following modules, whose specifications can be found in the full specification [3]:

---

[1] Note that only the most common operations are shown here; the full definition includes additional functions.

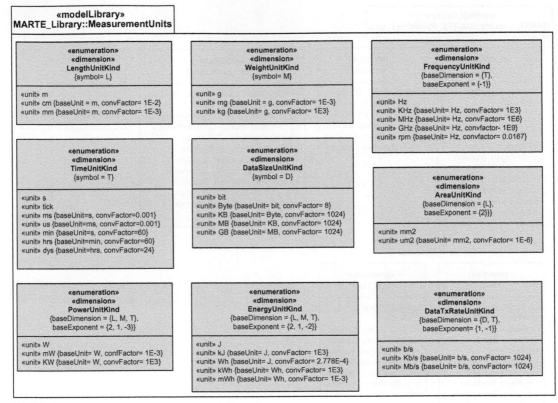

FIGURE B.3

MARTE library dimensions and corresponding measurement units.

- **MARTE_Library::GRM_BasicTypes** — This library contains a set of data types used for modeling schedulers and scheduling policies.
- **MARTE_Library::OsekVDXLibrary** — This library contains a set of elements for modeling the OSEK and VDX real-time operating systems and applications running on those platforms [4]. These operating systems are primarily intended for automotive applications.
- **MARTE_Library::ARINC-653**[2] — This library contains a set of elements for modeling the ARINC-653 real-time operating system and applications running on those platforms. This operating system is primarily used for avionics applications [1].

---

[2] http://en.wikipedia.org/wiki/ARINC_653.

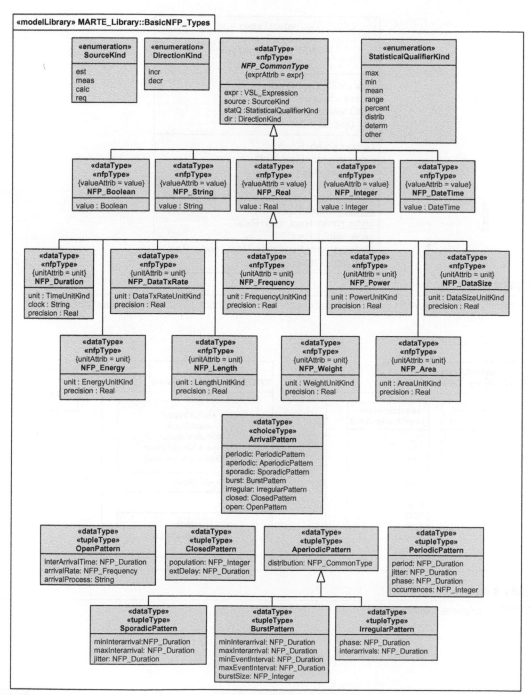

FIGURE B.4

MARTE library basic NFP types and arrival patterns.

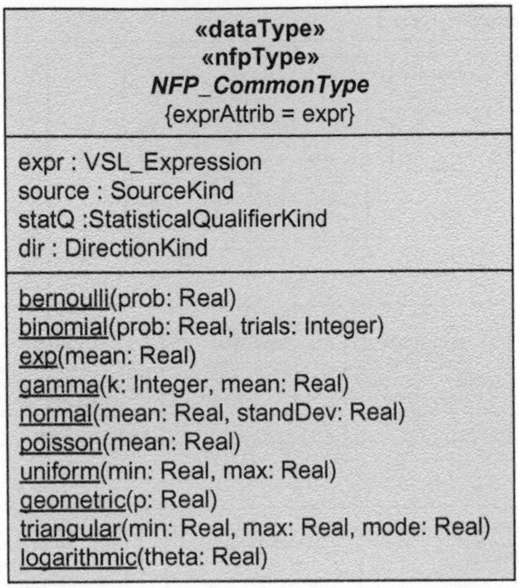

«dataType»
«nfpType»
NFP_CommonType
{exprAttrib = expr}
expr : VSL_Expression
source : SourceKind
statQ :StatisticalQualifierKind
dir : DirectionKind
bernoulli(prob: Real)
binomial(prob: Real, trials: Integer)
exp(mean: Real)
gamma(k: Integer, mean: Real)
normal(mean: Real, standDev: Real)
poisson(mean: Real)
uniform(min: Real, max: Real)
geometric(p: Real)
triangular(min: Real, max: Real, mode: Real)
logarithmic(theta: Real)

FIGURE B.5

The definition of common probability distributions as class operations of the **NFP_CommonType**.

«modelLibrary»
MARTE_Library::TimeTypesLibrary
«enumeration»
TimeNatureKind
discrete
dense
«enumeration»
TimeStandardKind
TAI
UT0
UT1
UTC
Local
TT
TDB
TCG
TCB
Sidereal
GPS
«import»
«modelLibrary»
MARTE_Library::TimeLibrary
«clockType»
IdealClock
{nature = dense,
unitType = TimeUnitKind,
getTime = currentTime}
currentTime() : Real
«clock»
idealClk : IdealClock
{unit = s}
«apply»
«profile»
MARTE::Time

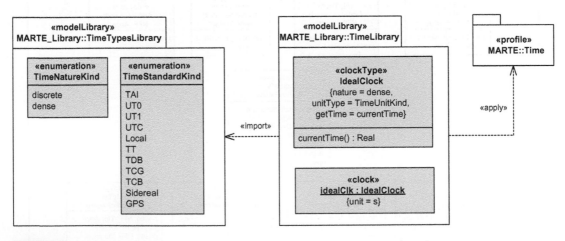

FIGURE B.6

MARTE library time related types.[3]

[3]Note that only a subset of the contents of these library packages are shown; the full complement can be found in the standard itself.

References

[1] ARINC-653-2 Specification (Avionics Application Software Interface, Part 1 — Required Services), 1st December 2005.

[2] Mallet F. Logical time @work for the modeling and analysis of embedded systems: foundations of the UML/MARTE time model. : LAP LAMBERT Academic Publishing; 2011.

[3] Object Management Group, The, Appendix D in A UML profile for MARTE: modeling and analysis of real-time and embedded systems, Version 1.1, OMG document no. formal/2011-06-02, 2011.

[4] OSEK/VDX Group. OSEK/VDX OS specification, Version 2.2.3, 2005. <http://portal.osek-vdx.org/files/pdf/specs/> os223.pdf.

References

[1] ARINC653-2 Specification (Avionics Application Software Interface. Part 1 — Required Services, 1st December 2005.

[2] Mallet F. Logical time @ work for the modeling and analysis of embedded systems. Foundations of the UML/MARTE time model. EDA LAMBERT Academic Publishing, 2011.

[3] Object Management Group. The Appendix D in a UML profile for MARTE: modeling and analysis of real-time and embedded systems, Version 1.1. OMG document formal/2011-06-02, 2011.

[4] OSEK/VDX Group. OSEK/VDX OS specification, version 2.2.3, 2005. <http://portal.osek-vdx.org/files/pdf/specs/os223.pdf>.

MARTE Stereotypes—Quick Reference

The two tables in this appendix provide a convenient guide for selecting suitable stereotypes for various modeling situations. Only the names of the stereotypes are provided here and the section in which they are explained; their definition, semantics, and method of usage of these stereotypes can be found in the appropriate chapters.[1]

Table C.1 contains the recommended stereotypes to be used when modeling applications, platforms, and deployment. The "Modeling Concept" column identifies the type of element that is being modeled. The three columns to the right are used to select the type of model being considered. "System Modeling" refers to models that are at a relatively high level of abstraction, where, for example, it may not be of interest to differentiate between software and hardware. "Software Application Modeling" identifies the stereotypes used for modeling real-time applications. Note that the entries here also include the stereotypes used for high-level modeling, and this is because users may choose to model some parts of the software in a more abstract manner. Finally, "Platform Modeling" lists the stereotypes used for modeling platforms. Note that this column includes all the stereotypes from the high-level column (to allow abstract modeling of some elements) and from the software modeling column (since platforms may be either software or hardware).

Table C.2 lists the stereotypes used for analysis situations. In this case, only those stereotypes defined specifically for analysis are included. However, for cases where the analysis profile does not define a specific stereotype for a concept, a suitable stereotype from Table C.1 can be used. For example, the PAM subprofile does not provide a special stereotype for representing mutual exclusion devices, but a high-level stereotype such as **MutualExclusionResource** can be used for that purpose, if needed.

---

[1]Note that *only stereotypes described in this book are included* in this appendix. The full set of MARTE stereotypes and their definitions can be found in the MARTE specification [1].

Table C.1 Recommended MARTE Stereotypes for Modeling Real-Time Applications and Platforms

Modeling Concept	System Modeling	Software Application Modeling	Platform Modeling
General resource	Resource	Resource, SwResource	HwResource, Resource, SwResource
Processing resource	ProcessingResource	ProcessingResource, SwSchedulableResource	ComputingResource, ProcessingResource, SwSchedulableResource
Storage resource	StorageResource	MemoryBroker, MemoryPartition, StorageResource	HwDMA, HwMemory, HwMMU, MemoryBroker, MemoryPartition, StorageResource
Communications resource	CommunicationEndPoint, CommunicationMedia	CommunicationEndPoint, CommunicationMedia, MessageComResource, SharedDataComResource	CommunicationEndPoint, CommunicationMedia, HwArbiter, HwBus, HwEndPoint, HwMedia, MessageComResource, SharedDataComResource
Concurrency resource (task)	ConcurrencyResource	ConcurrencyResource, Scheduler, SwSchedulableResource	ConcurrencyResource, Scheduler, SwSchedulableResource
Mutual exclusion resource	PpUnit, MutualExclusionResource	MutualExclusionResource, PpUnit, SwMutualExclusionResource	MutualExclusionResource, PpUnit, SwMutualExclusionResource

Timing resource	Clock, ClockResource, ClockType, IdealClock, TimingResource, TimerResource	Clock, ClockResource, ClockType, IdealClock, TimerResource	Clock, ClockResource, ClockType, IdealClock, TimerResource
Special device	DeviceResource	Alarm, DeviceResource, InterruptResource, NotificationResource	DeviceResource, HwComponent, HwDevice, InterruptResource
General resource service	GrService	GrService, SwResource	GrService
Acquire service	Acquire	Acquire	Acquire
Release service	Release	Release	Release
Constraint	NfpConstraint, TimedConstraint	NfpConstraint, TimedConstraint	NfpConstraint, TimedConstraint
Timed processing	RtFeature, RtSpecification, TimedProcessing	RtFeature, RtSpecification, TimedProcessing	RtFeature, RtSpecification, TimedProcessing
Timed instant/duration	DateTime, NFP_Duration, TimedConstraint, TimedInstantObservation, TimedDurationObservation	DateTime, NFP_Duration, TimedConstraint, TimedInstantObservation, TimedDurationObservation	DateTime, NFP_Duration, TimedConstraint, TimedInstantObservation, TimedDurationObservation
Timed event	TimedEvent	TimedEvent	TimedEvent
Deployment	Allocate, Assign	Allocate, Assign	Allocate, Assign

Table C.2 MARTE Stereotypes for Model Analysis

Modeling Concept	General Analysis	Schedulability Analysis Modeling	Performance Analysis Modeling
General resource	GaResourcesPlatform		PaLogicalResource
Processing resource	GaExecHost	SaExecHost	GaExecHost
Shared resource		SaSharedResource, SwMutualExclusionResource	
Concurrency resource (task)		SwSchedulableResource	PaRunTInstance
Communications resource	GaCommChannel, GaCommHost	SaCommHost	GaCommChannel, GaCommHost
Analysis context	GaAnalysisContext	SaAnalysisContext	GaAnalysisContext
Resource usage	ResourceUsage		
Workload	GaWorkloadBehavior, GaWorkloadEvent, GaWorkloadGenerator	SaEndToEndFlow	GaWorkloadEvent
Execution scenario	GaAcqStep, GaCommStep, GaEventTrace, GaRelStep, GaRequestedService, GaScenario, GaStep	SaCommStep, SaStep	GaAcqStep, GaCommStep, GaEventTrace, GaRelStep, GaRequestedService, GaScenario, GaStep, PaStep
Time constraint	GaTimedObs, GaLatencyObs, LaxityKind, TimedConstraint	TimedConstraint	TimedConstraint

Reference

[1] Object Management Group, The, A UML profile for MARTE: modeling and analysis of real-time and embedded systems, Version 1.1, OMG document no. formal/2011-06-02, 2011.

Index

Note: Page numbers followed by "*f*" and "*t*" refer to figures and tables respectively.

Printed and bound by CPI Group (UK) Ltd, Croydon, CR0 4YY

03/10/2024

01040324-0012